Get the Job (and Compensation) You Want

- - - It's All About The Process - - -

By Jim Grant

ISBN: 1-4392-1249-X
ISBN-13: 9781439212493
Library of Congress Control Number: 2008908824

Visit www.booksurge.com to order additional copies.

Introduction

The tone of this book is meant to be one of "tough love." I intend to tell you what you *need* to hear, rather than what you *want* to hear.

What you want to hear is that it will be <u>easy</u> to find the job and compensation you want. Sorry. It won't be.

What you want to hear is that you will find the job and compensation you want <u>fast</u>. Sorry. It will take more time than you think.

The good news is, I will tell you what <u>you</u> need to do and that will make it <u>easier</u> and <u>faster</u> than what other job seekers often experience. I'll also provide you with the tools and information you will need to pull it off.

Your fundamental choice is to use the "traditional" approach to finding a job or take the more "effective" approach I have laid out in this book. You will find the "effective" approach takes a little more time for each job you pursue, but your success rate at getting interviews will be much higher and you will land a job sooner.

The tactic I've taken in this book is to focus on the "process" and not upon the end result. This is consistent with the wave of management techniques that have rolled through American businesses in the last 20-30 years. They go by names like "Total Quality Management," "Continuous Improvement," "Kaizen," "6-Sigma Black Belts," and "Integrated Process Control." The essence is if you get the "process" right, good results (in business, product or service) will follow almost automatically.

When it comes to the job search, "process" means what you <u>do</u> and what you <u>say</u>. I have found that many job seekers aren't sure <u>what</u> to do, don't know the specific details as to <u>how</u> to do it, and are at a loss as to what to <u>say</u> to other people. In this book, I will focus on step by step and word by word details. Ultimately, this is what landing a job gets down to . . . . . knowing what to say and what to do (in a myriad of situations). <u>It's all about the process.</u> If you've got the right process, you'll get the right results.

There is one particular concept that far too many job seekers embrace which I would like to dispel from your mind, in case you believe it, or have gotten sucked into it. Too many job seekers think this is a "numbers game." That is, if you're going to only get an interview 1% of the time you send your resume in, then the more times you submit it, the more interviews. This is a self-fulfilling prophesy. If you believe this, you will act, accordingly. If you act accordingly, that is exactly what will happen. Don't fall into that trap. Use the more effective "process" that I describe in this book. It will get you an interview more often and an offer sooner.

You're probably like most job seekers. That is, you stay at home too much. You're waiting for someone else to do something that will lead to your desired job and compensation. You have negative thoughts constantly running through your head like, "This is taking too much time," "No one wants to hire me because I'm too old," "No one will pay me what I'm worth," or "I'm not good at this job-hunting thing."

How do I know? There are two reasons. First, I'm just like you. I've been on the job hunt at least four times in the last couple decades and I changed jobs among those four employers 15-20 times. Second, I've counseled over 2,000 job seekers through an organization I co-created in northeast Ohio, the Chagrin Valley Job Seekers (CVJS). I've been doing this for over six years and have 65-85 job seekers at our twice-a-month meetings. I encounter job seekers with negative thoughts all the time.

Searching for a job is stressful, psychologically and financially. I don't expect you to be inhuman and somehow avoid, ignore, or deny these stresses. I do want to help you rise above them.

There will be two things I'm asking you to do. First, <u>take action</u>. Second, <u>be</u> as <u>positive</u> as you possibly can be when dealing with <u>every</u> <u>person</u> you encounter.

In regard to <u>taking action</u>, I am surprised there is such a high proportion of job seekers who seem to be doing very little to help themselves. They are either waiting for someone else to do something or they're afraid to <u>take action</u>. Waiting for other people may work. However, it takes way too long. If you want to minimize the time you are out of work, then <u>take action</u>. Take control of your job search. I frequently get questions from CVJS members like "Is it OK if I ....?" It seems people are afraid to do something for fear that something bad will happen. Bad things can happen if you do nothing! If something bad happens, would you want it to be because you did something or because you did nothing? If it isn't illegal or offensive, it's very unlikely that <u>taking action</u> is going to be a bad idea. If by some chance it doesn't turn out well, it will at least be a learning experience and you'll do better next time.

The point of <u>taking action</u> is so important that I've written many of the sentences in this book in the imperative. They start, "Do this" or "Do that." Most of the chapter titles even start with a verb calling you to <u>take action</u>.

In terms of <u>being positive</u>, I'm sure you know this already. However, the key words to the second thing I'm asking you to do are to do it with <u>every</u> <u>person</u> you encounter. It's obvious when you are interviewing with a hiring manager that you need to <u>be positive</u>. But what about those people you normally ignore in your day-to-day activities? The custodian? The clerk at the fast-food spot? That nuisance neighbor? Who is to say one of these people doesn't have a brother or a sister who has exactly the job you are looking for? How are you going to find that out, unless you come off <u>positively</u> with these people and treat them with respect? Ask them how their life is going and they'll ask you how yours is going. Ask them how their job is going and they'll ask you the same. That's when you tell them what kind of job you are looking for. I'm frequently surprised that job seekers present themselves with a "chip on their shoulder." It's not that I don't think people have "chips on their shoulders." Heck, I frequently do, too. The point is, don't let anyone see your "chip." We all have "attitudes." Just don't let anyone see your "attitude." You must learn to view every person you encounter as the one who will get you started on the path to your next job.

Structure of This Book

There are three parts to this book. They are:

Part I – <u>The Job Seeking Process</u> – This part describes the entire process and provides you with step by step instructions for <u>taking action</u> in virtually everything you will encounter in your job search. Part I starts with an overview of the job seeking process. There is a chapter devoted to each of the key tasks of the process and the chapters are in the same sequence as you would typically perform the tasks.

Part II - <u>Special Cases & Issues</u> – This part addresses a variety of situations and considerations that frequently occur during a job search, although not with all job seekers.

Part III - <u>Appendices</u> – This part includes materials that will be useful in specific steps in your job search. It includes templates for communications (resumes, letters, etc.) and samples of questions and answers that will help you prepare for interviews.

How to Use This Book

I suggest a very specific approach to using this book.

- Go to the "Overview of the Job Seeking Process" in Part I. Read it over closely. Pay attention to the flow chart. This will give you an idea as to where you already are in the process and what you need to be doing.

- Read through the Table of Contents closely. You need to have a complete picture of what is in this book so when a situation occurs, you will know where to go in the book to get help.

- Read the rest of Part I. You will get a more complete sense of what it means to take action or how to handle things, when you get down and wallow around in the details. There are a few people out there who are tremendously successful at ad-libbing and reacting on the spur of the moment. That's not me and it probably isn't you. In the same sense that it took you at least months, if not years, to get really good at your profession, you need to spend the time to "practice" how to hunt for a job. . . . . . That is your new job.

- Use the materials in Parts II & III as the situations arise.

Alerts Used in This Book

I've used various buttons throughout the book to draw your attention to specific material. They appear as follows.

This indicates either a task or a step-by-step procedure for you to follow. This is what you should <u>do</u>. In some cases, sequence will be critical and will be noted as such.

This indicates what you should <u>say</u>, almost verbatim.

This indicates options for you to <u>do</u> or <u>say</u>. Pick one or more that fit your situation and personal style.

This indicates a high level concept that helps establish an understanding of the material in a particular section.

This indicates an idea or a tip for you to consider. It may be anything from enlightening, to uncommon, to a way to distinguish yourself.

This indicates one or more examples of what was discussed in the prior paragraph.

This indicates caution about some material that was just presented. It cautions against misinterpretation, overuse, or misapplication.

That's it for now. Good luck and happy job hunting.

If you get to northeast Ohio, certainly stop in and visit me at a CVJS meeting.

Jim Grant
Fall, 2008

Acknowledgements

Over the last several years, I have spent a large part of my personal time helping job seekers. I want to thank and owe a great debt of gratitude to my wife, Lyndy, for putting up with my lack of attention. I'm sure there were many times she felt job seekers were getting more help from me than she was. She has spent many hours proofreading my book and getting my language and grammar in order.

I also owe a great deal of thanks to Greg Reynolds. Greg is my cofounder and coleader of the Chagrin Valley Job Seekers (CVJS), a volunteer support group for job seekers. Much of what I have learned about the job search came from Greg. He has over 25 years experience in human resources management, executive recruitment and career transition services. He currently works for a regional wholesale outplacement firm. Over the years, he has helped a few thousand job seekers, both in his professional and personal capacity. He and I became good friends when I was last looking for a job and he agreed to a breakfast networking meeting. At the end of the meeting, he asked me if I would be willing to start up a job seeker group with him. As Greg says, I responded with those infamous words "Sure, I've got nothing but time!"

I also want to thank June Bolenbaugh. June is an educator, a writer, and writing coach. She reviewed my book word for word and made countless editorial corrections and enhancements. June also provided me with excellent feedback and insight as to how job seekers will interpret much of what I've written and better ways to present my ideas.

I can't leave out Bill King. Bill has helped hundreds of jobs seekers over the years and CVJSers for the last two. He "stalked" me during my efforts to get this book published, never letting me get away with any excuse about why I wasn't making progress. He gave me the "tough love" I hope to pass on to you as you read this book.

Finally, there are a variety of people who have endorsed my work and encouraged me to keep at it. In particular, I want to thank Dana Kachurchak, Nancy Patterson, Richard Heiser, Doug Cantlay, and Joe Jiamboi for their support.

Table of Contents

<u>Part III – Appendices and Forms</u>

Part I – The Job Seeking Process

Overview

In order to effectively search for a job, you need to have some context in which to operate. You need some guideposts to confirm you are doing the right things and are headed in the right direction. You need a check-off list. You need a sense of sequence. This overview is intended to provide all of that for you.

There are six phases to the job search.

Phase I - Separating	In this phase, there are two key tasks. First, you are going to have to deal with the shock of your job loss and the emotional challenges you will experience. Second, you need to take care of a variety of matters that are likely to be outstanding with your prior employer.
Phase II - Planning	This phase leads you to define the end result of a successful job search. If you don't know where you are headed, any road will seem okay!!! You may need to do some formal career planning and hold some informational interviews to define your desired job.
Phase III – Preparing	Prepare, prepare, and then prepare some more. This phase addresses creating the promotional materials you need, improving your job searching skills, and getting help for your search.

Phase IV – Seeking	This is where the bulk of your time will be spent. There are four fundamental job search methods:

- Pursuing specific, known job opening
- Pursuing target employers
- Networking
- Using recruiters

In this phase, you should be using all four methods, almost simultaneously.

Phase V – Acquiring	You've found a job you want. Now, it's time to land it. This phase focuses on interviewing and negotiating to meet your job objectives.
Phase VI – Wrapping Up	You've landed the job. Now it's time to bring closure to the process and appropriately thank people who helped you along the way.

A flow chart of the phases and the key tasks within each phase is shown on the next page.

Overview - The Job Hunting Process

The numbers in the boxes are the chapters where the details can be found for that task.

Phase I - Separating

Deal with the Shock	Separate from Your Employer
1	2

Phase II - Planning

Develop a Career Plan	Hold Informational Intervies	Define Your Desired Job & Comp.
3	4	5 & 6

Phase III - Preparing

Develop Your Promotional Materials and Job Hunting Skills	Get Help & Develop a Method to Record Your Activity
7 & 8	9 & 10

Phase IV - Seeking

Pursue Specific, Known Job Openings	Pursue Target Employers	Network, Network, Network	Work With Recruiters
11	12	13	14

Phase V - Acquiring

Interview	Negotiate
15	16

Phase VI – Wrapping-Up

Thank Everyone	Maintain Your Network
17	18

Typically, you will move from phase to phase in the vertical sequence shown in the flow chart. Try to resist your sense of urgency to jump ahead to a phase, before completing the prior phase. You may be excited if a job offer comes to you tomorrow out of the blue. However, if you don't know how to deal with it, at least three bad things might happen. First, the offer might disappear right in front of your eyes. Second, you might accept less compensation than the hiring manager is willing to offer. Third, you might land a job that, a month later, you find you don't really want.

Within each phase, there are multiple tasks. Sometimes tasks within a phase are overlapping or performed simultaneously. Also, if you move on to a task before finishing a previous one or you happen to perform tasks out of sequence, don't worry. It's not likely to be serious. Note it and make a judgment call if you need to go back to perform or complete a task.

The key tasks are organized and separated into chapters, where you will find details that explain how to do each task. Sub-tasks within each task are identified and they appear as sections or sub-sections within the chapters.

OK. That's the overview. Use it as a check-off list. Mark the page with a paperclip so that you can come back to it several times during your job search and make sure you are doing everything you should and doing it in the right order.

Now you've got the big picture and know what to do to make your job search a success. You're off and running! It's time to get at it.

Phase I – Separating

In this phase, there are two key tasks. First, you are going to have to deal with the shock of your job loss and the emotional challenges you will experience. Second, you need to take care of a variety of matters that are likely to be outstanding with your prior employer.

Chapter 1 – Deal with the Shock

Losing a job is typically a negative, emotional shock. It commonly leads to extreme personal and financial stress. The good news? I'm here to tell you I've yet to come across someone who didn't get through it. As a matter of fact, a large portion of the job seekers say it was the best thing that ever happened to them.

However, I don't want to minimize the emotional part of the transition you are probably going through right now. I want you to know there is nothing wrong with you and virtually all job seekers go through it. If I can explain to some small degree what typically happens, you will, hopefully, be able to cope better and get it behind you faster.

Professional psychologists will tell you the emotions you go through due to the loss of a job are much like those when you lose a loved one. They usually describe it as a set of emotions like shock, denial, anger, bargaining, and acceptance. You may not experience all these emotions. You may experience a different emotion. You may go through them in a different order. You may go through them quickly or slowly. The point is you are human and you are not likely to be immune to these emotions. It is OK to feel what you are feeling.

The trap you have to avoid is thinking there is something wrong with you. It is essential that you recognize the reason you were let go probably had nothing to do with you. The more likely reasons are the company was downsizing, profits were off, there was a merger, your boss wanted to bring in his/her team, or senior management had to find someone to blame. Tens of thousands of people are laid off in this country every day. Hiring managers, HR people, and recruiters know it and deal with people who were let go all the time. Every job seeker does find another job and there's no reason to believe your next job will pay less, have less prestige, or be less desirable to you.

The bottom line: Take it as it comes. Work your way through it. Stop looking backward as soon as you can. Be as positive as you can.

Learn to become as good at *searching* for a new job, as you were in *doing* your last job.

Chapter 2 – Separate Successfully from Your Last Employer

Very little is written about this activity. (I'm presuming you had a job and now you don't.) Many job seekers don't even think about it. They get terminated, think all the control and leverage rests with their last employer, and they roll over and play dead. As a job seeker, you have probably physically separated from your last employer and you're probably emotionally upset and mad. Stop..... Wait..... There's a bunch of things you need to look into and take care of through your last employer to make your separation successful.

(If it is too late by the time you read this chapter to do the things I suggest, just note the information presented here for the next time.)

Employer Benefits and Terms of Separation – Many states are "at will" states in regard to employing people. That is, unless there is an employment contract between your employer and you, your employer can terminate you at anytime, for any reason, and isn't under any obligation to give you a reason. Unless the employer has violated some law, such as the Americans for Disabilities Act or the discrimination laws, that's it. You have no recourse, except for what you can negotiate.

However, that doesn't mean you don't have anything coming. Severance is a good example. Virtually all large companies have a severance program. The amount of severance you get is typically related to how many years you worked for the employer and your base salary. Here's a list of pay and benefits to which you may be entitled to under your employer's human resource plan. Although not typically negotiable, the larger the employer, the more items you are likely to have coming to you. The smaller the company, the more likely you will be able to negotiate something.

Ideas

<u>Severance Pay</u> – This is cash you may be entitled to, if the company terminated you. If you resigned, you are not entitled to this, but you may be able to negotiate it.

<u>Base Salary</u> – You may think the last day you worked is the last day that you get paid. Well, it's not so black and white. Unless you were part of a mass layoff, it's going to be your boss who defines your last pay date and not the HR Department. This is particularly true, if you end up working for your prior employer for more than the standard two weeks. You may be able to negotiate your last paid date, which isn't necessarily your last work date.

<u>Commissions</u> – Part of your cash compensation may not have come from a base salary. You may have earned commissions as a consequence of sales you made. Commissions are commonly paid after-the-fact. Check your records to make sure you get all the commissions you already earned. You always want to read the terms of your commission program to determine whether you will have a right to commissions in weeks or months down the road.

<u>Unused Vacation</u> – Vacation is typically a benefit you earn by working. When you were terminated, you probably had accrued some vacation days that you hadn't taken. Because you already earned them, your prior employer will probably give you cash for those unused vacation days. Check your prior employer's benefits book to know for sure what you are entitled to.

<u>Health Insurance</u> – In 1985, the federal government established a program called **COBRA** (Consolidated Omnibus Budget Reconciliation Act). Basically, it requires that a group health care plan must offer health insurance coverage to each qualified individual, who would otherwise lose coverage due to termination of employment. You probably have the opportunity to elect to continue that coverage for a specified time period. That means your employer is likely to be

obligated to provide you with health insurance through its standard plan. The Act doesn't apply unless your employer has more than a minimum number of employees. The amount of time that your employer is obliged to do so is 18 months. In addition, you will have to pay the entire premium, plus perhaps 2%-5% administrative fee. As with most federal laws and acts, there are all sorts of exceptions and the devil is in the details. You'll have to research this for your employer's specific circumstances.

Use of Employer Resources – While employed, you were provided office space, administrative support, company cars, computers, in-your-home company assets, etc. by your employer. These resources are typically only offered to high-ranking officials of the company. However, for small items, your boss may have more latitude than you think to make something available for your personal use after your termination date.

Temporary Assignment – Although you may have a specific termination date, there still is likely work to be done and you may still be the best person to do it. You may be able to obtain a short-term assignment or an interim project assignment that will carry you for a few more weeks or months. This is more commonly the case when the requirement to terminate you was imposed upon your boss and he/she knows that there is still a lot of work that needs to be done.

A Referral Letter – Before leaving on your very last day, be sure to carry two to three letters of reference with you. Unless you were terminated for performance issues, you can often get a good reference from your boss. Other good candidates to ask for references are your colleagues, other managers, customers, and suppliers.

Outplacement Services – Many employers commonly pay for services provided by outplacement firms to employees they've laid off. If it is offered, be sure you understand the details, terms, and conditions in order to receive these services. If not offered, ask about it. If available, take advantage of these services.

For all the items above, there are two ways you are likely to obtain some benefits from your prior employer.

Action to Take – First, check if your employer has a standard plan that offers benefits to employees who have been terminated. Don't rely on the ex-boss or the HR Department to explain everything you've got coming. Get your hand on the current benefits package and/or personnel manual, read it, and become more of an expert on the terms and conditions than they are.

Action to Take – Second, negotiate whatever you can. Assume that everything is negotiable . . . . . and remember, if you don't ask, you definitely don't get.

Action to Take – If you are over 40, your employer is obligated to advise you to review the severance agreement with a legal counsel. Do so. Chances are good the document was written by a lawyer and the language is standard. However, for a fairly nominal fee, a good lawyer can give you some suggestions on what to ask for in the way of separation benefits and what, if any, statutes or laws may have been broken.

Your Employer Offers to "Allow" You to Resign, Instead of Terminate You (This is called "Constructive Discharge.") – Your first reaction might be to accept this offer. Having to tell anyone, much less show it on a resume or reveal in an interview, that you were terminated might sound ominous. But, be wary. By accepting this offer, you are probably giving up benefits that are based on government rules/laws, if not also your employer's rules. For example, as of this writing, employers are not obliged to provide health insurance through COBRA if you resign. Another example is state unemployment compensation. In most states, you do not qualify for benefits if you resign. (Again, the devil is in the details and there are all sorts of exceptions.)

Action to Take – The point is to think through this "offer" from your employer before you jump on it. Over the last 10-15 years, millions of people have been terminated. Many of them were good, competent employees and the reason they were terminated had nothing to do with them. Most employers these days know the environment and are comfortable hiring a person who was previously terminated.

Networking at Your Last Employer – In addition to benefits through your last employer, there is one other thing you need to do before you finally separate. That is to "network" with people within, and related to, your last organization. Examples of people to talk to are your colleagues, managers, customers, and suppliers. Tell them that you are leaving the organization and let them know what kind of job you will be looking for. Ask for their phones numbers, help, and referrals. Details on "How to Network" are provided in Chapter 13. Just remember that when you are terminated, you may not have many days to contact these people and it will be more effective and convenient to you if you jump on this right away.

Action to Take – (1) Become an expert on your employer's benefits and get everything to which you are entitled, (2) Negotiate / ask for other benefits, (3) Network, network, and network.

Caution

When you do these things, you are more than likely to be in a negative emotional state. You are probably upset, mad, and/or bitter because you were terminated. These are common and normal reactions. However, try to set these feelings aside during the last few days within your employer's organization. You're going to have to talk to a variety of people. You need their help, information, and advice. If all they get from you is a negative emotional reaction, they'll be less inclined to give you what you need. When you are completed separated, let your emotions out in the privacy of your home.

Public Benefits - There is another source of benefits for you and that is the unemployment compensation available through your state. The laws, rules, and procedures for any one state are complicated and the number of states makes it impossible to even try to summarize for you what your benefits might be. Suffice it to say that, if you are terminated, you likely are entitled to unemployment compensation.

Action to Take – You're going to have to contact your state agencies, talk to their representatives, figure out what you're entitled to, and play the game. It's a beast and again, the devil is in the details.

Phase II – Planning

This phase leads you to define the end result of a successful job search. If you don't know where you are headed, any road will seem okay!!! You may need to do some formal career planning and hold some informational interviews to define your desired job.

Chapter 3 – Develop a Career Plan

Do you have a clear idea of the kind of work you want to do?

Some job seekers, right out of the gate, know that they want to make a career change. My experience has been that the vast majority of job seekers do know the kind of work they want to do, at least at the start of the job search. Unless you just graduated, you are more than likely to want to do the same type of work you previously did. However, after a couple of months into the hunt, you may start asking yourself whether you might want to consider a career change.

Here are a couple of additional questions to help you decide:

- Can you say your 30-second commercial (described in "Promotional Material" in Chapter 7) with conviction and without variation?

- Are you able to fill out the "Job Desired" form (described in "Job Desired" Chapter 5) completely and easily?

If not, you need to seriously undertake a Career Planning effort. Career Planning is a mature process that many organizations offer. They test your capabilities, your aptitudes, and your preferences. They also have databases of job descriptions and salary information that give you insight into jobs you are considering. Because of the elaborate nature of the testing and personal counseling in this process, I recommend consultation with the professionals. There are many organizations that provide this service throughout the country. Here is a list of places and resources where you can obtain career planning.

- Government agencies (commonly provided for free)
- Private companies (typically not free)
- Your ex-employer's HR Department
- Your city/county library system
- College career centers
- Outplacement firms

There are also a variety of good books dedicated to this subject.

The result of this career planning process will be one, two, or perhaps three specific careers in which you are quite interested. You then research them more closely in the "real world" for confirmation of which one you will pursue.

Idea

There is a specific case that I need to address. That is the person who has worked for several years and has decided to make a career change. One very important and helpful thing a job seeker in this situation needs to do is to demonstrate to prospective employers how his/her experience and skills are "transferable" to the new career. This can be done more effectively by using a "functional" resume, which I discuss in Chapter 7.

When you have completed a formal Career Planning program, move on to Chapter 4, "Conduct Informational Interviews."

Chapter 4 – Hold Informational Interviews

Informational interviews are ones in which you are the interviewer. Your goal is to obtain information about jobs, industries, and specific companies to help you firm up your career plans. This is entirely in contrast to a job interview in which you are the interviewee and you're pursuing a specific job.

Career planning organizations, professionals, and books can provide you with a lot of good advice and information about a career you are seriously considering. However, after you start to focus on a specific career or two, you also need to get out and find out what those careers are really like. The best way to do that is to interview people who really know. Let me explain how to go about it.

Goal of the Informational Interview - First, you need to crystallize in you mind what the goal of an informational interview is. It is not to land a job. It is not to ask about a job. The goal of an informational interview is to obtain information about an industry and about a job type that will help you define your desired job. You're at the point where you have identified a type of job in which you are interested and may want to consider pursuing, but you need more information before you commit.

Prepare for the Informational Interview – The most important task is to prepare a list of questions that you will ask during the interview. During your career planning, you did research on a variety of industries, companies, and job types. During that research, you had questions in the back of your mind. You were looking for information that would give you insight. Start jotting down those questions all over again. Make them specific to the job type for which you're doing informational interviews.

Here are some subjects to consider for your list of questions for the interviewee.

- How did you get into this line of work?
- How do you spend your time, day to day, week to week?
- What words are used to describe the functions that you perform?
- What portion of time do you spend with other people? With machines? With materials?
- What particular work experience is required for this type of job?
- What special skills are required?
- What particular education is required?
- Are any specific certifications required?
- What personal characteristics are needed for this job? (high energy, very verbal, fast paced, analytical, etc.)
- Does a person with this type of job typically supervise other people?
- Does a person with this type of job typically manage a budget?
- What are the typical work hours & days?
- How much travel is required?
- What's the best thing about this type of job?
- The worst?
- What is the typical compensation structure? (base salary only, commission only, bonuses, or combinations thereof)
- What is the typical base salary range for this type of job?
- What are typical benefits? (health care, vacation time, use of company facilities)
- Where does this type of job lead, in terms of career advancement?
- What types of organizations typically have jobs like this?

<u>Who to Interview</u> – Here's a list of the type of people to interview, listed in the order of preference, with the best choice at the top of the list.

- People you <u>do not</u> know who currently do this type of job.
- People you <u>do</u> know who currently do this type of job.
- People who used to perform this type of job.
- People who manage the people who perform this type of job.

<u>How to Find People to Interview</u> – There are a variety of ways to do this.

- Tell everyone you meet that you are considering a particular type of job and you are currently researching it. Ask everyone you meet if they happen to know someone who performs that type of job. If they don't, ask them if they know someone who may know someone. If they name a person for you, ask them if they will call this person in advance, let them know that you will be calling them, and ask them to accept your call.
- Contact organizations that you think have the type of job that you are researching. If it is a reasonably large organization, ask for the HR Department. Tell them exactly what you are doing, what your motives are, and if they could refer you to someone.
- Go to seminars, trade association meetings, and professional organization meetings where you think people with this type of job may be.

<u>Setting Up the Informational Interview</u> – OK, so you've identified a person with whom want to do an informational interview. How do you get them to agree to meet with you?

Here's what you tell them:

- You were referred to him/her by _____ (name the person).
- What your recent situation has been. (1-2 sentences)
- You recently did some serious career planning. (1-2 sentences)
- You've decided to focus on a certain type of job, but that you're looking for insight from people who actually perform this job (or manage these people).
- You understand that he/she performs this type of job.
- You would like to meet with him/her for 20 minutes max, at a place of his/her choosing, to go through your list of questions.
- You know that he/she does not have a job opening to offer you.
- You will not ask about job opportunities.

Ask the person if you could meet with them on _____day or _____day. (Offer more than one day, three to four days down the road.)

If the person agrees to meet with you, you are all set. If not, he/she will verbalize a reason. Here's a list of possible reasons and what you say to overcome the objection.

Reason He/she Can't Meet with You	Your Response
I'm too busy.	That's fine. This is not urgent. How about if I call you next week and see if things have calmed down for you?
My employer isn't paying me to meet with job seekers.	[Referring person] said you are a very helpful person. How about if we meet for coffee, before work, or over lunch?

How about if we talk right now?	Well, we can. However, I do have a specific set of questions which I don't have with me. I would prefer to obtain my list and meet with you later when I can be prepared and effectively use your time.
We're not hiring and I don't know anyone who is.	Right now, I'm not seeking this type of job. I'm in a career planning mode and am hoping that you can help me understand the nature of this type of job, so that I can firm up which direction I want to take.
No, I don't do that kind of work.	Oh, I'm sorry. I was led to believe that you did. Any chance that you know someone who does?

If the person continues to object to meeting with you and you can't overcome the objections, express your appreciation, but *be absolutely sure that you ask the person if he/she could refer you to someone.*

Holding the Informational Interview – By now, hopefully, you think this is the easy part. Remember, you are the interviewer, not the interviewee.

Here is a list of "Must Dos" during the informational interview:

- Arrive on time.
- Be courteous to everyone you encounter, not just the interviewee.
- Be sure to take your list of questions out of your pocket so that it can be seen.
- If you are not finished when the 20 minutes is up, tell the interviewee that 20 minutes is up and that you intend to honor your promise not to take more than 20 minutes of his/her time. More than likely, the interviewee is going to tell you it is OK for you to stay. Otherwise, leave.

- When you are out of questions, tell the interviewee such and express your appreciation for his/her time.
- Ask the interviewee if he/she has any final thoughts / advice for you.
- Ask the interviewee if he/she could suggest another person who does this job that might be willing to meet with you. If yes, ask the interviewee if he/she would be willing to contact that person in the next couple of days and let them know that you will be calling him/her.
- Ask for the interviewee's business card. Shake hands and leave.

Do <u>not</u>, under any circumstances, ask about the existence of any job opportunities. This would be a violation of the basis on which you set up the meeting. You are likely to be escorted out early, if you ask about job opportunities.

<u>Follow-Up After an Informational Interview</u> – Never think of a meeting with a person as the "be-all-end-all," extent of your relationship with that person. Your goal is to establish relationships with people, so that they will remember you, so that you may contact them again in the future. This takes follow-up work.

Follow-Up by doing these things:

- Send the person a thank you note within 24 hours of the meeting. Handwritten thank you notes are much more preferable to typed ones. Typed ones are much better than emails. Emails are OK, unless you have reason to believe the person is computer illiterate or would frown on an email.

- The note should:
  - Thank the interviewee for meeting with you, answering your questions, and everything else that he/she did for you, which might include giving you advice or giving you a referral.
  - Also, refer to comments made by the interviewee during the meeting.
  - Tell him/her what your next steps will be.

- Consider adding this person to your list of people to periodically notify about your job search progress, including when you land a job, even if you do not end up taking a job that you talked to him/her about.

- Send a thank you note to the person who referred you to the interviewee. Tell them that you did meet with the person, what transpired, and what your next steps will be.

Chapter 5 – Define Your Desired Job

The point of this chapter is simple. You must take time to write down the definition of your desired job.

I can hear you already. You're thinking "That's easy" or "My resume already says it." Not true. You will find that your resume only answers about three of the roughly 18 questions that I'll provide you that people will ask you about the kind of job you want. Typically, only 5%-10% of a resume explicitly indicates the kind of job a person wants to do. Also, your resume primarily describes what you did in the past. By default, it is assumed that you want to do the same kind of work in the future that you did in the past. If that is the case, it is helpful . . . . . but what if you want to make a change?

There are very good reasons to write down the definition of your desired job:

- You need to have prepared answers when someone asks you what your desired job is. You don't want to be ad-libbing when they ask.

- It will help you prioritize during your job search. You will, hopefully, encounter a handful of advertised or posted jobs at any one time which you think might be interesting. Compare them to the description of your desired job and pursue the ones that match it the best.

- Suppose you are lucky enough to have two job offers. How will you know which one to pick? You may think that it is simply the one that offers the biggest paycheck, but it may not be that simple. It is unlikely that the two jobs are exactly the same in all aspects. If you are in this situation, you don't want to be glib about making this decision. While you may consult with others, it would be best to fall back on your description of your desired job. *Your* opinion is the most important one.

• The description of your desired job might change, possibly more than once, during your job search. That's OK. However, you need to explicitly acknowledge to yourself it is changing and adjust your search, accordingly.

You need to write down the definition of your desired job.

Do it Now!!!

The good news is that I've provided a framework for you to do so. Refer to Appendix A. It's a document named "Form – Your Desired Job." Sit down in a quiet setting and fill it out. It comes with instructions that will tell you how to fill it out and, perhaps more importantly, how to use it.

After trying to fill out the form, you may conclude you are not able to define the job you want. This may be because you have many different ideas. It may be because you are planning a career change. In that case, get some career planning advice. It may be because you just don't have the information. In that case, arrange some "Informational Interviews" (described in Chapter 4).

Chapter 6 – Define Your Desired Compensation and Benefits

The point of this chapter is simple. Take the time to write down the definitions of your desired compensation and benefits.

I can hear you already. You're thinking "as much money as I can get" and "as many days off as I can get." . . . . . Wrong . . . . . You do not want to settle for too little and, in fact, you don't want too much (because it won't last when they find out the mistake they made).

There are a couple of very good reasons to write down the definition of your desired compensation and benefits:

- You need a basis of comparison for offers that you get.

- You need to be very clear about your desires in your mind and in the words that you speak when negotiating compensation and benefits, after an offer is received.

- You need to be fairly specific to ensure that your expectations are close to local the job market's level and trend.

You need to write down the definition of your desired compensation and benefits.

Do it Now!!!

The good news is that I've provided a framework for you to do so. See Appendix B. It's a document named "Form – Your Desired Compensation and Benefits." Sit down in a quiet setting and fill it out. It comes with instructions that will tell you how to fill it out and, perhaps, more importantly, how to use it.

After trying to fill out the form, you may find that you are unable to fill out all the parts. In that case, you need to do some research. Arrange some "Informational Interviews" (described in Chapter 4) and/or search the Internet for facts.

Phase III - Preparing

Prepare, prepare, and then prepare some more. This phase addresses creating the promotional materials that you need, improving your job searching skills, and getting help for your search.

Chapter 7 - Develop Your Promotional Materials

I know what you are thinking. What else do I need other than a resume? The answer is multiple documents, including: (P=Paper version, E=Electronic version, V=Verbal version)

- A. Resume (P and E)
- B. T-Letter (Cover Letter for a Specific Job) (P)
- C. Marketing Plan (P)
- D. Cover Letter (No Specific Job) (P)
- E. Thank You Note / Letter (P)
- F. Job Interview Follow-Up Letter (P)
- G. Your 30-Second Commercial / Elevator Speech (E and V)
- H. Business Card (P)
- I. Your References (P)
- J. Portfolio of Your Work Examples (P)
- K. Your Performance Appraisals (P)

The good news is that you won't have to develop these materials from scratch. I've provided examples of most of them in the appendices.

I'll take them on one-by-one in the rest of this chapter.

A. Resume

I believe that most job seekers put too much emphasis and confidence on the resume. I'm not saying that you should forget about your resume. Just don't believe that using a resume is the best way to get a job, or that waiting for someone to read your resume and decide to interview you is a good idea, or that the amount of information that you put in your resume is all that important. I will spend several pages providing details about what your resume should include and look like. However, I am concerned about reinforcing your preconceived impression of the high importance of a resume. At best, I think it is the second most important piece of promotional material for your job search. (A T-Letter is more important than a resume. More on that in the next section.)

Let's start with purpose. What is the purpose of a resume? It is specifically one thing: To get you an interview. Its purpose is not to lay out your employment history. It's not to brag about everything that you accomplished. If you're not getting interviews, it's your resume. When a hiring manager reads your resume, you want him/her to think "I've got to get this person in here and find out what he/she is like." That's the trick. You need to provide enough information to get that reaction without trying to answer all the hiring manager's questions with your resume.

There are basically two types of resumes: the chronological type and the functional type. The chronological one is the most common. Most HR people and hiring managers want to see the chronology of your work experience. A functional resume is a better way to go when you are planning to make a career change. What I am going to propose to you is a blend of the two, leaning towards the chronological.

Resume size is a controversial subject. I've heard all sorts of opinions from "Keep it to one page" to many pages are OK for a person with 25+ years of experience. I'm biased. One page is not quite enough. The reader will think that you have not done enough (even if you just graduated from college). More than two pages is not only a waste of your time, it also provides more information upon which the reader can screen you out. One and a half pages are just right. Remember, your resume is a piece of sales literature. Did you ever spend more than two to three minutes reading a sales brochure? Of course not. If you can't capture the reader's attention with one and a half pages, you're either missing the point of the resume or you need writing skills enhancement.

Resume content is fairly straightforward. You've probably seen or used the standard content before. Here are the primary sections that you should include:

- Your Identification and Contact Information
- Your Profile / Professional Summary
- Employment Record
- Education
- Special Skills, Certifications, Awards
- Associations / Professional Memberships

The names of the sections are not critical. The above sequence is best for a variety of reasons which will become apparent in the next few pages. If your Education is your best attribute, then place it before your Employment Record.

Here is material that you can optionally include:

- Your community involvement
- A statement like "Additional details are available." If you have a long career, such as 20 years or more, you do not need to cite your oldest employers and jobs. If you don't, include a statement like this one in quotes so that you cannot be accused of covering something up.

Here is a list of things that you definitely should <u>not</u> include:

- Your list of references. Don't even include a sentence that says "References are available upon request." Everyone presumes that already.

- Any reference to an organization you belong to that is oriented towards a specific religion, race, ethnic background, age, or anything else that you expect employers not to use as a basis for discrimination.
- Never, never, never include anything about your past compensation.
- Reasons why you left an employer. (Don't worry. They'll ask during the interview and you can explain it then.)

OK, I've moved down to the <u>details</u> of what appears in your resume. Where do they come from? Well, it shouldn't be too hard putting together a list that describes your education. You can probably also list the organizations that you have worked for and maybe even the specific jobs that you had.

However, the second most important thing that you should include in your resume is a list of your accomplishments. If you're one of those rare folks who have been maintaining a list of your <u>accomplishments</u> over the last five, ten, or twenty years, then pull it out. If you're not one of those folks, then start the habit when you start your next job. (More than likely, you will look for a job one or two more times in your life.) Given that you don't have a list now, pull out a piece of paper (a computer is even better) and begin making your list. Each accomplishment should be one to three sentences. Here is a list of tips for writing them:

- Focus on accomplishments, not responsibilities / duties.

- Avoid first person (I) or third person (he/she) references. Start each sentence with an action verb in past tense. Examples are "Developed," "Implemented," and "Raised." Use of verbs reveals that you are a person of action.

- Use sentences structured around "PARs." First, describe the (P)roblem. Then, describe the (A)ction that you took. Finally, describe what good (R)esults occurred because of what you did. Boil the PARs down to one or two sentences.

- Quantify absolutely as much as you can. State dollars, volumes, ratios, percentages, or any number that indicates the magnitude of what you did, how often you did it, and the favorable results. Don't be afraid to estimate or give ranges.

- Avoid using uncommon technical terms or mnemonics, unless you are absolutely sure that hiring managers will know what you are talking about.

All right, it's time to fill out your resume. I've concluded that a large portion of job seekers get hung up on resume format and trying to type into a computer. To overcome this, I've provided a document called "Form – Resume Template." (See Appendix C.) This is a template in which the structure and format are already laid out for you. It includes a variety of explanatory information and placeholders for you to insert your own information. Now, I'll walk you through each piece of information and explain what to include. Follow along.

Your Identification and Contact Information – Include this in the document heading that should appear on each page. Use your official name. If you go by a common nickname (like "Jim" for "James"), then put that in parentheses after your official first name. I've seen a lot of job seekers using special fonts and styles to make their name stand out. Maybe design it in a somewhat larger font, but don't get too carried away with this.

Put your address on the second line and your phone number on the third line. If the phone number you provide is where you are still employed, then change the word "Home" to "Work." If you want a caller to be discrete as to why he/she is calling, then keep the word "Confidential."

Include your email address. Make sure it is a professional sounding one. (Believe it or not, we had a woman join our job seeker group who used the email address "SexyBaby" for her job search. That may have gotten her some interviews, but maybe not for the job she was seeking!)

Enough with the heading. Check out the footer. Include your name and phone number. Yes, again. You want the reader to be able to find you easily. (It's not uncommon for copy machines and fax machines to not handle paper perfectly and either the top or bottom of a page gets cut off.)

Profile / Professional Summary – I previously told you what the second most important section of your resume is. This is *the* most important. Why? Because you've got 10-15 seconds to catch the reader's attention. If the reader doesn't think he/she wants to interview you in 10-15 seconds of reading, your resume goes into the "B" pile. Picture this image. You're the HR or external recruiter responsible for filling a job. You advertised it and now you have 100 resumes piled up in front of you. How much time do you think you're going to spend on each one? That's why you, the job seeker, have 10-15 seconds to catch the reader's attention.

Another title option is "Career Summary." Pick something that fits your circumstances and implies a "summary."

Include a job title that best represents the type of position that you are seeking. If there two common ones, then include both, separated by a slash. Here's an example: **CFO / Controller**. If may be unfair, but everyone who reads your resume wants to put you in a box. They're asking themselves "What are you?" So tell them. They've got a job with a title. They are looking for a near-immediate confirmation that you are, or at least close to, what they need. On one hand, you need to be specific. On the other hand, if you're too specific, you may get screened out. Here's an example of possibly being too specific. Suppose your title at your previous employer, which was a very small company, was "VP Marketing." Also suppose you are applying for a job with a huge company. Maybe at that large company, you fit best into a different title. (Vice versa is, of course, an issue, too.) If you are applying to both small and large companies, you may want to use multiple job titles like "VP, Director, or Manager of Marketing."

Now, fill in the paragraph right after the job title. Put three to six sentences here that summarize what you do, the kind of work that you have done, and your key strengths and/or accomplishments. Where can you get good ideas for this paragraph? Go back and read over your accomplishments. Go back and read "Your Desired Job" form. (You did fill it out, didn't you?)

Do not use the term "job objective." (I see this a lot on the resumes of new and recent graduate students. The college career centers must be teaching this.) Candidly, no one cares what your job objective is. In this section, you've got to tell the readers what you can do for them. Their job is not to help you satisfy all your needs and wants.

Under that paragraph are two four-item bulleted lists. These are key words and phrases that describe what you have done, what you are capable of, and special skills that you have, all of which the reader is looking for. You probably used some in the paragraph above. There are likely to be more. If your resume gets scanned, then the employer's computer probably does electronic searches for key words and phrases. Type these in here. Examples are Black Belt, Project Management, Customer Service Oriented, Microsoft Office Expert, Benefits Administration, Staff & Line Responsibility, Inventory Control, Fashion Design, Fluency in German, and Direct Marketing. If these key words and phrases occur later in you resume, that's fine. Just make sure they also appear up here in the "summary" section, as well.

It is essential that you rid yourself of the thought that you have one, and only one, resume. When applying for a specific job, you must customize the resume around that job. (Fortunately, with computers this is fairly easy.) One way to customize it is to leave the last four to five sections intact and modify the Profile / Professional Summary to include things that you have done or accomplished that will help convince the reader that you are qualified for the specific job for which you will be sending in the resume. One way to perceive and do this is to read the job description and requirements closely and include in your resume your experiences and accomplishments that qualify you for the job. Remember, you will only get the interview if the reader believes that you can fulfill the specific business need. Generic resumes do not typically do that.

Employment Record – This section should list your jobs in reverse chronological order.

> Your Prior Employers – Include the city and state where you worked, not the employer's home office. Include "from" and "to" dates. (If you don't, it will be interpreted suspiciously.) Month and Year are sufficient. If you are still employed, use "To Date" as the end date. If there has been a long time since you last worked, don't worry. It bothers you more than the recruiter or the hiring manager. There is a debate out there among job seeking advisors as to how to handle gaps in the dates from employer to employer. I tend to be less concerned about having a resume with gaps. Given the millions of people who have been laid off in the last 10-20 years, I think recruiters and hiring managers see this all the time and hire people with gaps. Finally, do not include reasons why you left an employer. (Don't worry. They'll ask during the interview and you can explain it then.) If you feel that it is valuable to describe the primary business of an employer, then keep it to a few short words or a phrase, like "multi-billion dollar manufacturer." This section needs to focus on you and less on your prior employers.

> Job Titles – Put the specific job title that you had here. It is not necessary to show different levels (like Analyst I, Analyst II, Analyst III), unless you conclude that it is important to show job progression. Write a sentence or two that describes the respon-

sibilities and duties you had for this job. Be careful not to write too much here. Hiring managers are more interested in your "Accomplishments" than your responsibilities and duties. It is not necessary, but certainly OK, if you want to include start and end dates for a job.

Accomplishments – Indented under each job is where you type your accomplishments. The minimum number to show for a job is two. Avoid listing more than five, if you have more than one employer or job to cite. Again, this is the second most important part of your resume. Spend lots of time thinking about which accomplishments to include and how to word them. Again, quantify as much as possible. Write the statements as PARs. Keep each accomplishment to at most two sentences.

Education – List your education in reverse chronological order, too. If you did not go to college, that's OK. List your high school. Name degrees and/or diplomas earned. If you graduated, include the date. If you did not, remove the word "graduated" and the date and include the words "In Progress" or "Not Completed." Most employers (definitely the large ones) now do background checks. They will contact your college(s) and confirm whether or not you graduated. If you didn't and you do not include the words "In Progress" or "Not Completed," some prospective employers will allege that you misrepresented your education on your resume. In addition to naming your major area of study, you can also list key achievements during your education, such as papers published or awards, to the extent that they are relevant to the job for which you are applying.

This is also a good section to list classes, seminars, and/or formal education that you attended / received while you were employed.

If your education is a key part of what you have accomplished or a special degree is critical for the job you are applying for, then it is OK to put the Education section before the Employment Record section.

<u>Special Skills / Certifications / Awards</u> – Describe and/or list anything here that an employer would consider valuable. Example skills are technical, language, and public speaking. Example certifications are CPA, 6-Sigma Black Belt, and CE.

<u>Associations / Professional Memberships</u> - Describe and/or list organizations you lead or are a member of. If you have an official capacity in the organization, such as treasurer, indicate so. If you lead or are a member of an organization that would contribute to your job performance, name it for sure. If you lead or are a member of an organization that reflects your virtues or character, then consider naming it. If you lead or are a member of an organization that is racial, national origin, gender, age, etc. specific or restrictive, don't name it.

Here are a bunch of tips for writing your resume:

- Avoid the trap of putting large amounts of unrelated items in your resume with the intent of spreading a wide net. People who read such resumes cannot get a good idea of what you do and will put your resume in the "B" pile.

- Avoid the format that places the section titles down the left hand side of the pages. It creates too much white space that you should use for your accomplishments. Then again, if you just graduated and have little or no work experience, use that format.

- When complete, use your computer's spelling and grammar checker. (Then, have someone who is good with English check your resume. Computers still don't catch everything.)

- Unless your profession is in graphics arts, use standard paper (white, 8 ½ by 11, 20-24 pounds), without special designs or folds. Use black ink, standard fonts, etc.

- When you think you have completed your resume, go back and read what you wrote in the "Your Desired Job" form. Seriously ask yourself whether this resume will help you get that job. Do the things you wrote in your resume convince the reader that you can handle "your desired job?" If not, go back and revise your resume, accordingly.

When you've finally completed your resume (that is, it is at least version 3, you're convinced that it will help you get "your desired job," and you're happy with it), it's time for you to get some feedback. Send/give a copy to at least five people experienced in hiring people or advising job seekers and ask them to review your resume. At the same time you give them a copy of your resume, give them a copy of "Your Desired Job" form. They should evaluate your resume in light of the job you want. Now, the first thing you need to know is that when you ask five people for feedback, you will get five different responses. Don't be deflated by that. Listen closely to what they say and identify those few suggestions that all of them made in common. Those are the important changes that you should make to your resume.

Preparing Your Resume for the Email or the Internet – There are several cases in which you will need a special version of your resume to use on the Internet, including:

- A recipient person or organization who will not accept attachments.
- You need to paste your resume into an Internet-based application that doesn't accept formatting.
- You need to paste your resume into the body of the text of an outgoing email.

The problem goes like this. Word processing programs, like Microsoft Word, are marvelous at creating documents with formatting that varies from paragraph to paragraph, even from word to word. Examples of formatting are font size, underlining, italics, and indenting. However, many computer systems still will not accept electronic documents with special formatting. Hence, you need a version of your resume that does not have any special formatting. The easiest way is to create one right after you complete your resume in your favorite word processing program. "Save" your resume as a new document in "text" format. This, by itself, will remove the bulk of the formatting. However, go through it line by line and word by word and remove any formatting remnants that might be left over. In particular, you will need to add manual blank lines where you want them.

My final suggestion about your resume is to get rid of the thought that you have only one resume. I mentioned this before and it warrants repeating. It is essential that you customize each resume that you send out when applying for a specific job. The good news is that with computers, it is fairly easy to customize a resume. In addition, I structured the "Resume Templates" to facilitate customization. I suggest that you focus on modifying the "Profile / Professional Summary" section for a specific job and add, enhance, or delete accomplishments as you determine is appropriate.

B. T-Letter

Far, far <u>more important</u> than the resume is the T-Letter. Why? Well, here is the most common scenario. If you're like most job seekers, you identify a job that you're interested in applying for. The source is almost always an advertisement or a posting on some job board. It says to send your resume to a certain place (usually the HR Department). You make a copy of your "standard" resume, write up a "standard" cover lever, and drop the material in the mail or send it through the Internet. At the other end, a person receives your cover letter and resume, along with probably a couple hundred other resumes. (Don't worry. 95% aren't qualified for the job. I'll talk more about that later.) Now, this person's job is to screen out the 95% and he/she has only been given a couple of days to do this (and this is just one of the jobs that he/she is working on). This person is more than likely an internal or external recruiter, who doesn't know anything more about the job than you do. (If you're really unlucky, the person is a recent college graduate who is still green behind the ears and doesn't have any idea what a good resume looks like.) This screener grabs a resume off the pile of a couple hundred resumes, probably ignores your cover letter, and spends 15-30 seconds scanning your resume to determine if you're qualified for the job. Imagine, your future is in the hands of this person!!!

How do I know they only spend 15-30 seconds on your material? Because I've met many of them and that's what they tell me.

You don't want to depend upon someone else to determine if you are qualified for a job. How do you avoid it? Develop a T-Letter. Here's how.

> **Procedure**

Before sending any material, read the job description closely. Write down the four to six key requirements of the job. Then, for each of those four to six requirements, write down your qualifications. Incorporate this into your cover letter. (Note: As stated in the section on writing your resume, it will be a good idea to customize your resume for this specific job.)

Good news. I've provided such an electronic document in Appendix D. Its name is "Form – T-Letter Template." Look it over, create one, and send that off, along with your resume. You will find that the percentage of time that you get a response to your material will be three to four times higher than if you don't use a T-Letter.

While it is acceptable in today's world to send such a letter via email, the reader recognizes that it takes more of your time and effort to print the letter, put it in an envelope with a stamp, and take it to the post office. Doing so will suggest to the reader that you really are interested in his/her organization and that will increase the chance that he/she will meet with you.

C. <u>Marketing Plan</u>

This is the third most important document for a job seeker. It is needed because your resume doesn't answer (and you don't want it to answer) some basic questions about the kind of job and employer that you are seeking. Examples of these questions are:

- Where do you want to work?
- What type of employment situation are you looking for?
- What size of employer do you want?
- How much travel are you willing to do?
- What specific companies are you targeting?

The point of the Marketing Plan is to answer these and other basic questions and provide a description of the kind of job and employer that you are seeking for the people who are willing to help you in your job search.

I provided a template in Appendix F. It identifies what to include in your Marketing Plan. Customize the content and/or format to your circumstances. (Be sure to delete the "instructional" information in the template before you use it.)

Your Marketing Plan explains the focus of your search. By deduction, it also describes what you're not willing to consider. By inference, if you don't rule it out, you would consider it.

This causes a dilemma. On one hand, you need to focus your job search. By the same token, the more you restrict the kinds of work and employers you're willing to consider, the longer your job search is likely to be. You need to find the right balance. You also may find that, over time, you need to make your Marketing Plan more flexible or more restrictive. Time will tell.

Work hard to keep it to one page. If you run over one page, you are providing your helpers with too much information. You will either confuse them or they will forget most of it.

How do you use it? You give it to people who are willing to help you with your job search. This includes your spouse, relatives, friends, neighbors, other members of groups that you belong to, and, arguably the most important, networking contacts that you make. Specifics on how to use it are provided in Chapter 13 on "Networking."

D. Cover Letter to a Target Company (When No Specific Job Has Been Identified)

While it is common to apply for specific jobs, there are going to be specific organizations that you want to work for. You target them, even if you are not aware that they currently have a job you are interested in. You do some networking and identify a person (preferably a hiring manager, rather than an HR person) within the organization you'd like to meet with. This person does not need to have a job for you or even be familiar with the function that you perform. While you could call him/her on the phone and ask for an interview, more than likely, you will be inclined to send him/her an introductory cover letter.

Below are the key paragraphs that you need to include in such a letter. I've provided a template in Appendix E. You may want to look at that as you read this explanation of the paragraphs.

Paragraph #1 – Explain why you are sending the person a letter. This is typically because you want to work for his/her organization and you are looking for information and help. (2-3 sentences)

Paragraph #2 – Explain what you want from the person. This typically requests information about the organization and help as to how to land a job there. When the person reads the letter, he/she is going to think that you are going to press them for a job. This will make them resist meeting with you. You need to defuse this thought, so also include a sentence that effectively says you know he/she doesn't have a job for you (literally). (2-3 sentences)

Paragraph #3 – Provide information about your work experience. Include a job title and your career profile statements from your resume. If you can keep it brief, describe some of your key accomplishments. (4-6 sentences or lines)

Paragraph #4 – Explain what you will do next to arrange to meet with the person. (Do not expect the other person to take the next step. If you do, it will never happen.) (1-2 sentences)

Paragraph #5 – Express your appreciation for the other person's time and consideration. (1 sentence)

It is important that you keep this letter brief and one page in length. Remember, the other person is only going to spend a minute or two on your letter. You've only got that much time to catch his/her attention. The goal of this letter is to arouse the interest of the reader enough that they would be willing to meet with you. (Remember, this is not an interview, since there is no known job.)

Most job seekers will be inclined to attach their resumes to this type of cover letter. *Don't do it*. The detail in your resume will give the reader a basis for not meeting with you, either because he/she finds something in your resume to screen you out, or because he/she is not familiar with the type of work you do. You can take your resume to the meeting and leave it as your sales brochure if you determine that it is appropriate.

While it is acceptable in today's world to send such a letter via email, the reader recognizes that it takes more of your time and effort to print the letter, put it in an envelope with a stamp, and take it to the post office. Doing so will suggest to the reader that you really are interested in his/her organization and that will increase the chance that he/she will meet with you.

E. <u>Thank You Note / Letter</u>

You absolutely must write and send a thank you note / letter every time someone meets with you or gives you something (including just information). It doesn't make a difference whether the meeting was an interview for a job, an informational interview, or a networking meeting.

Every job seeker needs and should want to distinguish him/herself from the other job seekers. An easy way to distinguish yourself is to write a thank you note / letter. As a hiring manager, I interviewed 35-40 people over a two year period. Of those people, only four sent thank you notes. I remember who those people are to this day. I hired one of them. It seems as though thank you notes / letters have gone out of fashion. When you send one, you will be distinguishing yourself for sure.

As there are a variety of cases in which you need to send a thank you letter, it is a challenge to develop a generic example that might apply to most situations. However, I have provided one sample in Appendix G. Look that over as I describe the contents.

Paragraph #1 - Open with a statement of appreciation. Briefly describe what the other person did for you. Also reference when it occurred, like "last Tuesday."

Paragraph #2 – Describe something specific that the other person suggested that you should do, what you did or will do, and the outcome. This will reassure that person that you were listening and followed through. This will help convince the person that he/she didn't waste personal time with you and will be inclined to respond to you if you contact him/her again.

Paragraph #3 – Include a sentence or two about what you will do to sustain your relationship with that person. It may be as simple as keeping the other person appraised of your job search process. It may be that you let them know when you land a job. It may be that you will see them at someone's graduation party in a couple weeks.

Paragraph #4 – Include a sentence or two that indicates that you would be glad to return the favor.

Paragraph #5 – Re-express your appreciation.

The thank you note / letter does not need to be long. In fact, avoid making it too long and keep it to one page.

The thank you note / letter needs to be sent promptly, best within 24 hours, 48 hours at the max.

The job seeker who I've come across who best handled thank you notes / letters was a middle aged woman who joined our job seeker group. She carried thank you note paper with her in the car. After the interview, she wrote the thank you note in her car before leaving the parking lot. On the way home she stopped at the post office and dropped it off. That ensured that the note arrived quickly and impressed the recipient even more.

While it is acceptable in today's world to send such a note / letter via email, the recipient recognizes that it takes more of your time and effort to print the letter, put it in an envelope with a stamp, and take it to the post office. Doing so will suggest to the reader that you really are interested in his/her organization and that will increase the chance that he/she will sustain a relationship with you.

To get an even more favorable reaction from the person, handwrite the thank you note. If you do, use one of those smaller cards and envelopes. It will distinguish itself in the person's in-basket when it arrives and they will read it as soon as they see it.

F. Job Interview Follow-Up Letter

Within a couple days of a job interview, you <u>must</u> send a letter to <u>each</u> person who interviewed you. The one that goes to the hiring manager is a special one and is described in detail in this section. More than likely you interviewed with two or three other people on the day of the interview with the hiring manager. Some may have been your potential boss's peers, your potential boss's boss, your potential peers, or an HR person. To those other people, you can send the more-generic thank you note / letter that I described in the previous section. However, don't hesitate to reference specific subjects that came up during the interview with these other people.

The follow-up letter to the hiring manager is special because it alone may move you to the top (or keep you at the top) of the candidate list in the hiring manager's mind. This is something you need to spend a couple hours on. Because of other diversions (hopefully, other interviews), it may take you two to three days to get it well-written and into the mail. If it takes that long, that's OK. However, if that is the case, send a thank you note as I described in the previous section to the hiring manager within 24 hours. Include an extra paragraph that says that you will be sending a more elaborate follow-up letter within a couple of days.

```
Ideas
```

I've provided a follow-up letter to the hiring manager in Appendix H. Follow along as I explain the paragraphs.

Paragraph #1 – Open with a statement of appreciation to the hiring manager for meeting with you.

Paragraph #2 – This is the key section of the letter. You want to reference and elaborate on two to five subjects that came up during the interview. There can be a variety of objectives for this paragraph and the sub-bullets. You may want to reiterate your qualifications for what you now understand is the key part of the job. You may want to amplify your understanding of the job. You may want to enhance a response that you made during the interview that you feel was inadequate. (We all can think of better answers later.) Regardless, spend your time and best thinking on this section of the letter.

Paragraph #3 – State your high level of interest in the job and willingness to go to the next round, whatever that might be.

Paragraph #4 – Include a sentence or two that indicates the next step you will take in regard to landing the job. If the hiring manager told you what to do, state that. Otherwise, indicate that you will call him/her in about a week.

Paragraph #5 – Re-express your appreciation.

Here are a couple more specific ideas as to what to include in this type of letter.

- If, during the interview, the subject of examples of your work came up, consider attaching some to the letter and include a paragraph in the letter indicating such.

- If you have anything to offer the hiring manager (like a reference to another person who could help the hiring manager professionally or articles about his/her field or industry), definitely include that, too.

While it is acceptable is today's world to send such a letter via email, the recipient recognizes that it takes more of your time and effort to print the letter, put it in an envelope with a stamp, and take it to the post office. Doing so will suggest to the reader that you really are interested in his/her position and organization and that will increase the chance that he/she will take you to the next round.

G. Your 30-Second Commercial / Elevator Speech

Concepts

Let me explain the point of this. You use a 30-second commercial / elevator speech when you are hoping to get a referral to a person who may know someone who has a job for you. Your 30-second commercial / elevator speech is no small matter. More than likely, this is what will lead to your next job.

How does it come about? In the course of your job search, you will encounter a variety of people in informal circumstances. You may be at a picnic, a graduation party, a wedding, your card group, an association meeting, (or in an elevator), etc., etc. You find yourself standing / sitting next to someone you don't know. You introduce yourself and strike up a small-talk conversation with this unfamiliar person. Eventually, he/she asks you "And what do you do?" (If the other person doesn't ask, you ask that question first. He/she will answer and then ask you, if for no other reason other than out of personal courtesy.) This is no longer an informal situation. You are on the job. Your job is to get a referral to someone who can lead you to a job. This may be the person who has a referral for you.

The first few words out of your mouth have to catch the other person's attention before you bore him/her to death and he/she walks off. This isn't the time to ad-lib. You need to have two to four sentences prepared, memorized and at-the-ready. They will describe the kind of work that you do. (This is called your "30-second commercial" or your "elevator speech.")

An excellent source for the information for your 30-second commercial / elevator speech is your resume. Read through your "Career Profile" / "Professional Summary." Now, re-cast the information there into your normal, common, everyday language – the way you speak to people. Write it down. Polish it off. Memorize it. That's right. Memorize it. Again, when the opportunity comes to use it, you do not want to be ad-libbing.

Here are some real-world examples.

- "I run a business helping companies increase their revenue through strategic manufacturing alliances, market development, and cost cutting services. I am looking for senior contacts in chemical, polymer, and glass companies who want to utilize their core competencies more effectively."

- "I am a seasoned Customer Service Representative with extensive experience in the retail and collection industries. Throughout my education and prior employment, I have demonstrated strong communication skills, mathematical abilities, and have excellent experience in Microsoft Office applications. I have used this experience in the companies that I have represented to save time, make money, and improve overall company image. I am looking for a customer service managerial position in a company that would put my skills and education to good use."

- "I am a Human Resources Professional whose purpose is to satisfy shareholders, customers, and employees, thus leading organizations to profitability and continuous improvement. I possess demonstrated expertise in diverse disciplines, with specific emphasis on organizational development/ design; succession planning; performance management; compensation and position evaluation, employee relations, and human resource/asset management and retention. I partner with senior management to accelerate success."

- "I am a well-qualified professional with proven expertise in commercial credit and risk management within a sales based portfolio management environment. I have an MBA and 20 years of cumulative experience in this area. I am proficient with receivables management and the financial analysis of current and potential customers, with a special affinity for loss avoidance. Additionally, I have a demonstrated record of fostering positive customer relationships and account retention, as well as the capacity to grow the business through account acquisition. I am looking to employ these skills within the banking or manufacturing industries in the Cleveland / Akron / Canton area."

- "I manage analysts who determine what caused the past and predict the future." (This is called a "grabber" that's intended to prompt a question from the listener.)

- "I am in technical sales and sell equipment for making tires. I'm currently employed but am always interested in a good technical sales opportunity in manufacturing or a service company that sells to manufacturers. I have twelve years in the rubber industry and also have experience in the aerospace and automotive industries. Feel free to contact me. Here is my card."

- "I am a buyer/purchasing agent with experience in retail management, distribution and manufacturing environments. My organizational skills will keep inventory levels low. By negotiation with the vendors I have saved money and lowered the number of discrepancies. Communication with the sales staff led to increased sales and customer service."

- "I am a purchasing/supply chain senior manager who adds value by improving the total cost of goods sold. My achieved results have reduced costs by $10 million per year, which has produced a sustainable profitability for the company. I have been successful with automotive and aerospace corporations by creating a strategic seamless integrated supply system. I am looking for a senior level management position in supply chain management."

Concepts

Most of the example 30-second commercials above are long to be presented all at once. The less the listener is familiar with the kind of work you do, the shorter the opening of your 30-second commercial needs to be. A one sentence 30-second commercial is fine. Remember, <u>the goal of your 30-second commercial is to sustain a dialogue with the other person that, hopefully, leads to a referral to you.</u> Don't overwhelm the other person with details about your work that they can't relate to.

Please note: Your opening couple of sentences do <u>not</u> include anything saying that you are looking for a job. Remember, you're trying to create some dialogue with this other person.

Whatever you say should also be packaged to prompt a question from the other person for more information. The other person will respond with something. Most likely, it will be a question. If the question is seeking elaboration about what you do, great! Provide the information. However, at the end of your response, ask a question to keep the conversation going. Your question can be as simple as "Are you familiar with this kind of work?" or "Do you know others who do this kind of work?"

If the other person responds with the question "And who do you work for?" respond with "I'm looking to make a change to another employer." but, again, end with a statement that will prompt another response from the other person. Examples are "I've been focusing on the _____ _____ industry, but haven't identified any opportunities, yet." or "I'm trying to identify organizations that use these kinds of skills." Make a statement like one of those and give the other person a chance to respond. If the other person doesn't ask "And who do you work for?", then you ask him/her and the question will come back to you.

The longer you can keep the conversation going and the more questions the other person asks about you and what you do, the more chance that he/she will give you a referral.

```
Procedure
```

If and when you get the referral:

- First, express your sincere appreciation.
- Then, ask the person if, when you contact the person that he/she named, you can use his/her name.
- Better yet, ask the referring person if he/she would be willing to call the person he/she referred you to and tell them that you will be calling, so please take your call.
- After you contact the referral, let the referring person know that you did, what came of it, and re-express your appreciation.

If, in the course of the conversation, the other person doesn't offer a referral, then ask for it. A simple question like "Do you know of anyone who might be interested in a person who does this kind of work?" or "Can you refer me to someone who might know of anyone who is looking for a person with my background?" is all it takes.

Try out your 30-second commercial/elevator speech over the next couple of weeks. Listen closely to the kind of responses you get. If people don't understand it, are confused or turned-off, it doesn't generate a dialogue, or people just walk away, then recompose it.

Also, keep track of how well you think your 30-second commercial / elevator speech describes the kind of work that you do. If you're not sure or uncomfortable about what it says, you need to recompose it. If you go through several cycles of recomposing it, maybe you're not sure what kind of work you want to do and you should get some serious career planning.

Your 30-second commercial / elevator speech can also be used in an email. An email won't facilitate the dialogue that a face-to-face meeting will. However, there are going to be a variety of cases in which you send emails to people and it becomes clear that it's not appropriate to send them your resume. They don't want that much information. All they're looking for, or willing to accept and read, is something like your 30-second commercial / elevator speech. Type it up and have it ready to send in emails.

H. <u>Business Card</u>

Yes, job seekers should create, carry, and hand out business cards. Why? For a variety of reasons:

- Another person may ask for one.
- Most people have business card storage units, but not resume storage units. People are more inclined to pitch resumes,

because of their size. They will be more inclined to save your business card.

- Another person may want to pass it on to someone else.
- You may decide that it would not be effective to give someone a copy of your resume, but you want them to have your name and contact information.

What should be on your business card? The same types of information that you see on the business card of employed people. As a matter of fact, that's how you want it to look. Here's a brief list of what to put on your card:

- Your name
- Your contact information (phone #, email address, address, street, city, state zip)
- A job title that is common for the kind of work you want to do.
- Two to five key phrases or key words that identify what you do.
- A logo, an icon, or some abstract art or lines to enhance the appearance.

Here are some other tips about your business card:

- Don't go overboard with logos or designs, unless you are a graphics artist and you want to provide a small demonstration of what you can do.
- Put your name at the top in larger font than the other items on the business card.

- Spell out your whole name, unless you want to be called by your initials (like C.J.).
- Include your job title (the one you are seeking) under your name.
- Be sure to use a large enough font for all items that everyone can read. 12-point is best.10-point works OK, but 8-point is getting pretty small for a lot of people.
- Be sure not avoid words or pictures suggesting that you support or participate in any groups that restrict membership.
- The format / layout of the business card is not all that important. If you see 100 of them, you'll see 100 different layouts.
- Size is important. Make your business card 2 inches by 3 ½ inches. That way, it will fit in the standard storage boxes and folders that people already use.

If you can't overcome the urge to provide a lot of information, then use the back of the card.

Where can you get business cards? Check out the Internet. There are numerous sites that provide you the capability to design one on-line and provide 500 for free or a nominal amount. You can also find specially designed forms and software that allow you to develop a business card on your own computer.

Here are some examples of business cards for job seekers. (Note. They are not to the proper scale.)

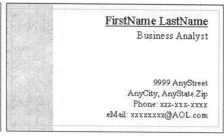

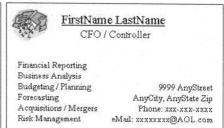

I. <u>Your References</u>

Concepts

Every job seeker knows about the need for references . . . . right? The time to develop this information is before you start looking for a job.

Who should your references be? The best choice is a person who previously had authority over you. That could be a boss, a teacher, an officer in an organization. Not only can these people testify as to what you can do and how well, but being able to cite them will reassure the people checking your references that you left your prior jobs on good terms. Other acceptable people to use as references are colleagues, customers, and suppliers. Do not include family members or relatives as references. No one will put any credence to references from people so close to you.

There are two types of reference material. One is a list of your references and one is a reference letter.

Let me start with the list of references. It needs to be more than a list of names. It needs to include contact information and a brief statement or two as to your relationship to the person referenced and what they can speak to as far as your background, skills, and capabilities. Two references is the bear minimum. More than four is an over-kill. Keep it to one page. Always have it at-the-ready.

A reference letter is much more valuable than merely naming a person and providing his/her contact information. The fact that someone was willing to take the time to write a letter and promote you enhances your value in the eyes and mind of the reader.

Here's what to ask the person to include in the reference letter:

Salutation – This is typically "To Whom It May Concern."

Paragraph #1 – An introductory statement indicating that the writer is providing a reference for you.

Paragraph #2 – A description of the relationship of the writer to you. This should include the circumstances, the organization, and time frame.

Paragraph #3 – This is the key paragraph. It should include the description of three to five things that demonstrate the writer's familiarity with your background, skills, and accomplishments. The more this information relates to the kind of work that you are seeking, the better.

Paragraph #4 – An explicit statement that recommends you to the reader. A simple example is "I highly suggest you consider _____ [insert your name] for jobs for which you feel he/she is qualified."

Paragraph #5 – This is an offer to the reader to contact the writer with additional questions about you. The person giving the reference needs to include his/her contact information in the letter.

You do not need to rely on the reference to compose the reference letter from scratch. Guide them through it. Review the list of above paragraphs with them. More importantly, explain to them the kind of work that you are looking for and how the work you did under their leadership is similar to that work to help reassure a potential hiring manager that you are qualified for the kind of job you want.

Just like all your other promotional material, carry your reference material every where you go.

Use your references and the material that you have from them, and about them, proactively to help you land a job. I elaborate on this in a Chapter 15.

J. Portfolio of Your Work Examples

During interviews, you will, of course, have to describe the kind of work you do. Better than describing is to show examples. Examples can be in the form of paper, physical props, or pictures of your work. If you're an artist, sculptor, graphics designer, or the like, it seems obvious that you should bring examples of what you produce, but here is a list of work examples for other types of jobs:

Job Type	Work Examples
Financial Analyst	Budgets, analyses, graphs
Salesman	Pictures of products

Purchasing Agent	Materials bought
Customer Service Rep	Printouts of computer screens that you used
General Managers	Organization charts of the groups that you managed
HR Generalist	Proposals that you wrote
Teacher	Pictures of bulletin boards, copies of lesson plans.

Example

The two best stories I ever heard about someone taking something to an interview go like this. The first one was about a high school teacher who took a brick to the interviews. When he walked into the interviewer's office, he took out the brick, set it on the desk/table, but he didn't say anything about it. Usually, the interviewer(s) would ignore it, but curiosity would get the best of them and by the end of the interview, they would ask what the point of the brick is. The teacher would then explain that the brick came from one of the buildings where the Kent State riots occurred in 1970. He would take the brick to his classroom when he discussed that event. This was an example of the way he made history "real" to the students.

The second story is about a middle school Spanish teacher. He developed a CD that he carried with him to interviews for teaching jobs. On the CD, he had placed a variety of Spanish lessons, Spanish vocabulary and grammar material, and links to web sites that taught Spanish and would serve as resources for students. For each school where he interviewed, he customized some of the material by adding the school's motto, mascot, or logo.

There is a valuable side-benefit to bringing examples of your work to an interview. I commonly hear job seekers express apprehension about talking about themselves during an interview. One easy way to get over that is to show the examples of your work. As soon as you do, you will find that you forget about yourself and start thinking about your work, as though the interviewer is already your boss. This will have an extremely positive effect on your comfort level and also how you are perceived.

K. Your Performance Appraisals

Most organizations do at least annual, written performance appraisals on each employee. (You saved copies of yours, didn't you?) Pull them out, read through them, and highlight what you consider key, positive comments. Create a separate file of those comments to pull out at an appropriate moment during interviews.

While performance review documents are an obvious choice, more than likely over your working career, you received some letters / notes of appreciation from customers, suppliers, colleagues, or other people you worked with, who were kind enough to take the time to express their appreciation for how you helped them or about the good work that you did. Pull them out, too and add them to the file.

Chapter 8 – Enhance Your Job Seeking Skills

```
┌─────────────────┐
│  Concepts       │
└─────────────────┘
```

After holding a job for a couple of years, you became pretty good at it. The job probably required five to ten different skills and, even if you hadn't mastered them yet, you were getting there. You need to start recognizing and thinking that searching for a job *is* a job. It requires a variety of skills and they're probably ones that you haven't developed much. More than likely, you need to get some training and practice with these skills.

What are these skills?

- Communicating verbally
- Communicating in writing
- Selling yourself
- Using a computer
- Identifying jobs, companies, and networking contacts
- Networking
- Interviewing
- Negotiating

While I will explain how to perform most of these skills in later chapters, this chapter is devoted to giving you ideas as to how to become proficient at them.

While practicing is the only way to master anything, there's a lot to be said for formal training. Go through this list of skills, evaluate yourself, and have another person evaluate you, too. Use a simple evaluating scheme such as 5 = a strength, 4 = Above average, 3 = Average, 2 = Below average, 1 = a weakness. For those skills which are a weakness for you, get some formal training. Formal training can be obtained through courses, seminars, one-on-one sessions, or books.

```
Ideas
```

Here are some specific ideas for how to enhance these skills.

Communicating Verbally – This is absolutely the most difficult skill to develop. It seems like some people are born with it and some die without it. While there may be some formal courses out there to help you, the best thing you can do is to ask for candid feedback from people who know you and know the types of communication which are needed in your job. Your prior bosses, colleagues, customers, and suppliers are good choices of people who might be willing to give you feedback.

Here is a starting list for questions to ask them:

- Do you speak too much or too little?
- Do you speak too fast or too slowly?
- Is your English grammatically correct?
- If English is your second language, is your accent so strong that you are hard to understand?
- Do you seem to be able to focus on a specific subject or do you seem to wander all over the place?
- Do you get too personal or do you get too cut and dried?

Communicating in Writing – This is arguably the form of communication that is the second most difficult skill to develop. Again, while there may be some formal courses out there to help you, the best thing you can do to enhance your writing skills is to read good examples of resumes, cover letters, and all of those other job seeking documents. I've gotten you started by providing a variety of them in the appendix. Look them over. Read them closely, out loud. Use various sentences, phrases, and key words in unique documents that you create.

One important thing you need to acknowledge about this subject is that I am not just talking about correspondence that you put in the mail. I'm also talking about emails. For every correspondence that you put in the mail, you will probably send 10-20 emails. The fundamental problem I commonly see in emails is that wording tends to be informal and abbreviated. While that is fine for personal emails, you want to make sure your job seeking emails sound professional and are complete with the relevant information. In general, approach composing an email in the same manner you would a letter. However, there are also some aspects of emails that are unique and do not apply to correspondence. Here are some specific suggestions and a variety of tips.

1. Use the "To" box for those people whom you expect to take action. Use the "CC" (courtesy copy) box for those people who may benefit from the email content, but are not required to take action. Use the "BC" (blind copy) box for those people that you want to anonymously know about your email.

2. Consider filling in the "TO," "CC" and "BC" boxes after you have completed the email. That way, if you accidentally hit the "send" button before you are finished, you won't embarrass yourself by sending a partial email.

3. Fill in the "Subject" box with a "grabber" . . . . . something that will get the recipient to open your email. Do not leave it blank. An example is your name and the name of the third party that gave you the recipient's name. For example: "Betty Jones, Referred by John Smith." Do not presume the recipient will recognize who you are by reading your email address.

4. In the body of the email, start by addressing the person to whom you are sending the email. Doing so confirms that your email is definitely for your recipient and for him/her alone. If you don't name the recipient and there isn't anything in the rest of your message to indicate otherwise,

the recipient will likely assume you have sent this email to many people. The recipient will be more impressed if he/she thinks you've written this email specifically for him/her.

5. Use a standard font style that is easy to read. Choose one which has rounded letters, rather than one with hard, angular lines. Rounded letters are easier on the reader's eye. "Times New Roman" and "Arial" are good choices.

6. Use a medium font size of 10 to 14 – something that comes close to what people read in books, newspapers, and magazines.

7. Avoid using graphics, unless that is an important part of your profession.

8. Do not use some of the email abbreviations that have almost become standards (like BTW for "by the way"). Doing so implies laziness.

9. Do not use emoticons. Those are the clever little faces constructed with the special characters on the keyboard. For example, here is a smiley face :-). While you may know what you mean, the recipient might not have any familiarity with these or, worse yet, might misinterpret the emotion you are trying to convey.

10. DO NOT CAPITALIZE THE LETTERS IN YOUR EMAILS. This is the email equivalent of shouting. Certainly, capitalize the first letter in the first word in every sentence and follow other, standard writing rules for capitalization.

11. Use punctuation. Failing to do so suggests laziness. Yes, you may not be as adept as others at the keyboard. However, no one is watching how slowly you type.

12. Structure emails just as though you were going to send a piece of paper in the mail.

13. In the opening paragraph, provide information about yourself and why you are contacting this person. You need to give information before you receive. The more you reveal, the more the recipient may reveal.

14. Now, tell the person what you would like them to do.

15. Use paragraphs and line breaks to separate ideas and subjects. If you don't, the reader will wear out before completing a long email.

16. Add a sentence at the end, expressing your appreciation to the recipient for providing whatever help you have requested.

17. End every email with your name and contact information. (Include your email address, so that the person can copy it easily into his/her email address book.) This will help you establish a connection to the recipient and send a signal that you are open to being contacted.

18. Grammar-check and spell-check every email before you send it. (Note: I have yet to come across a computer grammar-checker or spelling-checker that catches everything. Use them, but don't rely on them. Read your email over very closely yourself.)

19. Attachments are good. However, if the attachment is only text, consider copying the text into the body of the email. Remember, there are still a lot of people out there who are new to email and attachments can be just one more complicating thing for them to deal with.

20. "Threads" are the prior history on emails exchanged between you and the other people. Consider including any relevant threads if you feel they have information that will help the recipient. Otherwise, don't send them, for fear of inundating the recipient.

21. While communications requirements vary with each job, a minimum expectation is that you check and respond to email at least <u>twice</u> daily.

Here are a couple of web sites with additional email tips.

- www.emailreplies.com/#rules
- www.dynamo.com/technical/etiquette.htm

<u>Selling Yourself</u> – I elaborate on how to do this in Phase V, but let me offer some ideas as to how to enhance your ability to sell yourself. First, you absolutely must acknowledge that seeking a job is now your job. Most of us are not sales people. Some of us are not comfortable selling ourselves. <u>Get over it, fast.</u> Now is the time to "toot your own horn." A hiring manager is probably not going to figure out what you can do for him/her unless you tell him/her.

How can you enhance this skill? Here are some ideas.

- Go to a seminar in which a professional sales person explains to prospective sales people how to sell. (Recognize that selling yourself is just like selling a product or a service.)

- Read a book written by a professional sales person on how to sell. (A good one is The Red Book of Selling" by Jeffrey Gitmor.)

- At the end of a networking meeting or even a job interview, ask the other person for feedback on how well you communicated your background, experience, skills, and what you could contribute.

- When you get a turn down letter, contact the hiring manager or the recruiting person and ask for feedback.

<u>Using a Computer</u> – Let's face it. People either take to computers or they don't. It's rare that I come across someone in the middle. If you

are not comfortable with computers, you have a major disadvantage. A huge portion of the communication going on between job seekers and organizations is via computers . . . . . and that goes for the job search, too. If you don't have one at home, you must get a computer. You must develop some rudimentary computer skills . . . . . two, in particular: emailing and word processing.

How can you enhance this skill? Here are some ideas.

- Go to your local county government job support agency. More than likely, they offer a variety of computer classes for free.

- Your local city government may also offer the same. Try them.

- Local community education departments, libraries, and even senior centers often offer computer classes.

- Meet with a relative or friend who is good with computers on a couple of occasions and get some one-on-one instructions. Contact that person over the next couple of months when you encounter some problems.

- Get a book on using a computer.

- Buy a CD or DVD computer training course. (It will run on your computer.)

If you're relatively new to computers, there are a couple of issues which you are going to encounter early on in your computer experience. Here they are and suggestions for resolving them:

- Windows or Macintosh? – Don't worry about this. For the rudimentary computer skills that you need for your job search (emailing and word processing), the differences are immaterial for the beginning or intermediate computer user.

- Which email service? – There are thousands. (Yahoo, AOL, MSN, Hotmail, gMail, juno, netzero, AT&T, just to name a few.) Don't worry. For your job search, virtually any of them are OK.

- Which Word Processing Program? – There are hundreds of these. (Microsoft Word, Word Perfect, Microsoft Works, Quattro Pro, Apple Works, on and on.) They all work basically the same, at least for the basic computer functions that you will need for your job search. The issue is compatibility - that is, whether the person you send a word processing document to is going to be able to open it with his/her computer. He/she may not have the same word processing program that you do. If the other person cannot open your word processing document, it is at least going to cause you some headaches and, worst case, it will cause you to lose a job opportunity. Therefore, do what you can to ensure that your word processing documents are compatible with the word processing programs of the people to whom you will send your documents.

  Here are some guidelines. If you are in a field in which the people tend to use a specific word processing program, then you should use it, too. The business world continues to use Microsoft Word more and more. Use that, if you will be seeking a job in business. Use a word processing program that is a well-known brand name and has been around for at least ten years. That will ensure that it has been enhanced well enough so that it is highly likely that the program will open any word processing document that someone sends you and they will be able to open yours.

Identifying Jobs, Companies, and Networking Contacts – Here, I provide some basic ideas as to how to enhance your skill in doing them. In later chapters, I describe in detail how to do these things.

Identifying Jobs & Companies – On one hand, you might think identifying jobs and companies is what hunting for a job is all about and no description is needed. On the other hand, I have surveyed over a 1,500 job seekers and asked them what their biggest, single challenge in the job search was. 32% say "Finding Job Openings" is the biggest challenge, almost twice as high as the second most frequently named challenge. Here are some ideas as to how to get better at this.

- In general, you need to start thinking of yourself as a professional information researcher. There are jobs out there now that require specialized training in research. Library professionals are the most common examples. These people commonly have master degrees in research. You need to pick up and employ some of their techniques. Go to a large library and meet with their senior research person. Ask him/her to do a couple specific job searches for you. Watch closely. Take notes. Write down the names of the sources that he/she uses. The devil is in the details as to how to do this. Ask for books and courses on information research.

- Get computer training. Many of the job openings are only posted on the Internet.

- Meet with other job seekers and ask them how they identify jobs. Share your best ideas with them, also.

Identifying Networking Contacts – The idea here is to find a person who would be willing to meet with you, help you in your job search and perhaps, even identify a job opportunity. The good news is that this is easy to do. Tell everyone you meet "I am looking for _____ type of job" and ask them "Do you know someone who I could contact and speak about that type of work?" Do it over and over again. The vast majority of people like to help other people. The fact that all they have to do is to refer you to someone else takes the pressure off them. They will typically think hard to come up with someone for you. (Of course, when they do, ask them if they would call the other person, tell him/her that you will be calling, and to please take your call.)

Networking – This is commonly a difficult skill to develop because it is usually not understood by job seekers. Here are some ideas as to how to become better at networking.

- The first thing to do is to read the chapter on networking to learn what it is.

- Talk to other job seekers and job search consultants to get their ideas on how to network.

- Ask your mentor arrange a meeting for you. Have your mentor attend it with you and a networking contact. During the meeting, you will do your networking. After the meeting, ask your mentor for feedback on how you did.

- Do some real networking and screw it up. Take notes afterwards and list what you did well and what you need to improve on.

- At the end of each networking meeting, ask the other person for some feedback as to how you communicated and interacted.

Interviewing — OK. I can hear what you're thinking. "I know how to interview." Sure you do. You've done it before. But are you really good at it? Did you ace your last couple of interviews? Did you have outstanding answers for every question that you were asked? Did you get all your questions answered? Did you "connect" with the hiring manager? And the most important question: Did you get the job offer?

How do you prepare? Practice, practice, and practice. Here are some ideas as to how to get better at interviewing.

- Attend job seeker support group meetings where they teach and hold role-playing interviews.

- Have your mentor play the role of a hiring manager and role play an interview. Afterwards, ask your mentor for feedback as to what you did well and what you need to improve.

- Arrange a meeting with a job search advisor who you do not know and ask him/her to role play an interview with you as your did with your mentor.

- Have your role-playing interviews video-taped and watch them. Listen to how you speak, what you do, and in particular, to your body language. Again, make notes as to what you did well and what you need to improve.

- Go to interviews for jobs that you are not sure you are interested in. Even if the interview confirms that you were right, you will get more real interviewing experience.

Negotiating – You need to learn how to negotiate with facts, emotion, logic, and passion. Negotiating is a fairly well-defined process. There are some very sound principles that all the professional negotiation consultants promote. Here are some ideas to get better at negotiating.

- Attend job seeker support group meetings where they teach and explain how to negotiate.

- Go to seminars on generic (not necessarily job) negotiating strategies.

- Get books (paper and audio) on negotiating.

- Negotiate the purchase and sale of various items (car, house, TV, etc.) in your personal life.

Chapter 9 – Get Help

I've found that most job seekers think of the job search process as a solitary one. That is, you take it on all by yourself. Dispel that in your mind right now! You're going to make out a whole lot better and land a desirable job a whole lot sooner, if you acquire some helpers who stick with you throughout your entire search. You need a handful of people, whom I describe below, who provide different kinds of help. There are also a variety of other things, which are also covered in this chapter, you need and sources to help you in your job search.

A. <u>Get a Mentor</u> – A mentor is a coach. It's a person who doesn't participate in the job search, but practices with you and stands on the sidelines watching your search. Here are important characteristics you should look for in a mentor:

- A person who has experience in the job search and/or the placement process and has also looked for a job him/herself sometime in the last few years.
- A person who is good at job hunting skills (communicating, using a computer, selling, finding jobs, interviewing, negotiating).
- A person with whom you feel comfortable having candid conversations.
- A person whose advice you are willing to follow.
- A person who can commit to an hour or two a week to you for an extended period.

Good possibilities are professional job search advisors who will help you for free, prior bosses, prior customers, suppliers, teachers, and even one of your references.

Bad choices are spouses, relatives, and close friends. If you pick one of these people, you get bogged down in maintaining your personal relationship and neglect proper focus on your professional relationship.

Meet with your prospective mentor. Explain what kind of job you are looking for. Offer copies of your promotional material. Explain what you want your mentor to do and how much of a time commitment you are looking for. If he/she agrees to be your mentor, provide details of what you have done so far in your job search and where things stand at the moment.

Use your mentor regularly. Talk on the phone with him/her at least once a week. Meet with him/her for coffee at least once a month. (You buy.) Explain what is going on. Ask for feedback and ideas. After you have networking meetings, interviews, and negotiating sessions, contact your mentor and discuss them.

B. <u>Get an Advocate</u> – At first look, you may think that an advocate performs the same role as a mentor. There is a key distinction. An advocate gets active in your job search and does things for you. A mentor doesn't. A mentor only advises you. Here are examples of what your advocate can do for you:

- Set up a networking meeting for you.
- Find a job for you.
- Call a hiring manager for you and tell him/her that you would be a good candidate.
- Write letters on your behalf.

The previous descriptions regarding good and bad choices for a mentor also apply to your advocate.

Your mentor and advocate can be the same person. However, you need a person who understands the distinction between the roles, perform each effectively, and can commit double the amount of time for you. Since you can use as much help as you can get, you will be better off if your mentor and advocate are not the same person.

C. <u>Hunt in Pairs</u> – My Chagrin Valley Job Seekers (CVJS) partner is Greg Reynolds. One of his colleagues for several years was Tim Slager. Tim is a former professional in the placement field. One of the great concepts that Tim promotes is to "Hunt in Pairs." The vast majority of job seekers think that the job search is a solitary activity. Au contraire. You will find you get better and faster results by teaming up with another job seeker. Tim has spoken at our CVJS meetings on a couple occasions and elaborates on his concept. He has worked it out in sufficient detail that he has now written it up as a ten-page article. The article can be found on the Internet at http://www.lulu.com/content/151390. Read it for more specific information.

D. <u>Develop Your Sales Force</u> – The more people you have marketing you, the sooner you will land the job that you want. In the spirit of Amway and Mary Kay, develop a sales force for yourself. Good candidates are your family, close friends, prior colleagues, bosses, customers, suppliers, and teachers. You need to train and manage them. Here's how:

- Meet with each of them individually over coffee. (You buy.) Tell them you are looking for a job. Give them a copy of your marketing plan and talk them through it. Give them a chance to ask questions to confirm that they understand what you are looking for.

- Give them multiple copies of your promotional materials (like your resume and business card).

- Teach them how to network. (They initially won't know how any better than you do.)

- Tell them what you want them to do, which is:
  - Let anyone they encounter know that you are looking for a job.

- Tell these people that they meet what kind of job you are looking for (a simple job title, like Controller or Customer Service Rep, is sufficient).
- If they encounter someone who might be able to help you in your job search, have them ask that person if you can call them.
- Have them ask people they encounter if they know someone who might be willing to help you out and get his/her name, title, phone #, and email address.
- Pass out your resume and/or business card to anyone who might want to see it or be willing to pass it on.
- Report back to you about their encounters.

- Send your sales force an email every four to six weeks about your progress in your job search and what you have been doing. This will bring you back to the front of their minds and remind them that they are on your sales force.

- When you land a job, be sure to let them know, express your appreciation for all their help, and offer to reciprocate.

E. <u>Train Your Spouse</u> – After you, your spouse has the greatest vested interest in you landing a job, so he/she should be willing to help. At the opposite end of the spectrum, I hear of spouses who only cause emotional stress on job seekers. If that is your situation, then bringing your spouse into your job search and becoming partially accountable for the results will, hopefully, mitigate the emotional stress. Either way, your spouse probably doesn't have any more of a clue than you used to as to how to find a job. He/she is going to need some training. He/she is an excellent candidate for your sales force, so follow all the steps in the previous "Develop Your Sales Force" section with your spouse.

The great advantage of your spouse as part of your sales force is that you get to talk to him/her frequently. Use that time to continue the training process. This job hunting process and networking are not necessarily obvious and require practice and refinement . . . . . and, in the course of training your spouse, you will become better at it, too.

F. <u>Pursue Other Sources of Help</u> – While I have described a variety of specific people in the prior few sections who can help you in your job search, there are also a variety of organizations that are set up to help job seekers for free. I've identified 26 in northeast Ohio alone. Examples are:

- City, county, and state government agencies.
- Job seeker groups (the Chagrin Valley Job Seekers in northeast Ohio is a good one!)
- Colleges, particularly community colleges
- Local chambers of commerce.
- Outplacement firms
- Churches
- Libraries

Research these, visit them, and find out what services they offer. Pick and choose which ones you will spend some time with. Regularly attend meetings of a couple of them. At a minimum, these groups provide an opportunity for you to network with other people.

One of the categories above requires some elaboration. That is out-placement firms. There are "retail" ones and there are "wholesale" ones. "Retail" ones charge job seekers for services, commonly thousands of dollars. Arguably, the most consistent thing that I hear from job seekers is that "retail" outplacement firms over-promise and under-deliver. With the vast source of free and helpful other alternatives for help out there, I highly recommend that you avoid "retail" outplacement firms, unless you have some extremely uncommon circumstance or absolutely no other alternative.

On the other hand, "wholesale" outplacement firms are paid by the employers who laid off the worker. There are many excellent national and regional "wholesale" outplacement firms. I highly suggest that you take full advantage of these services, which are available to you for free.

G. <u>Don't Pay for Help</u> – There are organizations and individuals who provide services to job seekers for a fee. No doubt, most of them can help. However, with the large number of organizations out there that provide services for free, plus job seeker books, plus the people I named in prior sections to help you, you shouldn't have to pay anyone or any organization to help you in your job search unless you have an extreme case and have already exhausted all the sources of free help.

Caution

I want to add a word of caution here. There are organizations that over-promise what they will deliver to a job seeker and charge huge fees (thousands of dollars). Beware of organizations that tell you they have a huge database of contacts and jobs and promise to find a job for your. It isn't likely to happen. I've heard many stories from job seekers who feel ripped off.

Also, there are recruiting firms or temporary agencies that charge job seekers to find a job for them. Don't sign anything that says you will pay anything. Don't pay any such fees. The employer who hires you virtually always pays the recruiting firm for finding you.

H. <u>Get Health Insurance</u> – One of the almost immediate issues that a job seeker typically has to deal with is health care/health insurance. I've provided a fair amount of information on this subject below. However, please recognize that (1) I am not a health care / health insurance expert and (2) the information and the related laws may have changed since I wrote this. Certainly check with an insurance or health care expert, before taking any action on the information below.

The first thing you need to know about is COBRA. COBRA stands for Consolidated Omnibus Budget Reconciliation Act of 1985. It requires that a group health care plan must offer each qualified individual, who would otherwise lose coverage due to termination of employment, the opportunity to elect to continue that coverage for a specified time period.

COBRA applies to all employers with 20 or more employees.

COBRA still applies, even if your employer was "self-insured."

It does not apply to plans sponsored by the federal government or certain church-related organizations.

COBRA is not free and the terminated employee typically pays for it in total. You must pay the full group premium plus a 2%-5% administrative fee.

COBRA ends after:

- 18 months.
- 29 months, if you become eligible for Social Security disability during the first 60 days of COBRA continuation
- 36 months, if you were covered under your parent's or spouse's plan and the parent or spouse became eligible for Medicare, died, divorced, or separated.
- Your prior employer goes out of business.
- You prior employer stops offering a group plan.

If COBRA is not an option for you or you can't afford it, there are other, less expensive alternatives, such as high deductible coverage that may be a good choice.

Dental and vision coverage may also be available through COBRA. It may depend upon whether the employer who terminated you offered them and whether you already had them.

Some health insurance carriers will allow a terminated employee to obtain an individual policy apart from COBRA.

The next thing you should understand is HIPPA. HIPPA stands for Health Insurance Portability and Accountability Act 1996. (It is also known as the Kassebaum-Kennedy Act.)

One of the features of HIPPA is that it established "Portability" for an employee that leaves his/her employer. "Portability" means you carry your "eligibility" with you, though not your previous "coverage," to your new employer, if your new employer offers health insurance.

HIPAA applies if you are covered by your employer's health plan and you move to another employer that offers a health plan.

This is a federal Act that requires insurance companies that provide individual health insurance in an area to make their insurance available to people who meet federal eligibility requirements. In general, in order to meet these requirements, a person must demonstrate that he/she had "creditable health insurance coverage" immediately prior to purchasing the new coverage. This Act prevents insurance carriers from denying coverage to an individual because he/she has pre-existing conditions.

You may be able to obtain a "Certificate of Creditable Coverage" from the employer that terminated you.

Your new employer's plan must accept any family member who was covered under your old employer's plan.

You cannot be turned down or charged higher premiums because of a family member's health problems. Even so, your new group plan may cost more.

If the new plan has a waiting period for pre-existing conditions, you will get credit for any time those conditions were covered under the old plan, as long as you enroll within 62 days of leaving the old plan.

If you or a family member is pregnant when you switch jobs, the new plan will cover pregnancy only if the new plan includes maternity coverage.

There may be a waiting period before you can enroll in the new plan.

If you enroll a child within 31 days of birth or adoption, the plan must cover all pre-existing conditions.

If you move from a group plan to an individual plan, you will need to know if you are a "federally eligible individual" (FEI). (Contact your state's Department of Insurance for qualifications.) If you are an FEI, no insurance company that offers individual coverage can reject you or exclude pre-existing conditions. If you are not an FEI, "conversion" (see below) may be your only choice.

Here are some other ideas for you to consider in regard to health care / health insurance:

- Unless your employer was self-insured, you have the right to convert ("conversion") your group insurance certificate into "Basic" or "Standard" coverage provided by the group's insurance company, if you were previously covered in the group for at least a year. This right also applies if you are a family member of a covered person who died, you reached the age limit of your parent's policy, or were divorced or separated from the certificate holder.

- Another alternative is to buy Catastrophic Health Insurance. It has high limits on what is covered, but you pay a hefty part of your medical costs out of your pocket. In addition, the deductibles are quite high.

- There are also a variety of "limited purpose" coverages.

- If you were enrolled in a "Managed Care" program under your previous small employer (2 to 25 workers) and you were laid off, you may have the right to continue under your old employer's group coverage for six months.

Current information on health care / health insurance can be obtained by contacting the Department of Insurance in your state. They will be able to provide more details and specifics that apply in your state.

I. <u>Get Cash</u> – Another critical issue that job seekers commonly experience during the job search is financial stress. Cash flow from week to week can become an extreme challenge, particularly if you have a big mortgage, kids in college, or ill parents whom you help support.

Below is a list of 28 ways to improve your cash flow during your job search. Skim the list, determine the ones that make sense for you, prioritize them, and make it happen. (Please note: I am not a financial planner or a tax accountant. *I highly recommend that you check with your financial advisors, before taking any of the actions below.*)

1. Take out a loan against your 401K, 403b, or IRA.

2. Withdraw money from your 401K, 403b, or IRA. (Rule 72T provides for circumstances - for example: "hardship", age 55 & over - in which you can withdraw money from some tax qualified plans - like a 401K - before age 59 ½, without the 10% tax penalty.)

3. Take out a loan on your life insurance policy.

4. Refinance your home.

5. Get a reverse mortgage.

6. Sell your house to someone and rent it back.

7. Get quotes on all insurances (auto, life, home).

8. Raise deductibles on your home and auto insurance.

9. Ask grandparents pay for college tuition for your children. (It may reduce the taxes on their estate.)

10. Ask grandparents pay for premiums of medical insurance for your family. (It may reduce the taxes on their estate.)

11. Ask "gifting" relatives to move up the delivery date.

12. File for unemployment compensation.

13. Get part-time work.

14. Shift a greater portion of your capital appreciation investments into income generating investments (for example: high dividend paying stocks).

15. Ensure that you receive all income that your prior employer typically gives terminated employees (for example: commissions on sales, unused vacation pay, severance).

16. If you were pressed into resigning, it may have been because your employer did not want to make payments to the state for unemployment. Consider going back to your employer and negotiating a financially better separation agreement.

17. Skip your vacation. (Hey, you're already on a long term vacation, right?)

18. Reduce or stop any quarterly estimated tax payments.

19. Become a coupon maniac.

20. Pay off credit cards. (Yes, it requires cash to do so, but it will eliminate the future cost of finance charges.)

21. Get a credit card that builds up points towards purchases or offers cash back.

22. Buy on credit. (This is, of course, dangerous.)

23. Get a loan from a relative.

24. Sell unused personal and household goods.

25. Move next year's tax deductions into this year. (For example: Pay your real estate taxes in the last couple of days of December, rather than the first couple of days of January). Yes, this requires some upfront cash, but it will get you a tax reduction now.

26. "Bundle" uncovered medical expenses into the same year to increase your itemized expenses on your federal taxes.

27. Consult your financial / tax advisor in those cases which require special knowledge of investment options and laws.

28. Develop an expense budget and stick to it!

Here are some income tax related tips for job seekers. (Note: I am also not a tax advisor or tax expert. *Consult with your own tax advisor before acting on any of these ideas.*)

What is Deductible?

According to IRS Publication 529, you can deduct certain expenses you incurred looking for a new job in your *present* occupation, even if you do not end up getting a new job. However, you cannot deduct these expenses if:

- You are looking for a job in a *new* occupation.

- There was a substantial break between the ending of your last job and looking for a new one.

- You are looking for a job for the first time.

The following are examples of job search expenses that can be deducted:

- Employment and outplacement agency fees - You can deduct employment and outplacement agency fees you pay in looking for a new job in your present occupation. (Of course, I earlier told you not to pay any of these.)

- Resume -You can deduct amounts you spend for typing, printing, and mailing copies of a resume to prospective employers if you are looking for a new job in your present occupation.

- Travel and transportation expenses. If you travel to an area and, while there, look for a new job in your present occupation, you may be able to deduct travel expenses to and from the area. You can deduct the travel expenses if the trip is primarily to look for a new job. The amount of time you spend on personal activity, compared to the amount of time you spend in looking for work, is important in determining whether the trip is primarily personal or is primarily to look for a new job.

- Even if you cannot deduct the travel expenses to and from an area, you can deduct the expenses of looking for a new job in your present occupation while in the area.

- Education Expenses - There are IRS regulations that let you save money when investing in education for yourself.

- Subscriptions - Magazines and journals related to your profession are also tax deductible.

Where can you find more Information?

- IRS - To find out about the specific regulations for deducting education and other career-related expenses, take a look at IRS Publication #529. Go to http://www.irs.gov/pub/irs-pdf/p529.pdf to view the guidelines in PDF format.

- Tax Preparation Services - H&R Block and Jackson-Hewitt can also advise you on deducting career advancement expenses from your taxes.

- Tax Software - Check out tax software like TurboTax and Tax Advisor, which use a computerized approach to help you discover expenses that can be deducted.

Chapter 10 – Develop a Method for Recording Your Activity

During your job search, you are, hopefully, going to encounter many people, identify many organizations, and come across many jobs that you are interested in. After just a couple weeks, you are likely to have done so much that, unless you've got a memory more extraordinary than the average person, you will start forgetting most of it. Yet, as the weeks and months roll by, you will find that you will want to refer to this information more and more. The obvious solution to the problem is to record this information as you go along.

A. <u>What to Record</u> - There are six major categories:

- People
- Organizations
- Jobs
- Web Sites
- Events
- To Do List

Here are details on what data elements to record for each category. You don't need every piece of information listed, but the more you can get, the better off you will be down the road when you want it.

<u>People</u>

- Name (last, first, middle)
- Mailing address (number, street, city, state, zip) (professional and personal)
- Email address (professional and personal)

- Phone number (professional and personal, office and cellular)
- Name of his/her employer.
- Name of person who referred you to this person. (*This is very important.*)

Organizations

- Name (the official one)
- Mailing address (number, street, city, state, zip)
- Web site address
- Main phone number
- Type of organization (like employer, recruiters, trade association, etc.)
- A brief description of its business.
- Name of person who referred you to this organization. (*This is very important.*)

Jobs

- Job title
- A brief job description
- Name of the employer
- Source where you found the job (like employer, recruiter, Internet job posting site)
- When found
- Where located
- Salary range
- A description of how to apply (name and email address of person to send a cover letter and resume to.)

Web Sites

- Name of web site
- Its web address
- Purpose of site (for example: job postings, resume help, career planning, company information, multi-purpose)
- A brief description of the information at the web site.

Events

- Date / Time of the event
- Who did you talk to / meet with
- What was said
- Who takes the next step
- What is the next step

To Do List

- Date logged
- Description of what you need to do
- Target completion date
- Priority

Now, lets talk about how you storage, reference, and maintain this information. There are two basic methods: a paper-based system and a computer-based system.

B. Paper-Based System - I recommend 3x5 index cards. Why? Because (1) they are easier to keep in order and, hence, find, and (2) it is easier to sustain the conceptual understanding that one index card is one entity (a person, an organization, etc.) The sequence in which you keep the 3x5 index cards varies by category. Here are my recommendations to help you find card when you need it.

- People – (sort by the person's last name)
- Organizations - (sort by the organization's name)
- Jobs – (sort by the job title)
- Web sites - (sort by the web site name)
- Events - (sort by the date the event occurred)
- To Do List - (sort by the task priority)

Keep the set of cards for each category in its own rubber-banded batch. As you create new 3x5 index cards, insert them in the right spot within the right batch. If you can obtain them, use cards of a different color for each category above.

In the top left corner of each 3x5 index card, write the data element by which you are going to sort each batch. That will make it easy to scan through the batch. In the top right corner, write the date that the card was created or last updated. That will tell you how old the information is when you reference it.

Ideally, you will have one person card for each person named in another batch, one organization card for each organization named in another batch, etc. Finally, you don't need to include all the detail for an entity on every 3x5 card where the information appears. For example, a particular person may be named on many cards. However, the detail information about the person only needs to be included on that person's "people" card.

Here's an example of what a "people" card could look like.

Mr. John Smith				
			Last Changed	
			Aug 22, 2007	
Professional	XYZ Corporation	999-999-9999	Off 1	
	HR Director	999-999-9998	Fax	
	987 Any Street	888-888-8888	Off 2	
	Any City, Any State Zip	777-777-7777	Cell	
		JSmith@XYZ.com	eMail	
Personal	123 Main Street	666-666-6666	Home	
	Any City, Any State Zip			
		JSmith@AOL.com	eMail	

C. Computer-Based System - The other method is computer-based. One approach is to use a PDA (Personal Digital Assistant) like a Palm, Blackberry, or a Windows device. The advantage of this approach is that you can carry it with you and update it as soon as you encounter new people or events that occur. The disadvantage is that it will take you a fairly large amount of effort to customize the screens to include the types of information that a job seeker needs to keep track of.

The other approach is to use your personal computer. There are a couple of pieces of software that you can find on the Internet that are already customized for job seekers. They will cost you $25 to $50. They are typically Excel-based. The advantage of Excel is that a large portion of people are familiar with it and it is relatively easy to use. The disadvantage is that you need to type in people and company names every time you want to refer to them. The alternative is a database program. Its advantage is that you need to type in a person or company name only once. When you need it again, you just pick it from a list. The disadvantage is that a database is somewhat more complicated to use and requires special software. (I have developed such a database, named the CVJS Job Seeker Database, and I offer it to all our members for free. It requires Microsoft Access.)

Ideas

Finally, here are some tips for managing this information:

- Continually maintain your system. You may think it takes too much time. However, as the weeks and months of your job search roll by, you will refer back to it more and more.

- Do not think of this data base of information as only applying to your job search. Keep it going after you have landed a job. It will serve you while you are working and, more than likely, you will need it again in the future when you are looking for a job again.

Phase IV – Seeking

There are four fundamental search methods that you need to be using, basically simultaneously:

- Pursuing specific, known job openings   _____
- Pursuing target employers   _____
- Using recruiters   _____
- Networking   _____

These are discussed in detail in the following chapters.

On the blank line at the end of each line above, write down an estimate of the percentage of your job search time you have already spent using each of these four methods. A range such as 5%-10% is fine. The total of the percentages should add up to about 100%.

Don't go to the next page, yet.

Below are the percentages for which jobs are found with each method. These numbers are roughly the averages that have been reported in various surveys over the years.

- Pursuing specific, known job openings   10%–15%
- Pursuing target employers   20%–30%
- Using recruiters   5%–10%
- Networking   65%–75%

Compare your percentages to the percentages that produce results. To reduce the elapsed time until you land a job, you need to allocate your search time, according to the above percentages.

Chapter 11 - Identify and Pursue Specific, Known Jobs

This chapter is devoted to the process of you, as a job seeker, pursuing specific, known job openings directly with an employer. This is probably the most common perception of the way to look for a job.

A. Find Jobs

The obvious sources of job postings are newspapers, magazines, and web sites. The fundamental problem with these sources is that there are so many. While there may be only a couple newspapers local to you, there are hundreds, if not thousands, of web sites that can help job seekers. It takes time and energy to determine which are the best sources for the kind of job that you are looking for. How are you ever going to figure out which are best for you? Let me provide some guidelines.

- First, you need to make the distinction in your mind of the difference between generalization and specialization, regarding the kind of employer you are looking for. If you are a salesman, it is likely you can sell any product to any customer. If you are a financial person, any employer is likely to be able to use your experience and skills. That's generalization in terms of employers. However, at the other extreme is specialization. What you do and the type of employer that you have worked for, and want to work for, may be quite specific. You may be limiting your prospective employers to specific industries or geographies. Very simply, to the extent that you are specializing, you will need to use newspapers, magazines, and web sites that address your specialization. (By the way, my observation of job seekers and my own job seeking experience indicates that we all start out the job search with a specialized focus. However, as the job search drags on for months and months, we become more and more open to the kinds of jobs, employers, and geographies that we will consider. It's just human nature, but the sooner and more generalized you become, the sooner you will land a job.)

- Over the last ten to fifteen years, there has been a transition in the proportion of jobs which are posted in newspaper, magazines, and the web. Like so many things, more postings are going to the web. But now, there is an additional extension of this transition. Large companies are now posting their job openings on their own web sites because they have the resources and skills to develop their own job posting functions. Be sure you check out the web sites of large companies.

- Go to the HR Department of a company and ask to see their list of jobs available. In today's world, that seems old fashioned. However, at least two good things might happen if you do this. First, you may be informed about a job that isn't posted yet, and you'll have a leg up on other candidates. Second, you will hopefully meet one of their recruiters and establish a relationship with this person. If you apply for a job there, you will probably work through this person and, even in today's world of the Internet, people still respond more often to people they have met.

- City, county, state and the federal governments also maintain lists of available jobs. Consider those, too.

- Join job seeker groups and county-level job support organizations. They typically share job leads.

The simple guideline is to initially try many sources and then spend more of your time perusing the sources that have the kind of job you are looking for.

Somewhere between 65% and 80% of the jobs available are not posted anywhere. The only way you're going to find out about these jobs is to talk with someone in the organization where the job is or talk with someone outside the organization who knows the job opening exists. That's called networking. I discuss that in detail in Chapter 13.

B. <u>Answer Ads and Postings</u>

The conventional thing that a job seeker does when he/she finds a posted job of interest is to grab a copy of his/her resume, slap on a maybe-customized cover letter, and mail it to wherever the posting said to send it. Well, that's a lazy and ineffective way to go about it. Why? Let me repeat exactly what I said back in Chapter 7 under "T-Letter":

> At the other end, a person receives your cover letter and resume, along with probably a couple hundred other resumes. (Don't worry. 95% aren't qualified for the job. Now, this person's job is to screen out the 95%, he/she has only been given a couple of days to do this, and this is just one of the jobs that he/she is working on. This person is more than likely an internal or external recruiter, who doesn't know anything more about the job than you do. If you're really unlucky, the person is a recent college graduate who is still green behind the ears and doesn't have any idea what a good resume looks like. This screener grabs a resume off the pile of a couple hundred resumes, probably ignores your cover letter, and spends 15-30 seconds scanning your resume to try to determine if you're qualified for the job. Imagine, your future is in the hands of this person!!!

Therefore, the first unconventional thing you have to do is to make your cover letter a "T-Letter." Go back to Chapter 7 and read up on how to construct a "T-Letter."

The second unconventional thing you need to do is not to send to wherever the posting asks you to send it. The posting probably says to send it to the HR Department or fill out the on-line form. Both are black holes and worse, neither is the hiring manager, who is the decision maker. You need to find out who the hiring manager is and send you material to him/her. This is discussed in sub-section G, later in this chapter.

Now, what's better than sending your material to the hiring manager? Call him/her. Tell him/her you are interested in the job and ask for an interview. (More than likely, the hiring manager will ask you to go through the standard channels. However, you have increased your chances of getting an interview.)

Now, what could be better than calling the hiring manager? Go see him/her. Don't wait for an invitation. . . . . . Let me give you an example. Napoleon Hill wrote a book entitled <u>Think and Grow Rich</u>. In it, he told the story of Edwin C. Barnes. Edwin wanted to work *with*, not *for*, Thomas Edison. He didn't know Edison and he had to travel a great distance to see Edison. When he got there, he went straight in to Edison and informed him that he "intended", not "wanted" to work with him. Did Edison take him on board? No. Barnes sat outside Edison's office day-in, day-out for almost a month, until Edison gave him a job that eventually led to Barnes becoming a partner of Edison's.

Are you likely to be as committed to a specific job as Barnes? Probably not. Are you going to come across a job that you think you are perfect for? Probably. When you come across it, don't let anything stand in the way of landing it. Go see the hiring manager. Good things will happen in his office area, even if you can't get to see him/her (the first time).

A couple of final points about responding to job postings are warranted. First, many postings ask you to send your material to an unidentified post office box. Count to 100 before your do so. Many of these postings are just market research attempts by either employers or recruiters. There probably isn't an actual job opening and all you are doing is providing information for their research. The chance that you will get a response is nil.

The final thing to mention is that troubling statement at the end of most job postings "Include your salary history (or requirements)." You want to fight the urge to provide this information. (See the section "Don't Answer the Salary Question" in Chapter 16.) Include a statement in the material that you send in like "Salary requirements are negotiable" or "Salary requirements are discussable at the time an offer is made." Say something that will give them the impression they will get the information later, just not now. Don't worry. If they think you are well qualified when they review your material, they'll call you anyhow and, of course, ask you over the phone "What are your salary requirements?" Again, read Chapter 16 for ideas about how to continue not explicitly answering this question.

C. Go Around the HR Department

This was discussed in the previous sub-section, but it warrants repeating. Most job postings will tell you to send your material into the HR Department. *Don't do it*, at least not initially. Again, find out who the hiring manager is and approach him/her directly.

Will the people in the HR Department get upset? Not likely. That's not just my opinion. I've had HR Managers and HR Directors participate in our CVJS panels and they say it's OK. They say that only really insecure HR people will get upset that you went around them. Most of these panel members said they would even give you extra points for your initiative.

If you still feel squeamish about going around the HR Department, then copy them on the material that you send the hiring manager.

D. Apply for a Job

When I say "apply," I mean filling out the employer's application form for the job. It may be a paper form. It may be an electronic form on the Internet. Either way, the suggestions below apply.

As I said in the prior couple of sub-sections, you should try to deal directly with the hiring manager. He/she doesn't really care that much about application forms and filling one out just slows you down in your pursuit of the job.

More than likely, though, you will at some point find yourself in a situation where you will end up filling out an application. Understand that you are not under any obligation to fill out applications. When you are hired, you will likely have to provide a variety of personal information like your race and social security numbers. The former is needed by the employer to demonstrate to the government that they are not discriminating on the basis of race. The latter is needed for withholding taxes from your paycheck. However, all the information that you put on an application is voluntary. You should fill out the application to demonstrate that you are a cooperative person. However, you do not need to fill out every box and answer every question. In regard to you salary history, I strongly urge you not to provide this information on an application. As soon as you do, you've lost Round 1 of the salary negotiations. Put an asterisk (*) in the boxes or questions about salary history. Then, in the footnote, say something like "Salary requirements are negotiable" or "Salary requirements are discussable at the time an offer is made."

Every time I tell this to a group of job seekers, one of them always says "Well, what about when you are filling out one of those on-line applications. They won't let you get passed the salary box, unless you fill in a number. What do I do then?" Well, fill in an obviously ridiculous number (like $11,111) and then in the "Comments" box (there's almost always a "Comments" box), fill in one of the suggested statements in the previous paragraph so the readers will know that you weren't trying to deceive them and, more importantly, you didn't lie on your application.

When I say that, a job seeker will then ask "What do I do when the on-line application won't allow me to fill in a ridiculous number and/ or there's no "Comments" box?" My response at this point is "Why are you wasting your time filling out on-line applications? You will increase your chance of getting an interview if you first contact the hiring manager."

Which brings me to the last, possibly the most important, suggestion: Don't lie on these applications (or on your resume, for that matter). Why? Two really good reasons. First, it's unethical. Second, you will likely be asked to provide written documentation on anything you write or say.

E. <u>Tips for Using the Job Boards</u> – Peter Tuttle, creator, CEO, and President of CareerBoard.com spoke at one of our CVJS sessions on this subject. If there was anyone who has the statistics as to what works and what doesn't, it will be Peter.

<u>Here are 18 of his tips for job seekers.</u>

1. Before using any job board, firm up / get clear on what your job objectives are. (Sounds like the "Job Desired" form, doesn't it?)
2. If you are willing to relocate anywhere in the USA, then focus on the large, national boards.
3. If you want to stay closer to your current residence, then focus on regional boards.

4. If your occupation is a specialty, then find a niche board that focuses on that type of job.

5. Read the "instructions" page at each board. It will save you time.

6. Once you have selected the job boards you plan on using, stick with them.

7. New jobs are uploaded to the boards from Wednesday to Saturday. Spend more of your time searching the boards on these days. (Interestingly, most job seekers search the boards on Monday through Wednesday.)

8. The best times to search job boards are evenings and weekends.

9. Most jobs get seven to ten responses, most in the first seven days that they are posted. Time your response, accordingly.

10. Post your resume on the boards. (Not for the hiring organizations. Only about 5% of direct employers search resume databases. However, about 95% of the recruiters do search resume databases.)

11. Re-post your resume every 30 days. (Any minor change will get its "last update date" updated and your resume will then pop up higher on lists that hiring managers and recruiters look at.)

12. If you get a call from a recruiter based upon a posted resume, ask "Do you have a specific job that you are looking to fill?" If the answer is. "No", this is a "red flag" and they may be trying to market you. Avoid them.

13. Sign up for the same job posted on different job boards.

14. Put keywords in the first 15-30 lines of your resume. (Why? Because many computer scans of your resume in these boards don't look any farther down your resume than that.)

15. Sign up for more than one "notifier." Using only one may not catch all the jobs that might be of interest to you.

16. Don't just sit back and wait for responses from the "notifiers." Continue to search the boards.

17. Figure out what search string works best for you. Also, your best search string may vary from board to board.
18. Learn how to use "Boolean" operators. (A good description can be found at most boards or check out SearchEngineWatch.com.)

F. Get the Job Interview

No hiring manager has ever hired a person without a face-to-face interview. When you identify a job that you want to pursue, your initial objective is to get an interview with the hiring manager.

| Procedure |

Here is the "traditional" way and a more "effective" approach for getting that initial interview.

The "Traditional" Approach. (The estimated probability of getting the interview is up to 3%.)

1. <u>Identify</u> a job you want to pursue in a newspaper ad or an Internet posting.
2. <u>Make</u> a copy of your resume and a copy of your generic cover letter that says (a) I'm applying for the _____ job, (b) attached is my resume, and (c) call me.
3. <u>Send</u> in your resume and cover letter, either by U.S. mail to a nebulously defined place, an email black hole, or fill out an on-line application, none of which names a specific person.
4. An internal HR person or an external recruiter spends ten to thirty seconds looking over your material trying to figure out whether you're qualified for the job, concludes that you aren't, and throws your material in the "B" pile with the other hundred "un-qualified" people.

5. Five to seven days go by, <u>get</u> frustrated, and perhaps angry because no one calls you back.

6. Eight to ten days later, <u>decide</u> to try to contact someone. <u>Send</u> an email to the address that was in the job posting or, if you were lucky and it had a phone number, make a call. Regardless, you can't get anyone to talk to and, even if you are able to leave a message, no one calls you back.

7. Twelve to fourteen days later, <u>think</u> about trying to contact them again and whether you do or don't, when no one responds, get more frustrated and angrier.

8. <u>Give</u> up, find a posting for another job, go back to step #1, and start the same approach all over again.

The <u>"Effective" Approach.</u> (The estimated probability of getting the Interview is 20% to 30%.)

1. <u>Identify</u> a job you want to pursue in a newspaper ad or an Internet posting.

2. <u>Find</u> a person who works inside the organization (by either networking or calling people in the organization). Either <u>call</u> or <u>meet</u> with him/her and tell him/her:
   - There is a job opening you are interested in.
   - That you have prepared some material that you'd like to send to the hiring manager, but you don't know who that is.

3. <u>Ask</u> that person:
   - To identify the name of the hiring manager, his/her title, mailing address, phone number, and email address. (Identifying the hiring manager and working directly with him/her is so important that I have elaborated on this in the next section.)
   - To find out what the salary range is for the job.
   - To hand-deliver your material to the hiring manager.

- To tell the hiring manager that you are going to call him/her.
- To ask the hiring manager to look your material over and to take your call.
- If you can use his/her name when contacting the hiring manager.

4. Prepare the material that you are going to send to the hiring manager.
   - Go back and read the job description, identifying the key 3-5 requirements of the job, and write down your two to three qualifications for each of the job requirements.
   - Write a customized letter (a "T-Letter") addressed to the hiring manager that includes:
     - A statement that you are interested in his/her job opening.
     - The list of job requirements and your qualifications for each.
     - That you would like to meet with the hiring manager.
     - That you will call him/her in a couple days to arrange a meeting.
     - Copy the person who hand-delivered the material to the hiring manager.

5. Also write a letter to the person who is willing to hand-deliver the material to the hiring manager that includes:
   - An introductory paragraph that reminds the person of your prior conversation / meeting.
   - Name of the hiring manager and remind the person of his/her prior willingness to hand-deliver your material to the hiring manager.
   - A request that he/she pass the letter on to the hiring manager.
   - A statement that you will call the hiring manager in two days.
   - A closing paragraph that expresses your sincere appreciation for his/her help.

6. <u>Send</u> the material to the person by either by U.S. mail or email. If you send it by email, include your material as an attachment so that it will retain the appropriate formatting and look good when printed.

7. Two days after you think the person has received the material, call him/her and confirm that he/she had a chance to pass your material on to the hiring manager.

8. When you get the confirmation, <u>call</u> the hiring manager and arrange a meeting. (At this point, also refer to Chapter 26, "Overcome Objections to Meeting with You.")

9. If you do not reach the hiring manager, <u>leave</u> a message which:
    • States your interest in his/her job opening.
    • Names the referring person and indicates that he/she passed on a letter indicating your qualifications for the job.
    • You will call him/her back in two days again (but also leave your telephone number).

10. <u>Call</u> the hiring manager in two days. If you do not reach him/her again, either call again in two more days or contact his/her administrative assistant and find out when would be a good day and time to call.

11. When you reach the hiring manager on the phone,
    • Identify yourself and indicate your interest in his/her job opening.
    • Name the person that passed your material on to the hiring manager.
    • Suggest a day or two to meet with the hiring manager.

12. If the hiring manager says you should send your material to the HR Department:
    • Say that you will, but . . . .
    • Ask him/her if he/she has had an opportunity to review your material and what does he/she think?

13. If you can't get the hiring manager to talk with you, consider coming right out and <u>asking</u> "Have you reviewed my material and are you giving me a polite turndown?"

   - If the answer is effectively "Yes" (No one will explicitly say "Yes"), try to get some information to help you in your job search elsewhere. For example: Say "Fine, I won't bother you anymore about this, but could you give me some feedback as to what was it about my background that you found lacking?" or "I felt a reasonable salary range for this job was $XX,000 to $YY,000. Is that consistent with your view?"

   - If the answer is effectively "no", then say "Fine, I'll follow up with you in a couple of days" and express your appreciation for his/her time and consideration.

You will note that the "Effective" approach requires more time and effort on your part. However, the success rate is substantially higher.

G. <u>Identify the Hiring Manager</u>

Most job seekers will apply for a job by using the "traditional approach" (see the prior section) and send a resume to the HR Department. The more "effective" approach is to identify and contact the hiring manager directly. This section will describe four approaches for you to help identify the hiring manager.

Approach #1

1. <u>Make</u> a guess as to the title of the hiring manager.
2. <u>Call</u> the company, using the main number, and talk to the reception / phone directory person.
   - Give that person the title of the hiring manager. (You should be able to make an intelligence guess.)
   - Ask him/her for the hiring manager's name, mailing address, and email address. Confirm the title, too.
   - If that person either refuses to give the information or asks you why you want it, identify yourself, explain that the hiring manager has a job you intend to apply for, and that you would like to send your resume directly to him/her.
   - If that person says that you are supposed to send resumes to the HR Department, say that you will, but you would like to also send a copy to hiring manager and ask for his/her name again.

Approach #2

1. If the prior approach doesn't work, a couple days later, <u>make</u> a good guess of the name of the department where the hiring manager works.
2. <u>Call</u> the company, using the main number, and talk to the reception / phone directory person. Ask to be connected to the department.
3. When someone answers (probably a receptionist), follow the last four to five steps in the "effective" approach as I laid out a couple pages back.

Approach #3

1. Go to your local library (or try the Internet) and look for a directory that includes a list of all the companies in your state. (In Ohio, there is one called the <u>Harris InfoSource</u>

<u>Directory.</u>) Or ask the librarian about the availability of an electronic database of companies.

2. When you find the company, the entry will include the company's main phone number and the names, titles, and mailing addresses of the top five to ten people in the company. If your target company is a small company, there is a good chance the hiring manager is one of those people. If not, note the name and title of the person that the hiring manager most likely reports to.

3. <u>Call</u> the company. Tell them the likely title of the hiring manager, that you are trying to reach that person, and you understand that to be _____ [give the name of the person you found in the directory].

4. <u>Ask</u> the person to confirm that person is still with the company, in that capacity, and what his/her phone number and email address are.

<u>Approach #4</u>

1. <u>Find</u> someone (by networking) who knows the hiring manager.

2. <u>Ask</u> everyone you know and encounter if they know someone at the company where the hiring manager works. Ask for a referral.

3. <u>Send</u> out emails to your network. <u>Tell</u> them you have identified a job you are interested in. Name the company. Ask them if they know someone at the company. Ask for a referral.

Even when you have successfully identified the hiring manager, remember it is then better to contact someone else within the company and have that person hand-deliver your material to the hiring manager with, hopefully, a recommendation that the hiring manager review it and take your call when it comes.

Chapter 12 - Identify and Pursue Employers

There are going to be employers that you are very interested in and would love to work for. I'm now talking about one, two, or maybe three specific employers. More than likely, they don't have a job for you right now. This doesn't mean that you ignore them now . . . . . . actually, you should do just the opposite. Pursue them now. However, it does require some different tactics, which I now discuss.

A. Identify Employers to Target – This basically gets down to a two-step process.

1. Define the characteristics of an employer that you want to work for. The easiest way to do this is to go back and review "Your Desired Job." To the extent that it is appropriate, modify or enhance your description. To develop many alternatives, remember to describe your job on paper and in your mind in the most generic manner that you can.

2. Make a list of all the prospective employers in your desired area of employment. The easiest way to do this is to get your hands on a book or an Internet database of companies. Be sure to pick one that includes private companies. Do a search within the geography that you prefer. Make the list. There's a good chance that you're going to identify many, many prospects. You're going to need some criteria to whittle the list down to two to four or at least prioritize the list. You can do this by checking news sources and sending out emails to your support group(s), inquiring about companies on your list.

B. <u>Research the Employer</u> – The information that you're going to look for includes:

- The lead people
- Its organizational structure
- Its products
- Its customers
- Its suppliers
- Its competitors
- Its financials
- Its terminology

The goal here is two-fold.

- Find out everything you can about the employer before you approach them.
- Develop a list of facts about the employer's customers, suppliers, competitors, etc. that the leaders of the employer may not know about and that you will tell them about.

Ideas

Once you whittle the list down to two to four, <u>pick</u> one company from the list and start researching it. If it is a public company, this will be relatively easy. You will be able to find lots of information on the Internet and at your library. Also, <u>contact</u> the company's investor relations department and <u>ask</u> for copies of annual and quarterly reports and get on their mailing lists, if any. Finally, <u>keep up to date</u> on what is going on with the employer and keep records of events.

Here are some other ways to get information about the employer:

- <u>Identify</u> and meet with its customers.
- <u>Identify</u> and meet with its suppliers.
- <u>Go</u> to the employer's distribution or sales facilities.
- <u>Meet</u> with people who used to work for the employer.

- <u>Go</u> to trade shows where the employer has exhibits.
- Go to trade association meetings where the employer is represented.
- <u>Ask</u> your accountant, tax preparer, and financial advisor about the employer.
- <u>Hold</u> "informational" interviews with anyone who might have some knowledge about the employer.

Collect articles, papers, and reports about the company. <u>Keep</u> notes on what people said. <u>Catalogue</u> and <u>organize</u> everything.

C. <u>Meet with People Who Currently Work for Your Target Employer</u> – The first step is going to be to identify them. Use the approaches that I laid out in previous chapter as to how to identify the hiring manager for a specific job. Do not be picky. Anyone you identify is worthy of meeting with.

The next step is to compose a letter to send to these people. I've provided one in Appendix E. It is named "Cover Letter to Target Company." It is similar to the "Cover Letter (No Specific Job)." However, it is more focused and offers something to the recipient.

Paragraph #1 – <u>Identify</u> your role/function and explain why you are sending the person a letter.

Paragraph #2 – <u>Describe</u> the research that you have been doing and the reasons why you want to work there. If you have already met with other people who currently work for the company, name them.

Paragraph #3 – <u>Offer</u> to share what you have seen and heard. This sentence is the "grabber." Set it off in its own paragraph, so that it stands out.

Paragraph #4 – <u>Explain</u> what you want from the person. Be sure to include a sentence that acknowledges that you know the person does not have a job for you. If you don't explicitly say it, the person might assume you will badger them during the meeting about a job and that will reduce the chance that he/she will be willing to meet with you.

Paragraph #5 – <u>State</u> what you will do next to initiate a meeting. Put the onus on yourself. Don't expect the other person to take the next step.

Paragraph #6 - <u>Close</u> with an expression of appreciation.

<u>Send</u> the letter. <u>Call</u> the person when you said you would. (Don't email him/her.) Refer to your letter. Ask for the meeting. (At this point, also refer to Chapter 26, "Overcome Objections to Meeting with You.")

If you are unable to reach the person, <u>leave</u> a message that refers to the letter and close by saying that you will call again at a later time. You can also include a statement like "If you wish to contact me before then, my number is 999-999-9999." Just don't expect the person to call you.

If you are unable to reach the person after three or four tries, contact his/her administrative assistant, explain your goal and mention your letter. Ask for advice as to how to reach the person.

If you reach the person and he/she dismisses your request, re-state your intense interest in the company and ask if there is someone else in the company who might be more appropriate to meet with. (<u>Always</u> ask for a referral.) If he/she names someone else, ask for some details about that other person such as his/her title, location, phone number, etc.

Even if you are never able to reach this person or he/she dismisses your request, <u>send</u> a brief thank you note for his/her time and consideration.

When preparing to meet with a person, assemble and take all your promotional material, plus all your research material.

When you meet with this person, remember this is *<u>not</u>* a job interview. This is a give and take meeting. First, give. Then, take.

Tell this person:

- Your name / describe your role / job title.
- What your goal is (land a job with this company).
- Describe your research and name who else you've already met with.
- Offer copies of any material that you have obtained or developed about the company.

Ask this person:

- Anything you want to know about the company. (Remember, you are trying to become an expert on the company. Re-visit the list of information to obtain about a company in Part B, Chapter 12, entitled "Research the Company.")
- What department within the company has positions like those you are looking for?
- For his/her business card. At a minimum, get his/her email address.
- For referrals to other people in the company.
- For authorization to use his/her name when contacting the other person.
- If he/she would contact the other person and suggest he/she meets with you.

Within 24 hours of the meeting, send a thank you note / letter. Refer to points that came up in discussion during the meeting. Tell him/her what your next step will be. Express appreciation for his/her time and consideration.

Every two to three weeks, send out an email to every person at the company you attempted to contact (whether you met with them or not). Remind them of your intense interest to obtain employment there. Update them on any new research, your recent progress, and, in particular, any additional people you have met within the company.

"Job Fairs" are another place where you can meet people who work for companies and are recruiting people. They are typically arranged by local or regional cross-functional organizations and held in hotels. My own firsthand experience with job fairs and second-hand information from job seekers indicates that these are not particularly effective approaches to finding a job. It's not altogether apparent why. It may be because the jobs these employers are trying to fill are ones for which they have many employees performing the same job and there is constant turnover. Regardless, if you attend job fairs with low expectations, they still offer a good opportunity to meet people who can lead you to a job you want.

D. <u>Use Nesting to Get a Job with a Large Company</u> – The material in the prior sections in this chapter applies to both small and large companies. With large companies, there are some additional things you can do to help you out. You can apply the ideas below to small companies, but you will find that they are more effective with larger ones.

Here is a list of "standard" things to do:

- Check out the company's job web site at least once a week.

- Submit applications/resumes for each and every job that interests you. (Do <u>*not*</u> assume that your resume will get passed on to a second or third job, just because you submitted it for one job.)

- If the company's web site has a feature by which it will notify you of new job openings that match your desired job, use that, too.

- Get your resume into the company's resume database.

- Identify the recruiter who is responsible for the area that interests you. Contact that person every few weeks, let him/her know how much you want to work at his/her company, and that you are still pursuing a job there. Find out how he/she wants to operate and conform/cooperate.

Ideas

Here are the "non-standard things to do." (This is where "nesting" comes in to play.)

- Ask anyone and everyone you know or meet (at the grocery store, during poker night, on the golf course, etc.) if they know someone who works at your target company, could you contact that insider, and would that person let the inside person know that you will be calling and to please take your call. With large companies, there a good chance that one in five people you encounter in a casual setting will know someone at your target company.

- Contact <u>every</u> person at your target company who you identify as an insider. Take these insiders out to breakfast / lunch. (Yes, it takes money to make money.) Definitely return any favor with a favor.

- Unless you really are some type of "specialist," develop words, sentences, and paragraphs that explain the kind of job you are looking for in more "general" terms. (In other words, appear as flexible, as you can.) The reason for this is very often in large companies, the same kinds of jobs are performed in more than one group. If you present yourself as "too" specialized, insiders won't think of these other groups as something that you might be interested in . . . . . and you want their help identifying all the groups and hiring managers you might want to make a run at.

- Keep a list of the people you encounter at the target company, their contact information, and log / journal every encounter with them. That way, you will be able to refer to past discussions, when you contact them again . . . . . which you will. Referring to past discussions enhances the relationship with the person you are contacting and frequently increases the sense in the other person's mind that he/she should do something to help you in your job search.

- About every four to six weeks, send an email to all the insiders that you identified. Here is list of the kinds of things to include:
  - Confirm that you are still looking for a job with this employer.
  - Things you have recently done, trying to land a job with this employer. (For example: people you've called or met, job interviews, networking meetings, job training obtained.)
  - Things you are planning to do to land a job with this employer.
  - Requests for information about the organization or referrals to other people.
- When you send out your insider email, unless there is some clear reason not to, include the inside recruiter that you are working with on these status emails. (Note: This can become sticky, if the inside recruiter does not appreciate you going around him/her. If you get an ultimatum from the recruiter to stop going around him/her, you may need to make an important judgment call as to whether you are going to only work through the recruiter or around him/her.

The experienced, professional, psychologically sound inside recruiters will be OK with this, and probably even be impressed with your initiative. However, not all are like that.)

- Ask for, and develop, a short list of "key" insiders who are willing to identify hiring managers of jobs you want to apply for, are willing to pass on your resume to those hiring managers, and are willing to recommend you to a hiring manager and ask the hiring manager to meet/talk with you.

- Call hiring managers directly. Ask for an interview, whether they have a job or not. They may not have an opening today, but when they do, it's better if they already know you. If they have a job opening that you want to pursue, send your "T" letter and resume to them. Then, call them.

- When you are in the interviewing process for a job, ask your "key" insiders to contact the hiring manager and speak up for you. Also ask the people on your official list of references to call the hiring manager or send him/her a letter on your behalf. In other words, use the people who will stand up for you in a *proactive* mode.

- After you land the job, send out one last email to all the folks who helped and tell them about your new job. They will be glad to hear that they contributed to your success.

I used this "nesting" approach the last time I was looking for a job. My target was a large insurance company. I had identified 42 people in the company and I was able to meet with 38 of them. One of those insiders led me to a job that happened to be the opening for his boss's job, which I ultimately landed. (How's that for picking your boss!)

Chapter 13 – Network, Network, and Network

Concepts

In real estate, the three most important things are location, location, and location. In the job search, the three most important things are networking, networking, and networking.

The third way to look for a job is by networking. As a matter of fact, 65% to75% of jobs are found through networking. You should spend that much of your job search time networking.

I've surveyed over a 1,500 job seekers, asking what the most challenging aspect of their job search is. The second most frequent answer is "how to network." 18% of the job seekers say understanding networking is their biggest challenge. (The first most common response is "finding jobs." 31% say that is their biggest challenge. Well, networking helps that, too.)

There are many aspects to networking. If you talk to five people, you will hear five different approaches. If you read the chapters in three to four books on networking, you will get surprisingly different information. The material here comes from my reading, four to six experts who have come to our Chagrin Valley Job Seekers (CVJS) meetings and spoken on the subject, the experiences of job seekers that I have worked with, and my own experiences. In this chapter, I am going to pull it together, organize it, and provide you with step-by-step instructions.

Because of the large amount of detail that I'm going to provide, let me give you a roadmap of where I'm headed:

- Why (goals / purposes of networking)
- An Overview of the Process of Networking
- Who are these people you should network with?
- When do you do it?

- <u>Where</u> do you do it?
- <u>What</u> do you say? Do?
- Tips (some crisp ideas to enhance your networking skills)

<u>Why?</u> – There are three types of interviews. First, there's the "job" interview, in which you and a hiring manager are talking about a specific job. Second, there's the "informational" interview in which you are trying to obtain information about some subject (for example: the job market, a career, a field, an industry, an organization, a specific company). Third, a "networking" interview is one in which you have one or more of the following goals:

- To identify an organization or person who has a job you might want.
- To get a referral to another person who may know an organization or person who has a job you might want.
- To get a referral to someone else you could network with.
- To market yourself and your availability.

Note that during a "networking" interview, you may find that it drifts off into an "informational" interview. That's OK, as long as you bring it back around to your original goals for meeting with the person.

There is another aspect of a "networking" interview that you need to be cognizant of. That is, you are the interviewer, not the interviewee. Yes, you are going to sell yourself. Yes, you are going to share your promotional information. However, you want to focus on the first two goals of networking. From this standpoint, it is better for you to use the term "networking" interview, so you don't lose track of who is supposed to run the meeting.

Caution

Note: <u>Do not</u> perceive a "networking" interview as an opportunity to ask someone for a job. The networking process laid out on the next few pages is meant to pursue the goals stated above. If someone agrees to talk/meet with you on these terms and then you switch to inquiring about a job with that person or his/her organization, you misrepresented yourself and your credibility will be harmed going forward. It is possible that the interviewee will reveal a job opportunity and the conversation will shift to that. If that occurs, that's OK, because the interviewee started it.

A. Learn How to Network

An Overview of the Process of Networking – In simple terms, networking is merely talking to another person to achieve the goals outlined above, but let me get a little more specific.

Procedure

Here is an overview of the steps in the process of networking:

1. Determine whom to network with and prioritize them.
2. Set up the meeting.
3. Prepare for the meeting.
4. Conduct the meeting.
5. Follow-up after the meeting.
6. Update your records.
7. Keep the person informed of your job search progress.
8. Go back to step 1 and repeat.

I detail these in the next sections.

1. Determine Who to Network With

Concepts

Who are these people you're going to network with? Believe it or not, you already know many of them.

You may have heard about the "6 degrees of separation." It basically means that there are only five people between you and everyone else in the world. You know someone, who knows someone, who knows someone, who knows someone, etc. The idea is to work your way through the network to the person who is going to hire you. Hopefully, even though you don't know that person, yet, he/she is less than six degrees away from you.

In picture terms, it looks like this:

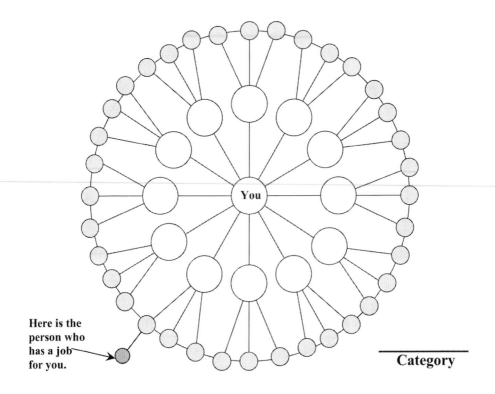

Here is the person who has a job for you. →

Category

You are in the center. Each circle is a person. Each ring of circles represents a "degree of separation," of which I have only shown two.

The idea is to start with people you already know. These people are represented by the first ring around you. Meet with these people, ask for referrals, and branch out to the next ring.

Ideas

Who are these people that you already know? Below is a list of categories and examples of people who you already know that you can start networking with.

1. <u>Relatives</u> (for example: your spouse, your parents, your children, your siblings)
2. <u>Friends / Social Acquaintances</u> (for example: neighbors, partying pals, golfing buddies, card playing group, country club members)
3. <u>Occupational</u> (for example: colleagues, bosses, customers, suppliers, competitors, your spouse's employer, customers, suppliers)
4. <u>Trade / Professional Associations</u> (for example: Chamber of Commerce, Financial Executives Network, Sales & Marketing Executives Association)
5. <u>School / Education / Alumni</u> (for example: your high school, college, trade school, your spouse's, your children's, conferences / seminars you attended)
6. <u>Civic / Service Group</u> (for example: PTA, Kiwanis, Jaycees, Rotary, Theatre, Symphony, Ballet)
7. <u>Service Providers</u> (for example: your CPA, your attorney, your insurance agent, your financial planner, your doctor, your dentist, retailers, bank branch managers, realtors, garage/ service station owners, barbers/hair stylists)
8. <u>Governmental / Political</u> (for example: your councilman, politicians, city hall administrators, civic center, military)
9. <u>Religious</u> (for example: churches/temples/mosques, mission activities)
10. <u>Community / Cultural / Ethnic</u> (for example: volunteer organizations, nationality, gender, or racial specific organizations, festivals, and fairs)
11. <u>Hobbies</u> (for example: sports teams, card clubs, health club, photography club)

12. <u>Job Hunting</u> (for example: job seeker groups, government agencies for the unemployed)

Pick a category and write down the names of the people in that category on the diagram. Put the name of the category on the diagram in the place provided.

This method of networking is taught to sales people who market services to individuals. Examples of these jobs are stock brokers, insurance salesman, financial planners, and tax accountants. Their whole livelihood depends upon constantly getting referrals to new customers by networking. (Did you ever wonder how they got your name, when they called you "out of the blue?")

One of the important tasks of networking is to keep track of who referred you to a person. You will find that easy to do if you use the diagram. As you meet with people, you will ask for referrals. When you get one, add that new person's name to the diagram connected to the person who gave you the referral.

When you meet with someone, write the name onto the diagram. This may seem like an unnecessary administrative task. However, when you attempt to contact someone, you will have much more success getting through if you can say something to the effect of "_____ {name the person] suggested I call you." If you don't come up with some type of scheme to record from whom you got a person's name, it will be difficult to do make an opening like that.

The important thing to recognize is that virtually _everyone_ that you know is a potential networking contact. For example, I got an interview with a large company in northeast Ohio by networking with the woman who cleans my home. She happened to live next to a vice president of a target company. She was willing to carry my resume to this VP and say something nice about a job seeker whom she knew. Sure enough, I contacted the company and the VP. The path had been greased and I got the interview.

A few months down the road, after many networking meetings, you are going to think that you have run out of networking contacts. Come back to these diagrams, pick one with some people that you haven't yet contacted or start a new category and diagram.

There is another source for identifying people to network with. That is an Internet networking group. There are many. *LinkedIn* tends to focus on business people. Other sites are *Ryze* and *Friendster*. *MySpace*, *Facebook*, *Plaxo*, and *Naymz* tend to have a more social orientation. Check out a couple of these sites and determine which might best fit your circumstances. When you join one or two, seek out people you know who are already members and ask them to connect to you. Picking people who already have many other connections will expand your network quickly, into the thousands and, perhaps, hundreds of thousands, of other people you can attempt to reach out to.

When to Network – This is easy. The answer is anytime . . . . . morning, afternoon, evening, seven days a week, 365 days a year. The important issue about "when" relates to specific instances. You should network with someone when it is convenient to the other person. Hey, aren't you the one who's got time on his/her hands? Aren't you the one who wants something from the other person? Then, meet with the other person when it best works for him/her. Bend over backwards trying to make it easy for him/her to meet with you.

Where to Network – This is easy, too. The answer is anywhere . . . . . in offices, at the coffee shop, the graduation party, the grocery store, anywhere. The important issue about "where" relates to specific instances. You should network with someone where it is convenient for the other person. Again, aren't you the one who's got time on his/her hands? Aren't you the one who wants something from the other person? Then, meet with the other person where it best works for him/her. Bend over backwards trying to make it easy for him/her to meet with you. . . . . . There is an additional factor to take into account, though, in regard to "where." That is, it is to your advantage to meet at the other person's place of employment. Why? Because good things will happen there. The other person may introduce you to other people within his/her organization. They probably won't have a job for you there, but you want to maximize the chance that you meet someone, who knows someone, who has a job for you.

2. <u>Set Up the Meeting</u> – OK, right now, you're probably starting to have some anxiety around the prospects of calling someone to ask them to meet with you. Good news. That's only the second best way to set up a meeting. The best way to get a meeting set up is to have someone else set the meeting up for you. Who is that person? It's the person who gave you the name of the person you want to network with. (Granted, if you're operating on the "first-degree" of connections, you will need to be the one to set the meeting up, but then, you already know those people.) Have the referring person contact the person you hope to network with, give some background on you, inform him/her that you will be calling, and ask *him/her to take your call.* The last part is clearly the important one. You want the person who makes the contact to "grease the path" for you. This is called a "warm-up call." It warms a person up to receive and accept you when you contact them.

Whether a "warm-up call" occurred or not, you will need to contact the person you want to network with in order to arrange the day and time of the meeting. Here are the ways to contact the person, in preferential order:

- Face-to-face (best)
- Phone
- email
- U.S. Mail (worst)

Before you make the contact, you need to script out what you are going to say. Here is an outline of what to cover with some examples.

Parts of the Message	Examples
Identify yourself.	"Hello, my name is John Smith."
Identify how you came to know this person.	"I got your name from Betty Johnson. She suggested I call you." Or "Sam Gerard called you a couple of days ago indicating I was going to call."
Explain what you are trying to accomplish.	"I am seeking an IT programming job in the health care field."
Defuse any apprehensions that the person may have for meeting with you.	"I recognize that you do not have any job openings and I have no intention of pressing you along those lines. I would only take up 15-20 minutes of your time."
Name / describe anything you have to offer the person that would give him/her incentive for talking/meeting with you.	"I did some research on your industry and thought you might be interested." Or, "I obtained a report on _____ {name a subject} and thought you might like to have a copy."
Tell him/her what you hope to accomplish at the meeting.	"I'd like to provide you with information about my background and work experience and inquire if you know of anyone or any organization that might be willing to meet with me." or "Betty said you were very knowledgeable about _____. I'd like to ask you about _____, _____, and _____."

The last thing you need to do before making the contact is to script out your response to the person's objections for meeting with you. Here are their possible objections and suggested rebuttals for you.

Objection	Your Rebuttal
"I don't have time."	"I promise to keep the meeting to only 20 minutes and we can meet at a place and time that is convenient to you. Would next Monday at 2 PM in your office work for you?"
"I don't know you."	Either "I got your name from _____ {name a person}." Or "We met at _____ ____ {name a place}." Or "We both attended _____ {name an event} back in October and met in the lobby."
"I don't have a job for you."	Repeat the example defusing statement suggested above. Or tell him/her what you have to offer him/her.
"I can't recommend you."	"Oh, I recognize that. I didn't intend to ask you to recommend me to anyone. I plan on talking about _____." {name a topic}.

It is OK to be aggressive when trying to set up a meeting. Being a pest or outright rude is not. It's sometimes hard to determine where to draw the line. It is my sense that job seekers give up too soon. Therefore, I suggest that you learn to be a pushier person than you normally are. If you push too hard with someone, they will send you a verbal signal and you can back off. Even if that happens, you'll probably never encounter that person again.

OK, it's time. You're ready. Make the call.

3. Prepare for the Meeting – I need to address this in general and for specific cases. In general, preparation means getting all your promotional material together. I addressed promotional materials in detail in Chapter 7. Go back and look at the list of promotional materials and get them together . . . . . not just one copy for a networking meeting, but two . . . . . one for you and one for the other person.

For each specific networking meeting, you need to make an outline of what you are going to talk about.

Ideas

The script described under "Set Up the Meeting" is a good place to start. It will refresh the networking contact's memory as to why he/she agreed to meet with you. It will get you started and, hopefully, passed those uncomfortable moments that are common to meeting start-ups.

There are three other items that you need to prepare. The first is any material, articles, reports, etc. which you have that the other person might find of value.

The second is a list of questions you want to ask the networking contact during the meeting. Here are some examples:

- Facts and opinions about the subjects you said were the pretext for the meeting when you arranged the meeting.
- Ask for information about your industry, your function, specific companies.
- Advice as to how to proceed in your job search.
- The kind of information you might come across in the future that the networking contact would like to hear about.

Last, make a list of what the contact can do to help you in your search. If you can't explain how he/she can help you, your contact isn't going to be able to figure it out on his/her own. Unless a person's job depends on networking, you will find that most people don't understand networking any more than you did before you started reading this chapter. You, effectively, have to train them in the process. Give them ideas as to how they can help you. Here are examples of what you can ask.

- Give you a referral to another networking contact (anyone who might be willing to meet with you or help you in your job search).

- Identify specific jobs for you.
- Identify organizations that may have a job like the one you want (even if they don't have an opening now).
- To call another person, let him/her know that you will be calling, and ask them to take your call.
- To keep you in his/her mind, in case they come across something that you might be interested in.
- To pass on your business card and resume.

4. Conduct the Meeting – During a job interview, it is typically the interviewer, and not the job seeker, who controls and conducts the meeting. In a networking meeting, **_you_** need to be the one to take charge.

If you read the last couple of pages closely, you now know how to conduct the meeting, but here is a brief outline of what to cover.

- Use your introductory script.
- Offer material of interest to the other party.
- Talk about yourself. Explain how you ended up in this situation and what your background, experience, and skills are. (resume-type stuff).
- Describe the kind of job you are looking for. If time permits, go through "Your Desired Job" paper, line-by-line. (very important)
- Give the other party your Marketing Plan (Appendix F). *Go through it in detail*. Make sure the other party understands the kind of work and employer that you are seeking.
- Go over the questions you prepared for the contact.
- Ask for a referral to someone else who might be willing to meet with you.
- Explain how the other person can help you after this meeting.

- Give him/her copies of your other promotional materials (resume, business card, etc.).
- Get his/her business card (email address, in particular).

Remember, you don't have much time. When you arranged the meeting, you probably committed to keeping it to only 15-20 minutes. The last three to four items on the list are the most important ones. Don't burn up too much time with the first four to six items on the list. It's not necessary to give blow-by-blow detail of your entire work history.

If people at companies or other networking contacts are named by the networking contact, be sure to ask how you should contact those people, whether you can use this networking contact's name, and whether he/she would be willing to call the referral and "warm" him/her up?

5. <u>Follow-Up After the Meeting</u> – Everyone knows that you send a thank you note after a job interview, right? Well, you should do exactly the same after a networking interview. In Chapter 4, I described how to pump out good thank you notes for Informational Interviews. The same applies for networking meetings.

6. <u>Update Your Records</u> – Do not develop the mind set that you meet with someone once and that's it. I've said in a couple places in this book that you should be trying to develop relationships, not contacts. You will speak with people you have relationships with more than once. Now is the time to take a couple of moments to log some notes about the person you just met with and what was discussed. Obvious things to record are his/her name, contact information, and the date and place of the meeting. Also consider noting any personal things like the type of wine the person likes, his/her favorite sports team or hobby . . . . . anything to connect you to the person when you contact him/her again.

7. <u>Updating Networking Contacts on Your Job Search Status</u> – Continuing with the theme of developing relationships, you want to periodically, say every four to eight weeks, update your network on your progress of your job search. The easiest way to do this is with emails. Examples of what you can cover are:

- Confirm that you are still looking for the same type of job or describe any change.
- Things you have recently done. (For example: job interviews, networking meetings, job training obtained.)
- Things you are planning to do.

<u>The Accidental Meeting</u> – The day is going come when you accidentally meet someone you know at the pharmacy or your work-out gym. You want to turn that into a mini-networking meeting.

Ideas

Here's how.

1. Ask the person how he/she is doing. He/she will ask you the same.
2. Ask the person how work is going. He/she will ask you the same. That opens the door for you.
3. Tell him/her that you are a "free agent," looking for a _____ _____ {name a type} job.
4. Ask him/her who is the _____ {name a function} manager where he/she works.
5. Go to your car and get copies of your promotional material, bring it back, and give it to your acquaintance.
6. Tell the person how he/she can help you. (Remember, they don't know how to help you.)
7. Ask for a referral.

Tips for Networking – Here are the best ones I've ever heard with some examples.

1. Dig your well, before you're thirsty. (In other words, even when you have a job, treat *every* person whom you encounter as a potential networking contact in the future. Update your records with their names and contact information.)

2. Make sure *everyone* you encounter knows that you are looking for a job.

3. Not only are you a sales person now, but you must turn everyone with whom you talk/meet into a sales person for you.

4. Train your spouse (the key member of your sales force) how to network.

5. Use an "Advocate" to develop and create networking opportunities for you.

6. Join several trade or professional organizations. Regularly attend their meetings.

7. *Always* ask a networking contact for a referral. (absolutely critical)

8. Get and stay organized. Capture all pertinent information about networking contacts and use a system that will work long after your job search is over. Remember, you want to build relationships, not contacts.

9. *Always* be able to quickly and clearly present yourself and what you're looking for. (You are going to accidentally encounter networking opportunities at social events and on errands.)

10. *Always* have your promotional documents with you when you're out of your house.

11. Do some volunteer type work, particularly types that give you a legitimate basis for meeting with people who might hire you.

12. Have a prepared list of questions/information you want from the other people. (For example: information about a target company, other contacts, information about your field.)

13. Make every effort to give as much as you receive (contacts, ideas, job fairs, articles, breaking news, etc.) and appreciate that networking is a two-way street.

14. More specifically, collect information and/or develop an analysis/report on a field, an industry, a company, a competitor, etc. that would be of value to a networking contact and give him/her incentive to meet with you.

15. If the networking contact suggests a course of action or someone to contact, after you follow through, let the suggesting party know the outcome. The helpers/advisors are dying to know if you follow their advice and what happened. Providing feedback will also enhance/sustain your connection to the other person. This is how you develop relationships.

16. If possible, meet in the networking contact person's office. Good things frequently happen there.

17. Do not tell the networking contact that you want to do some networking. Half of them don't know what you mean and the other half will feel that you just want to "use" them. The third half will think that you are going to badger them for a job. (three halves??? It's just a test to see if you're reading closely.)

18. Instead of networking on behalf of yourself, make contacts on behalf of another job seeker and promote / recommend that other person. This will give you experience in making

networking contacts and most people find it easier to talk about someone else.

19. Follow up with your "best" networking contacts (about every 45-60 days). Use the mail or email and send out updates on how your job hunt has been going.

20. Develop relationships, not contacts. (It bears repeating several more times.)

21. The more you give, the more you will get back.

22. It's not "What you know" or "Who you know" . . . . . It's "Who knows <u>You</u>."

23. Meet with anyone who will meet with you, especially in their office. Do NOT rule out anyone by virtue of their function, title, education, background, current company, etc.

Chapter 14 – Work With Recruiters

The fourth way to look for a job is through recruiters.

It is my view that job seekers place far too much value and importance on recruiters and many misunderstand the role of recruiters. In addition, too many recruiters mislead job seekers as to what they can do for a job seeker, some are unscrupulous, and a few just outright lie. Consequently, you are going to read a very candid view about recruiters in order to balance off the typical job seeker's view.

Recently, a job seeker told me an unfortunate experience he had with a recruiter. Basically, the recruiter abused him. She was condescending in her tone and treatment of him. It was her way or the highway. On one occasion, she asked him to change his resume. When she saw the changes, she said that was great. The next day, she called to say she didn't like the resume. Becoming suspicious and concerned, the job seeker indicated he wanted a commitment from her that she would not do something that negatively impacted his relationship with his current employer. She wouldn't commit. The job seeker final stopped working with her.

Note. All this isn't to say that recruiters don't provide value. They do. It's just that job seekers tend to over-rate the value. There are many excellent recruiters, who are of value to job seekers. Some of them have even participated on CVJS panels.

The goal of this chapter is to help you recognize the good, the bad, and the ugly recruiters and to show you how to maximize the value derived from recruiters, if you work with one.

First, I need to describe the types of recruiters.

148

- Internal Recruiters – People who are employees of an organization, typically in the HR Department, and only recruit for that organization.

- External Recruiters – People who work for themselves or a recruiting firm and recruit for many employers. There are two sub-types:

  - Retained Recruiters – People who typically have a contractual arrangement with an employer and get paid, regardless of where the hired person comes from. These recruiters typically work on higher paying jobs ($200K and up).

  - Contingency Recruiters – People who only get paid by the employer if the person hired comes through the recruiter. (This is the vast majority of recruiters.)

The rest of the material in this chapter focuses on the last type, Contingency External Recruiters.

As I said before, job seekers tend to misunderstand the role of recruiters. This has led to some commonly held myths about recruiters. They go like this:

Myth	The Truth
Recruiters find jobs for people.	They don't. They find people for jobs. (If you "get" this, you will have far more success working with recruiters.)
Lots of people find jobs through recruiters.	They don't. Surveys say only 5%-10% of the jobs are found through recruiters.
A job seeker should "seek out and select" a good recruiter.	It's a rare situation when it is worth a job seeker's time to do this. Recruiters will come to you with jobs. (Recall the first myth above.)
A job seeker is bound to one recruiter.	Not at all. It's OK to work with several to many recruiters.

It is worth a job seeker's time to "register" with a recruiter and fill out his/her forms and applications.	It rarely is. Give a recruiter your resume and answer his/her questions on the phone. They can fill out their own forms and databases.
The recruiter should be in control and on the lead when talking to the employer about the job seeker.	It's appropriate to allow the recruiter to submit you to the employer so that the recruiter can lay claim to his/her right to a fee. After that, you, the job seeker, should . . . . **Get control of your destiny!!!**

Here are some pros and cons for working with recruiters.

<u>Pros</u>

- A recruiter may know about a job that you want, but you don't know about, yet.

- A recruiter may know more about your field, your employer prospects, and the job market than you and offer good advice, accordingly.

- You feel that the recruiter is more competent than you in landing a specific job for you.

<u>Cons</u>

- Recruiters are not working on your behalf. (They work on the employer's behalf.)

- Job seekers typically lose control of their destiny when a recruiter is involved.

- If a hiring manager has two good, equally qualified candidates and you are one represented by a recruiter, and the other candidate represents him/herself, the employer may use the recruiter's fee as a tie-breaker to decide whom to hire and thus, go with the other candidate.

How to Select a Good Recruiter - Many job seekers ask how to "select" a good recruiter. ***It's the wrong question!!!*** If you had "selected" one, what would you want him/her to do for you? Remember, recruiters do not find jobs for people. A recruiter, "selected" by you, is not likely to know about any jobs that you are interested in and is very unlikely to do a search for you. After you "select" one, you will probably never hear from him/her for many weeks, if that.

Nevertheless, if you can't overcome your psychological need to "select" a recruiter, then here are some sources help you seek out a good one:

- Your colleagues and bosses.
- HR people.
- Trade & Professional association members.
- Other job seekers.
- The recruiting directory web publishers Kennedy Information or Hunt-Scanlon.

Seek out first-hand knowledge. Avoid second-hand knowledge and hearsay. Ask a referring person the "standard" questions (coming up shortly) about the recruiter.

In addition, during your job search, you will find that many jobs are posted by recruiters. You are likely to end up working with several, to many, recruiters. That's OK. (Just remember, when you find a job you want to pursue and it was posted by a recruiter, you should first attempt to identify the employer and apply for the job directly with the employer.) Also, be alert for a recruiter who specializes in jobs in your functional area or industry.

Standard Questions to Ask a Recruiter – Before committing to work with someone, you typically ask for some background information on the other person. The same should hold true for recruiters.

Ideas

Ask these questions, whether the recruiter contacted you first, or vice versa.

- How long have you been recruiting?

- How long have you been with this recruiting firm?

- Do you specialize in any industry, functional area, or geographic area?

- What kinds of jobs do you work on? (For example: Level: Entry, Manager, CEO, Term: Temporary, Full Time.)

- Are you a contingency or a retained recruiter?

- How many placements did you make last year? (If you hear a number larger than 20, that may well be a fabrication.)

- Where are you located?

- How do you prefer to operate with job seekers?

- Are you aware of any job opportunities for which I qualify?

How Recruiters Operate – To help you get the most value out of working with a recruiter, you need some insight into how they operate. Here's the gist of it.

- Their objective is to find people to fill jobs with employers.

- *They do not find jobs for job seekers.*

- They are paid by employers in various manners:
  - Typical – Fees can range from 25% to 35% of the employee's annual salary (and more).
  - Fixed Fees – More common with the highest paying jobs.
  - Hourly Rates – Uncommon.
  - Piecemeal – For temporary jobs, they may get a percentage of what the hired person gets.

- They may have contracts with the employers.

- They may not receive the full fee if the person hired leaves the job in less than a year (or some other time period). It depends upon the nature of the business relationship between the recruiter and the employer.

- Tenure
  - Many have been successfully in business for a long time.
  - Many are one-person businesses that disappear when the person finds the job that he/she really wants. (There are virtually no barriers to enter this business.)

- Their Scope
  - Some specialize in a particular industry or functional area.
  - Some focus on a particular regional area.
  - Some focus on lower paying jobs, some on higher paying jobs.
  - Some focus on just temporary or contract jobs.
  - Many / most are generalists. (There's no point to turning down any type of business.)
  - They establish relationships with employers, so that the employers will contact them when they want to hire.

- They look for job openings. Sources are employers, newspaper ads, Internet job posting sites, and word of mouth. (They commonly call job seekers about jobs that job seekers can find posted somewhere, too.)
- They look for candidates. Sources are their internal computer databases, Internet resume posting sites, referrals, other job seekers, and word of mouth.
- They may first talk to the employer to understand the job requirements or they may first find a qualified candidate. (Chicken or the egg?!?)
- They compare candidates' written qualifications to the employer's job requirements.
- The vast majority of candidates placed by recruiters are those "currently" identified for the specific opening for which they are recruiting, rather than from their files of "previously" identified candidates.

- When the job opening is in the public domain, it is a cut-throat business.
  - There are many recruiters working on the same job.
  - Speed in finding the "right" candidate that gets hired is crucial.
  - They commonly don't have time to respond to "status" inquiries from candidates.

- They may submit a candidate to an employer without revealing the candidate's identity or without notifying the candidate beforehand. (If a recruiter does that, consider it to be a "red flag.")

- They contact candidates they think are qualified and interview them by phone and maybe face-to-face.

- Then, they decide which candidates to submit to the employer that will maximize their chances of landing a fee. They may submit three to five candidates.

- If the employer indicates that he/she wants to interview a candidate, the recruiter may coach the candidate how to handle the interview.

- After you've interviewed with the employer, the recruiter typically calls the employer to find out how it went.

- If the employer is really interested in you, the recruiter will call you to see how you think it went.

- When an offer is made, the recruiter will attempt to control the communications and negotiations and convince the job seeker to accept the offer and/or convince the employer to accept the job seeker's counter offer. (Remember, a "contingency" external recruiter only gets paid if there is a deal. While an extra $1,000 or $2,000 may mean a lot to you, it means very little to the recruiter.)

- When business is slow, they may interview job seekers just to get to know them and load their databases for the future, when business picks up.

Characteristics of "Good" Recruiters – I said I'd give you insight into the "good", the "bad", and the "ugly" recruiters. Here's what you will see from the "good" ones.

- They provide you with a good description of the job _and_ the employer.

- They _ask_ you if they can submit you to an employer.

- They call you after they submit your name to an employer with either a date for an interview or they give you a good reason why you were not selected for an interview.

- They advise you not to answer the "What are your salary requirements?" question and coach you how to deal with the question when it comes up.

- They have high integrity and are very "up-front" and not deceptive.

- They do what they say they will do.

- They call you periodically with status on pursuit of a specific job.

- They give you advice to help you in your job search, even if it doesn't immediately help them out.

Characteristics of "Bad" Recruiters – Unfortunately, you're sometimes going to end up working with a recruiter who doesn't fit the "good" characteristics. Here's what you'll experience.

- They rarely call you back unless it is in their best interest.

- They lead you to believe that they have relationships with employers that you can't possibly match.

- They ask you to come to their offices and have you fill out their forms. (That's almost always a waste of your time.)

- They won't have good answers for why you weren't called in for an interview.

Here are some other things you may experience with a "bad" recruiter. These are serious "red flags" and you should be concerned, if it happens to you.

- "Red Flag" – A recruiter asks you where you have been interviewing. (This means the recruiter is fishing for jobs to fill. Answering this question will cause additional competition for you for jobs you were already pursuing.)

- "Red Flag" – You ask the recruiter for an employer's offer in writing and he/she balks for some obscure reason. (If this happens, the recruiter better have a really good reason why the employer won't provide the offer in writing.)

- "Red Flag" – A recruiter calls you and says he/she has a job for which you are an excellent candidate. You get excited and tell the recruiter to submit you to the employer. In a seemingly short time (a day or two), the recruiter calls back and says the job was filled by an internal candidate and starts talking to you about another job. (Bait & Switch)

Characteristics of "Ugly" Recruiters – I'm sorry to say that some of the recruiters out there are seriously unscrupulous.

| Concepts |

If you encounter any of the following with a recruiter, you should break off your connection to him/her and find another way to pursue the job.

- "Red Flag" – They outright lie to you about just about anything, in particular, that they know about a job that "you are perfect for" that doesn't exist.

- "Red Flag" – They try to get you to pay for their services.

- "Red Flag" – They say that you signed a contract that says only they can represent you to an employer (as though they have "exclusive" rights on you).

- "Red Flag" – They ask you to sign a contract that gives them "exclusive" rights on you.

What You Will Experience with Most Recruiters – There are a few other annoying things that you will experience with most recruiters. These are part of the "nature of the beast" and you will do well not to have an emotional reaction to them. Just work your way through it.

- They press candidates very hard for their salary history or salary requirements. (Employers commonly require this and/or the recruiter is trying to be comprehensive in his/her matching process.)

- They don't reveal the name of the employer until they get the sense that you want to pursue the job opening, that you are of high integrity, and you will not cheat them. (They need to protect themselves. They've been ripped off by job seekers too many times, too.)

- They won't return most of your calls.

How You Should Work with Most Recruiters – Now that you know how the recruiters operate, let me focus on how you *should* work with them.

Ideas

- You will hear good things and bad things about the same recruiter. Don't draw any conclusions unless you hear the same thing over and over.

- Distinguish between a recruiting person and a recruiting organization. There are good recruiters working for lousy organizations and vice versa.

- If you first learn about an employer who has a job opportunity that you are interested in through a recruiter and the recruiter identifies the employer, you have a moral and ethical obligation to initially work through the recruiter and give the recruiter the opportunity to lay claim on his/her right to a fee.

- *Never* pay a recruiter for helping you find or land a job.

- *Never* sign anything that says that you have any financial obligation with the recruiter or which restricts your job search in any manner.

- *Never* give a verbal commitment that you are giving the recruiter exclusive rights to you in any manner.

- Avoid answering the "What are your salary requirements?" question.

- Talk with a recruiter as through he/she will pass everything you say on to the hiring manager.

- You need to sell yourself to the recruiter, too.

- After an interview with the employer, contact the recruiter two to four days later and ask for feedback. Before calling, prepare your answer to the recruiter's question "What did you think?"

- If the recruiter is not willing to submit you for a job, ask "Why not?" Then, contact the employer directly, regardless of the recruiter's answer.

- If you aren't going to be invited in for an interview, ask "Why not?"

- Establish a relationship with three to five recruiters who you think are good. Send them a brief email every few weeks to remind them that you are still available. This list of recruiters may grow or shrink as you expand your network.

- (Last, but it should be first.) Avoid pursing a job through a recruiter. Try to determine who the employer is before you contact the recruiter and then approach the employer directly. This will save the employer from having to pay a fee to the recruiter and make you more attractive than another candidate who came through a recruiter.

<u>What to Do If a Recruiter Calls You Out of the Blue</u> – It's going to happen, hopefully many times. Be ready and prepared.

- Be sure to find out up front what the purpose of the call is. Ask "Are you calling me about a specific job or you are just trying to get to know me?"

- Ask "How did you find out about me?"

- If he/she says, "I found your resume on the Internet," ask "Which web site?" (You want to find out which resume posting site is working for you.)

- Listen to what the recruiter has to say and then ask the "standard" questions for a recruiter.

<u>What to Do If a Recruiter Calls You About a Specific Job Opportunity</u> – This too, is going to happen, hopefully many times. Be ready and prepared. (Note: The *sequence* of the bullets below *is* *important*.)

- Ask for details about the job and employer. Get as many details as possible about the employer (size, business, location, etc.) without asking for the employer's name.

- Ask the "standard" questions. (Found a few pages back.)

- If you are not interested in the job, try to help the recruiter by naming other people who might know of someone who is qualified. (Remember, what goes around comes around.)

- If you don't want to work with the recruiter, but want to pursue the job, then do so on your own. Do research to find out who the employer is.

- Ask the recruiter if he/she already submitted you to the employer. ("Red Flag", if he/she already did.)

- Ask the recruiter how many candidates he/she has already, or hopes to, submit to the employer. (Learn what the Demand/Supply situation is.)

- If you think you will be happy working with this recruiter and you want to pursue the job, then ask for the name of the employer.

- If you get the name, tell the recruiter it is OK for him/her to submit you as a candidate. (Again, once you have the employer's name, it is *unethical* for you to go around the recruiter and approach the employer directly.)

<u>Conflicts Between Your Objectives and the Recruiter's Objectives</u> – You want to get a job. The recruiter wants to get paid when an employer hires you. At a high level, and in most cases, your objectives and the recruiter's are aligned. However, that isn't always the case.

Here is an example.

- Suppose Recruiter #1 submits two candidates (A & B) for a job and you are Candidate A.

- Recruiter #2 submits Candidate C for the same job.

- The hiring manager concludes that you are the best qualified for the job, but only slightly better than Candidate C and Candidate B is last.

- The hiring manager also concludes you are much more expensive than Candidate C.

- Candidate C is now his/her first choice and he/she intends to make an offer to Candidate C.

If you were recruiter #1, what would you do now? (Before you read ahead, think about it.)

Here's the answer. Your recruiter figures out what the hiring manager's intentions are (recruiters are street-smart people) and concludes that he/she will not get paid, unless he/she starts promoting his/her Candidate B, aggressively. You'll never know what happened and why you didn't get the job.

How do you protect yourself? You've got to develop a trusting relationship with the hiring manager when you interview with him/her. Here's how you do that.

- At the end of the interview, ask the hiring manager how he/she prefers to handle future communications and that your preference is that they go between the hiring manager and you directly. (Paper communications can be copied to the recruiter.)

- Why? ___You___ need to control the situation.
  - There may be a conflict in objectives between the recruiter and you (as the example above portrayed).
  - Don't let someone else (a recruiter) control, censor, and/or embellish communications between the employer and you.

- If you land the job, it means 25% to 35% of your first annual salary goes to the recruiter. However, it means, hopefully, several annual salaries to you. (You have a lot more "skin" in the game.)

- To convince the hiring manager to communicate directly with you, tell him/her that you will not be badgering him/her every other day for feedback. Tell him/her this before you ask for direct lines of communications between the two of you.

- If the hiring manager wants to work through the recruiter, you'll have to concede.

When an Offer Comes Through a Recruiter – While this is not the preferred way (you asked the hiring manager to communicate directly with you, didn't you?), sometimes it is going to happen. Here's what you do.

Procedure

- Ask for the offer *in writing* from the employer. (Be sure to request that any contingencies related to the offer are included.) The reason to ask for the offer in writing is that experience has shown that verbal offers have a tendency to either change on the fly or sometimes disappear as though they never existed.

- Listen to the recruiter's advice as to how you should respond, but don't immediately act on it. (Remember, the recruiter's objectives and yours may not be aligned. It is not in the best interest of a recruiter to turn you into a tough negotiator. The recruiter is biased and wants you to accept the first offer.)

- Solicit the advice of your advocate / mentor as to how to proceed.

- Based on everyone's advice, decide how you want to respond. Formulate your response in bullet format. Write a letter to the employer and copy the recruiter. (A face-to-face meeting with the hiring manager is better. More elaboration is below.)

- If you accept the offer, restate your understanding of the offer along with any/all terms and conditions and in particular, your understanding of any contingencies.

- If you do not accept the offer, make a counter proposal, stating the terms and conditions that are acceptable to you. (Note: Making counter offers face-to-face with the hiring manager is more effective than a letter.)

If you can't get the offer in writing, that is a "red flag", but you will have to deal with it. In that case, here's what to do.

- Write down the terms of the offer as you understand them and list any contingencies as explained to you by the recruiter.

- Write a letter to the hiring manager. If it was the recruiter who told you what the offer is, include a sentence in the letter that says "_____ {Recruiter Name] told me that you've made the following job offer to me" and then include the description of the offer.

- Again, if you do not accept the offer, make a counter proposal, stating the terms and conditions that are acceptable to *you*.

Critical Note. While letter writing is OK, it is far, far more effective to negotiate compensation and make counter offers face-to-face with the hiring manager. This also is the best way to keep the recruiter from influencing the outcome.

Unless you feel that you are really an incompetent compensation negotiator, eliminate the recruiter and negotiate with the hiring manager directly. (See Chapter 16, "Negotiating Compensation.") If you don't feel you are competent enough to negotiate with the hiring manager yourself, then address the letter to the recruiter and ask him to present it.

The rest of this chapter is devoted to some specific questions that I've received from job seekers on working on recruiters.

<u>Job Seeker Question #1</u> - *Is it OK to go around a recruiter?*

<u>Answer:</u> If you didn't first learn about the job from the recruiter and the recruiter did not identify the employer, the answer is a simple "of course." Be sure to tell the recruiter such, so that he/she doesn't think you are ripping him/her off.

If the recruiter has already submitted you to the employer, then the recruiter is protected (that is, he/she will get the fee if you are hired). If you are unhappy with the recruiter, then you can pursue the job directly with the employer without harming the recruiter.

If the recruiter has not yet submitted you to the employer, but has revealed who the employer is, you have the moral and ethical obligation to keep the recruiter from being cheated out of getting paid, if you are hired. However, even in that case, if you are not happy with the way the recruiter is handling things, inform him/her of such, and tell him/her exactly how you want him/her to proceed. If the recruiter doesn't start operating to your satisfaction, inform him/her that you are through dealing with him/her.

<u>Job Seeker Question #2</u> - *Is it OK to work with two recruiters on different jobs with the same employer?*

<u>Answer:</u> Sure. You didn't sign a contract with either recruiter, did you? You didn't make any verbal commitments otherwise with either recruiter, did you?

But remember, you want to develop relationships during your job search. If you have a strong relationship with Recruiter #1 and do not want to negatively affect it, you may want to tell Recruiter #2 and release him/her.

Job Seeker Question #3 - *Is it OK to work with two recruiters on the same job?*

Answer: Yes, but not for long.

If a recruiter proposes you to an employer without your authorization, you are under no obligation to continue working with that recruiter.

When Recruiter #2 calls, get all the details about the job and employer. When you realize this is a duplicate effort, tell him/her that you are already working on this job with another recruiter. Then, compare what each recruiter intends to do to represent you.

The key questions for you to ask *each* recruiter are:

- Does he/she intend to submit you to the employer?
- Are you his/her #1 candidate?
- What is he/she going to tell the employer as to why the employer should hire you?

Once you hear the answers from each recruiter:

- Decide which one you want to have propose you to the employer.
- Call the other one and tell you've decided to work with other recruiter on this job.

Job Seeker Question #4 - *Is It OK to give a recruiter your references?*

Answer: This may be a "red flag." The recruiter may be looking for people to add to his/her database. Hiring Managers / Employers typically don't ask to investigate a job seeker's references until they've decided to make an offer. If you get a request from a recruiter to see your references, ask "Why?" If the recruiter says it's to pass it on to the employer, then say "I'll be glad to handle that when the time comes." If the recruiter presses and explains that, as part of his due diligence, he intends to check out a job seeker's references before submitting a job seeker to the employer, then you may choose to give the recruiter your references.

Job Seeker Question #5 - *How do you identify and work with a recruiter when you are pursuing a job in another state?*

Answer: Where can you find one? Go back to the section entitled "How to Select a Good Recruiter to Work With" and apply the suggestions there, generically.

Does the recruiter need to be in the desired location? Technically, no. There are recruiters around the country who are connected to other geographically distant recruiters who can help you. However, one would have to believe that local recruiters know about more local opportunities and a job seeker would do better working with a recruiter, who is located in the job destination area.

The challenge in working with recruiters when pursuing a job out of state is how to let enough of them know about your interest in relocating. Post your resume on large, national job search web sites. It's easier for the recruiters to find you than for you to find a recruiter in a distant state who knows about a job you would be interested in.

Finally, forget the recruiters and search the postings in the location where you want to work. Subscribe to newspapers in your target cities. Check out regional job posting web sites that focus on the geographic area that interests you.

Job Seeker Question #6 - *How much do you tell/trust a recruiter?*

Answer: Assume that whatever you tell the recruiter will be passed on to the hiring manager. Don't tell a recruiter anything that you wouldn't tell a hiring manager.

Remember, the recruiter gets paid by the hiring manager. You need to acknowledge the reality that the recruiter is not like a friend with whom you confide.

Pet Peeves that Recruiters Have About Job Seekers – In the interest of fair play, it seems only appropriate to list some of the things job seekers do that drive recruiters "nuts." Here's what I hear them say about job seekers:

- "Job seekers don't know what they want."
- "Job seekers aren't flexible enough in considering what jobs they would accept."
- "Job seekers don't know what they're worth."
- "Job seekers keep calling for status checks when there's no news."
- "Job seekers expect the recruiter to do all the work."

Asking good questions helps to discern the quality of recruiter with whom you're working. With well-defined goals and your promotional materials in order, you help a recruiter you're working with to facilitate your job seeking process.

Phase V - Acquiring

You found a job you want. You contacted the hiring manager or you submitted your resume and, lo and behold, they want to meet you. It's time to shift gears and move into the "acquiring" phase. This phase covers two fundamental parts: interviewing, which hopefully, leads to an offer and negotiating the terms of the offer (the job and the compensation).

Chapter 15 – Interview for a Specific Job

The excitement starts now. To learn how to successfully get through the interviewing process, it's helpful to understand the process from the employer's perspective. Let's start there.

```
Concepts
```

A. <u>Interviewing from the Employer's Perspective</u> – Imagine you're the hiring manager. You need to hire a person. You write up a job description and advertise the job opening. 100-300 resumes come in. You don't have time to go through the pile, so you ask someone in the HR Department to go through the resumes and screen out the ones that obviously don't qualify. You also review the job description with the HR person and provide any additional requirements for the job or qualifications you expect to see in a candidate. More than likely, you will also tell the HR person what you are willing to pay. You ask the HR person to find you the top five, or ten, or maybe even twenty best candidates.

The HR person then starts tackling the resumes. Screening candidates out is pretty easy. (There are lots of people who send their resumes in for nearly any job, even though they aren't even close to qualifying.) However, there are still lots of potentially qualified candidates and the HR person needs to reduce the list. He/she starts holding phone interviews for the long list of candidates. Eventually, the HR person gets it down to the short list that the hiring manager wanted and turns the candidates' material and his/her recommendations over to the hiring manager.

The hiring manager reviews the material for the candidates and decides which ones to invite in for Round #1 of face-to-face interviews. Round #1 of face-to-face interviews typically includes an interview by the HR person and the hiring manager. If the hiring manager is in a rush and/or the job is relatively high ranking, the hiring manager may include his colleagues as interviewers during Round #1 and may even include peers of the person who will be hired.

After Round #1, the hiring manager will get feedback from the other interviewers and decide on his/her next step. If really in a rush, he/she may immediately make an offer to a candidate. Otherwise, he/she will start arranging Round #2. During this round, the hiring manager will likely expand the scope of interviewers. He could include people in other departments who will work with the person who is hired. He also will likely include his own boss. (Few hiring managers want to hire someone that their boss doesn't like.)

If the position is a very senior level one, there could be a Round #3 and #4. The general practice that is the higher the level of the position, the more rounds of interviews there will be.

At some point, the hiring manager must decide who he/she is going to make an offer to. Some hiring managers use thorough and elaborate evaluation schemes. Some defer to their "gut" feel and can tell in five minutes with a candidate whether this is "the one" or not.

Now, the issue for the hiring manager is how much compensation to offer the lucky candidate. There may be a variety of elements to the offer, but let's focus on the salary. There are a variety of criteria that hiring managers take into account when deciding on a salary to offer a candidate, like:

- To what degree he/she may have to conform to a well-defined salary structure that defines minimums and maximums for each job in his/her organization. (The larger the organization and the lower the ranking of the hiring manager, the less flexibility he/she has in setting a salary offer.)

- Salary levels of other people in his/her group that are currently performing the same job.

- Any salary history information the HR person or one of the interviewers was able to extract from the lucky candidate.

- How many other, equally well-qualified candidates there are.
- His/her sense of urgency to fill the job.

If the hiring manager has lots of qualified candidates and/or a psychological need to dominate others and put another "notch in his gun," then the poor, "lucky" candidate is going to get a low-ball offer.

If the hiring manager is a reasonable person, then the offer will be reasonable, at least in comparison to the salary structure that the hiring manager needs to conform with.

More than likely, the hiring manager will not make his best offer first. He/she needs to be prepared to deal with the possibility that the candidate won't accept the opening offer. If that happens, he/she wants to be able to handle it without having to go to his/her boss for approval of more money.

The hiring manager then makes the offer to the candidate. In order to make it harder for the candidate to refuse the offer, the hiring manager will likely have the HR person present the offer. The hiring manager will also have the HR person present the offer if he/she is uncomfortable negotiating compensation.

Doesn't all that sound reasonable? Is that how you would handle it, if you were the hiring manager?

The question now is "How will you, as a job seeker, deal with this interview process?" Read on.

The next sixteen sub-sections focus on Round #1 of the interviewing process. Most of the suggestions apply to subsequent rounds, too.

B. Respond Effectively to Interviewers' Questions – Are you confident you can effectively answer all those crazy questions interviewers ask? You know the ones. "What are your strengths and weaknesses?" "What are you going to be doing in five years?" The two craziest ones I've heard were "How many gas stations are there in the USA?" and "What is your sexual preference?" Yes, really! You're probably thinking the first one is a stupid question and they can't legally ask the second question. Well, they do ask it. How are you going to respond to such questions? There are reasons they ask questions like this.

Most people get anxious about being interviewed. This is largely because they're concerned about getting asked a question for which they don't have a good answer. Answering questions is as much a science as it is an art. It is a matter of practice, understanding the point of the question, the type of response that is needed, and preparation. You have to be ready.

Concepts

First, let me provide some general ground rules for responding to interviewers questions.

- Make every one of your responses sound as positive as you can. You must not let negative emotions or negative thoughts about your past or present circumstances come through in either your words, expressions, or body language.
- If you get a question that stumps you, there are two tried and true ways to handle this. One is to respond with humor.

The second is to respond with a question. There's maybe only a small chance the question will go away, but those two approaches will give you a little more time to compose a response in your mind.

Next, review Appendix J. This is a valuable list of those crazy (and some serious) questions interviewers ask, the reasons they ask them, guidelines for how to respond, and in many cases, specific example answers. Prepare answers to many of the most common questions. Make written notes. Carry them with you. Review them before you go into an interview.

Finally, review Appendix K. This talks about "Behavioral Interview" questions. This is a special type that you will encounter some day. They require a specific type of response, which is explained in that appendix.

C. <u>Practice Your Interviewing Skills</u> – Most of us have apprehension about getting interviewed. However, it's just like anything else. The more you do it, the better you get at it. It took you years to get really good at your job. Isn't it worth some time and energy to enhance your interviewing skills?

I gave you ideas as to how to practice interviewing back in Chapter 8. Now is the time. It's almost too late. Go back and follow the instructions in Chapter 8.

D. <u>Sell Yourself</u>

Concepts

There are many sales experts in this country who have written excellent books on how to sell. Get one of these books and read it. The sales principles they describe apply perfectly when interviewing for a job. One of their common principles is to "know your product." When you are a job seeker, *you* are the product. You need to "tell the customer" (the hiring manager) about the product. Tell the customer about your education, experience, knowledge, skills, and accomplishments. You do this with your resume, but you also need to do this with your words. Don't rely on another person to have read your resume. One way to get your verbal explanation started is with your 30-Second Commercial / Elevator Speech that I discussed in Chapter 7. A brief statement by you will, hopefully, prompt the listener to ask a question and you can continue your verbal explanation by filling in details.

There are, however, a couple of key points that I want you to take into consideration. I learned of the first point from Dana Kachurchak. She has spoken at our CVJS meeting about once a year. Dana started and runs her own consulting company, Presentation Dynamics. Dana provides consultation services to executives at large companies, regarding how to present their proposals and get them accepted. That's called "sales." Dana is an expert on communications and how people take in information. The key point she makes is to "sell" your *benefits*, not your *features*. In the case of a job seeker, your *features* are your education, experience, knowledge, skills, and accomplishments. Now, the message here is not to avoid talking about these things. However, what you need to do is to explain to the hiring manager (or an HR person, or a recruiter, or a networking contact) how your *features* are of *benefit* to the listener and his/her organization. To make the distinction between *benefits* and *features* when she speaks to a room full of job seekers, Dana grabs a card-table chair and places it up on a table where all can see. She asks people to name the *features* of the chair. Well, the *features* are: the chair has a back, it's made of metal, it has four legs and a seat. Next, she asks what the *benefits* of the chair are. Well, the *benefit* of the back of the chair is that it allows a person to sit back and be more comfortable. A metal chair means that it is durable and will last a long time and you won't have to buy another too soon. The four legs are of equal length and provide a flat stable spot. The chair is lightweight and portable and can be moved to a place convenient to the person.

Dana then translates this distinction to the job seeker. When a job seeker speaks of his/her education, experience, knowledge, skills, and accomplishments, he/she should follow each example with "and what this means to you is _____ . [*benefit*]" You finish the sentence with the *benefit* your *feature* provides to the hiring manager. In simple terms, tell the hiring manager why it would be good for him/her to have you around.

This brings me to the second point, which links very closely to the first. During an interview, you want to listen closely to the hiring manager to determine what his/her problems are. Yes, the job posting included a description of the requirements of the job, but those are generic descriptions. They don't describe what it is that is causing anxiety in the hiring manager. You must listen closely and maybe even ask questions to find out what the problems are. The greatest *benefit* that you can bring a hiring manager is to make his problems go away. Figure out how you can do that and tell the hiring manager.

The next point I want to make is you don't want to leave an interview with the hiring manager until you *"ask for the job."* (Note: This may not be appropriate until Round #2 of the interviews. You will need to make a judgment call.) Maybe this sounds somewhat bold. However, it is the same as another principle in the sales experts' books. They call it "asking for the sale." Another term sales people use is "go for the close." You can creep up on "asking for the job" by asking the hiring manager a couple questions like "How well do you feel my qualifications match your job's requirements?" or "Have your learned anything about me which gives you concern that I may not be a good fit for the job?" It is essential that you not leave the interview until you know where you stand in the hiring manager's mind. If you are in good standing, asking will lead to an explanation of the "next steps." If you are not in good standing, you can then inquire what the hiring manager's concerns are and respond to them to improve your standing. In Section J of this chapter, I provide a much more complete list of questions for you to ask during interviews.

Finally, I want to refer you to the book <u>The Greatest Salesman in the World</u>, by Og Mandino (copyright held by Elizabeth L. Mandino). This is a marvelous, enchanting, almost ancient story of a set of selling principles that were passed down from one great salesman to another. The principles fit a job seeker like a glove. The challenges of a salesperson are the same challenges of a job seeker. The ten principles will help you overcome those challenges.

1. I will form good habits and become their slaves.
2. I will greet this day with love in my heart.
3. I will persist until I succeed.
4. I am nature's greatest miracle.
5. I will live this day as though it were my last.
6. Today I will be master of my emotions.
7. I will laugh at the world.
8. Today I will multiply my value a hundredfold.
9. I will act now.
10. I will pray for guidance.

E. <u>Take Something to the Interview</u> – I have found that many job seekers don't feel comfortable talking about (selling) themselves. Here's a tip that will easily get you over that. "Take something to the interview." Why? It gives you something to talk about, other than yourself. If you are a normal human, you will feel a sense of anxiety when you are asked to talk about yourself. However, as soon as you start talking about something that you brought to the interview, your anxiety will drop immediately. You will probably find that, as soon as you talk about an object, it will be just like talking with other people at your last job. Why? Because what you take should have something to do with the kind of work you want to do. Back in Chapter 7, I gave examples of a "Portfolio of Your Work." I also cited the two best, real stories of objects that job seekers took to an interview. Go back there and get some ideas as to what you can take with you to your interviews.

F. <u>Prepare for the Interview</u> — Are you clearly the most well-qualified person for the job? Are you one of those extraordinarily bright people who always comes up with the right answer off the top of your head? Or one of those people who has so much charisma that you own a room you enter in only a matter of minutes? Or does your fame proceed you so much that the employer is already lusting for you?

Well, if you don't meet any of the criteria above, you're going to need to prepare for each interview. While the generic items I describe below that you need to prepare are the same for each interview, the results of your preparation vary from interview to interview. I highly recommend you spend at least three hours of preparation for every one hour that you expect to be interviewing with the hiring manager. (That doesn't count the time needed to research the information and assemble it.)

You may be thinking right now that this is an awful lot to ask. But think about what the situation is. You are probably one of at least three, if not five or seven, candidates who are getting an interview. On paper, you are all well-qualified or you wouldn't have been invited in. The employer is planning to interview all the candidates to figure out who's the best of the lot. How are you going to distinguish yourself? What are you going to do to make the hiring manager conclude that you are "the one?" Oh, you may actually be much more qualified than the other candidates, but can you count on that? Remember, it is easier to train and educate someone on the technical skills and knowledge of the job than trying to get someone to modify his/her personal characteristics, traits, and style. Just like that dinner you had a couple of months ago at the fancy, expensive restaurant, "It's all in the presentation." . . . . . . You may say "Substance is more important than image." Well, even if it is, when the substances of the candidates are the same (or even close), image is going to win out.

How do you present yourself well? You prepare and display confidence. How do you display confidence? The easiest way is to be well-prepared, ready to handle whatever they throw at you. How do you get well-prepared? It takes two fundamental tasks: (1) Gather and digest a bunch of information. (2) Meet with your mentor and get his/her thoughts and encouragement.

Here's a list of information to gather and digest.

- Research the employer. Find out everything you can about their products, customers, suppliers, facilities, financials, and their competitors. (This could take a couple of days. Don't wait until the last minute.)

- Find out everything you can about the people who will be interviewing you. Get their names correct, their titles, their department names, their roles, etc.

- If an external recruiter is involved, contact him/her and ask for all the information he has about the employer's organization and the people with whom you will be interviewing.

- Assemble all the information about the job, particularly the job description.

- Pull out the "Your Desired Job" form. (You filled it out, didn't you?) Compare the job description to your desired job. Look for variances. Note them and inquire about them at the interviews. Pull out the "Your Desired Compensation & Benefits" form and read it again.

- Assemble copies of all your promotional materials. Make copies of those things that you may leave with the employer. (Be sure to take four to six copies of your resume. You can't assume that it was passed around to all the people who will be interviewing you.)

- Read through your resume again. Pay close attention to the "accomplishments" so that you can speak to them extemporaneously.

- Go through Appendix I (Interviewers' Questions and Answers) and Appendix J (Behavioral Interview Questions and Answers) again. Review / memorize answers to key questions.

- Prepare the list of questions you want to ask during the interviews. (This is so important that I elaborate on it in the next section. I provide lists of questions to ask various people you will encounter with the employer.)

- Go back and review the Chapter 16, "Negotiating Compensation" and "Don't Answer the Salary Question."

- Complete your salary research so you know what the salary range for the job you will be interviewing for is in this geographic region.

- Determine the appropriate attire and get it cleaned / prepared. Groom yourself as is appropriate for this interview.

- Re-read through all of the information above and digest it.

Arrange a meeting with your mentor. Take all your materials with you. At the meeting:

- Give your mentor the background about the employer, the hiring manager, and the job.

- Tell your mentor to what degree you are interested in this job.

- Tell him/her what your concerns are. Ask for ideas as to how to deal with them.

- Identify key materials you have.

- Ask your mentor to be a devil's advocate and ask you some tough interviewer-type questions.

- Ask for candid feedback in terms of how well-prepared you are.
- Keep at it until you feel confident that you're going to "ace" the interview.

That's it. If you spend the appropriate amount of time preparing and cover the majority of the items above, you should float through Round #1 of the interviews.

G. <u>Prepare Your Own Questions for the Interview</u> – This is an extremely important task for a job seeker. My sense is that too many job seekers think an interview is when you sit in a room with someone else, they ask you questions and you answer. If you're lucky, you get a job offer and you say "Yes."

Far from it.

You need to ask questions, too . . . . . for two very good reasons. Most importantly, you want to be sure this is a job you want. Secondly, you want to demonstrate to the interviewers that you are capable and are an intelligent, discerning candidate.

I've provided a list of questions for you to consider asking. There is a list for each of the different types of people you are likely to encounter in interviews. See Appendix K.

H. Maneuver Through the Phone Screen – It is now common for many employers, particularly large ones, to start the interviewing process with a phone screen. Phone screens are used when there are lots of candidates or there's a candidate they're not quite sure they want to bring in for an interview. If you get a phone screen, it probably means you're in the running, but not yet on the short list.

Phone screens are usually done by HR people. Occasionally, a hiring manager will do them.

Before the phone screen, HR may send you a list of questions and ask you to answer and return them beforehand. Use the suggestions I gave you for filling out applications to answer these questions. Be sure to keep a copy for your own records and to have on hand during the phone screen.

If an HR person is doing the phone screen, he/she is likely working from a standard list of questions. Most of the questions will be generic, used for all jobs. Some will pertain to the job for which you hope to get a face-to-face interview. It is very unlikely an HR person will know enough detail about the job to be able to ask a technical question you can't answer.

You will get questions about your background and work experience. This is largely a screen to confirm that you "fit" and the personal "chemistry" is fine.

Your goal for a phone screen is to convince the screener to recommend you to the hiring manager who will invite you in for a face-to-face interview.

When the phone screen is arranged, make sure you know the name, title, and role of the person who will be calling. Be absolutely sure of the date, time, and who is going to call whom. If someone is going to call you, be sure to give them a number where you will be able to be alone in quiet surroundings.

Prepare for it as thoroughly as you would a face-to-face interview with the hiring manager.

Thirty to forty-five minutes before the phone screen, go to your desired location. Make sure there won't be any distractions to you or the screener, such as chiming clocks, children playing, or pet noises. Go over the answers to the questions you sent in. Go over the questions you want to ask.

There are a couple of things you need to do during the phone screen. First, stand up. That will help you keep your energy and attention high. Second, use hand gestures and animated body language that will help you communicate your enthusiasm, positive attitude, and interest in the job.

At the end of the phone screen, be sure you ask several of the "Common Questions" in Appendix K, in particular, "How did you stack up?" "Is the screener going to recommend you for a face-to-face interview?" "What is the next step?"

Within 24 hours, send the screener an email expressing your appreciation for his/her time and consideration, and then re-state your interest in the job.

I. Dress/Appropriately for the Interview – Job seekers often ask what they should wear to interviews. Years ago, this question rarely popped up. However, with "business casual" in fashion, it becomes a somewhat more complicated issue. Most job search consultants advise dressing up. I, however, fall back to that old cliché "When in Rome, do as the Romans do." In other words, if you are going to be meeting with the CEO of a large company who you know regularly meets with his high-level customers, you can be highly confident that he'll be dressed impeccably. Therefore, you should have on your best outfit and groom yourself well. On the other hand, if you are pursuing the job of a motorcycle mechanic and you're going to be meeting with the local chapter president of the Hell's Angels, who you expect to be dressed in all black, with leather vest and pants, and long hair and beard, then that's the way you should look. Do you want to be accepted or not?

Of course, this response leads job seekers to ask, "What if I'm not sure how the other person is going to be dressed?" If you consider the possibilities, the answer is easy. Suppose you and your spouse plan on having a fancy house warming party and you invite a lot of influential people. You send out invitations that ask for an RSVP and indicate it is "black tie." (That means, dress-up.) Suppose someone shows up in jeans, a dirty wrinkled shirt, and running shoes. How are you going to feel? You're going to feel angry, insulted, and disrespected. You're going to conclude that this person isn't interested in fitting in at all. If you go on an interview unsure of how the other person is going to be dressed, and you guess on the under-dressed side, that's the way the other person is going to feel. Your error might be small, but the consequences could be big. If the opposite happens and you over-dress, your error is still small, but there aren't likely to be any consequences. (If there are, they'll be positive.) If you are asked back for Round #2, you will also have the chance to ask what dress / attire would be appropriate for Round #2.

J. Ace the Face-to-Face Interview

Concepts

You can't "ace" the interview unless you know what the objective is. It's to get a job offer, right? . . . . . *Wrong.* . . . . . It's a rare hiring manager indeed who makes an offer the first time he/she meets a candidate. The goal for you, as the job seeker, is to be invited back to Round #2 of interviews. But there is second goal, too. That is, for you to figure out whether you really want the job.

Although the second goal is probably more important to you, I suggest that you initially focus on the first goal. Why? Very simply, it's because you aren't going to get the job, unless you achieve the first goal. In addition, the day will come when you are so rushed through a set of Round #1 interviews that you never get a chance to ask the hiring manager much of what the job is about. Not to worry. If you achieved the first goal, you will get the chance to ask more questions during Round #2 and confirm that you really want the job.

The first goal in Round #1 is achieved by being "prepared" and "selling" yourself. I explained how to do that in previous sections in this chapter. If you've read though sections and followed my suggestions, you're going to do just fine. You will distinguish yourself and your chance of being asked back for Round #2 will be much higher than most other candidates. (Remember, many job seekers think all you do is just show up at an interview and answer some questions.)

There's one other background point I want you to understand. There is a high probability that the hiring manager's deciding factors are going to be your personal characteristics, the "chemistry," or the "fit" issue. Why? Think about what the hiring manager and his HR person have done, so far. They worked their way through possibly hundreds of resumes, whittled down the list to five or ten people, probably held phone screens, and reduced the number of candidates to a short list for face-to-face interviews. More than likely, every candidate on the short list appears qualified on paper, from a background and capabilities standpoint. So again, the hiring manager's deciding factors are going to be your personal characteristics. Do I mean that the hiring manager isn't going to ask you any questions to confirm you can handle the job? No. Am I implying you won't have to explain and demonstrate that you are capable? No. What I'm saying is that, unless there is one candidate who stands high above the rest in terms of background and capabilities, the hiring manager's deciding factors are going to be your personal characteristics. Note: This becomes even truer during Round #2 and #3. The higher ranking the people are who interview you, the more and more emphasis they place on your personal characteristics. They rely more and more on the hiring manager to ensure that you are technically capable to handle the job.

It keeps coming back to *"selling yourself."*

You start *"selling yourself"* the moment you meet an interviewer. Shake his/her hand. Give a firm handshake. No one likes a "dead-fish" handshake and few hiring managers want to hire a "wimp." Look him/her in the eye and introduce yourself. He/she'll reciprocate. Repeat the interviewer's name out loud. That confirms to him/her that you are listening and it will also help you to remember his/her name.

The interviewer is going to ask you one of those "opening" questions. I listed several of them in Appendix I, explained how to answer them, and suggested some answers. (You read and memorized those a couple of days before the interview, didn't you?)

Next, you will be taken to the hiring manager's office or maybe a conference room for a private discussion. (In Part II, I talk about the "tag-team" interview in which several people will interview you at the same time.) You will be offered a place to sit. Do so, but don't treat the chair like your recliner at home. Sit on the front edge of the chair. Doing so will help you appear to be attentive and energetic.

Now is the time to get the material ready which you brought with you. There are a variety of items, so let me review them.

- Make sure your resume and business card are readily reachable.

- In a prior section in this chapter, I talked about taking something to the interview for you to talk about. ("Show and Tell.") Pull that out now.

- Pull out the list of questions you want to ask.

- Also, pull out some blank paper or a notepad for notes. You don't need to start taking notes right away. You may not take many notes. However, you need to take some notes to reassure the interviewer that when he/she said something important during the interview, you recognized it. (I also learned a great tip from a job seeker about note taking. He said if you take notes during an interview and you suspect the interviewer is leading up to something confidential and key, but uncertain whether he/she should mention it or not, close your note pad at that moment. The interviewer will recognize that his/her next comments are not going to be recorded and he/she will be more inclined to share with you.)

The vast majority of the time, interviewers ask questions before offering the candidate the opportunity to ask questions. This is the point where you need to have memorized your resume and in particular, your accomplishments. You absolutely must demonstrate your qualifications to handle the job with examples and conviction. You are also going to get a variety of "generic" type questions. Again, I listed many of these in Appendix I, explained how to answer them, and suggested some specific answers. (You reviewed and memorized many of them, didn't you?)

There's one other question you need to have an answer for, but you can't really prepare an answer in advance. The question is "What do you think about the job?" It may come near the end of Round #1 or not until Round #2. The way to answer this question is simple to describe. Answer with as much enthusiasm as you can and mention two to four things you really like about the job. (If there is some aspect of the job that concerns you, don't mention it yet. See the next section for more details on how deal with that situation.)

During the course of an interview, you are likely to get a question that you're not sure how to answer yet. You need some time to think it through. The easiest way to get some time is to initially respond with a question that asks for clarification about the interviewer's question. After that, if you're still not sure how to answer, then consider offering two different answers and indicate you would have to think it through more closely to decide which way you might lean.

At some point during the interview, the interviewer is going to offer you a chance to ask questions. This isn't the time to "hum and haw." Pull out your list. Look prepared. Look like there are some things about this job and this company which are actually important to you to find out about.

Before you leave an interview, particularly with a hiring manager, you want to get a clear idea where you stand, if not actually coming right out and asking for the job ("Ask for the sale," remember?) Below is a list of closing statements. They start with "Timid" and progress up to "Aggressive." Use the one(s) that fit your style and circumstances. If there is clearly going to be a Round #2 of interviews, then it is probably not going to be effective to use the responses below that push for an offer.

- Timid – "Well, where are we?"

- Timid – "Well, what are the next steps?"

- Passive – "Do you have any concerns about my background and capabilities?"

- Passive – "Are you confident I can handle the job?"

- Pessimistic – "Would you like to initially bring me on board as a contractor in a 'try and buy' mode?"

- Direct – "Well, given that there will be another round of interviews, is there any reason why you wouldn't want to invite me back?"

- Challenging – "I feel that my qualifications match the requirements of the job quite well. What do you think?"

- Challenging – "Are you sufficiently confident about my capabilities that you would offer the job to me?"

- Presumptuous – "I would want to give my current employer two weeks notice. Does that work for you?"

- Presumptuous – "Would an offer from you be contingent upon anything?"

- Aggressive – "If you knew I was willing to accept $XX,000, would you offer the job to me?" (This is quite risky, too. I rarely, if ever, recommend that a job seeker be the first to name a number. However, if you think being aggressive is the right way to go, this is it.)

Regardless of where the close ends, you want to be sure what the next step is, who will be taking it, and when it should occur.

K. <u>What To Do If You Conclude You Don't Want the Job</u> – The material in the prior section presumed you have concluded that you want the job. What about the case in which you've decided otherwise?

Concepts

There are two sub-cases to talk about. The first is one if you largely like the job, but there are one, maybe two, aspects of it that you just aren't comfortable with. Do not say anything to any interviewer that suggests that you have great concerns and *definitely* don't say that you don't want the job. Maybe a better way for me to say that is "<u>Don't turn down a job which hasn't yet been offered</u>." Assume that the hiring manager has some latitude to re-configure the job to make it more acceptable to you. What you need to do is to get some sense as to whether he/she can. That's a judgment call that you need to make.

Do you start discussing this during "Round #1 or wait until Round #2? Here are some factors to consider to help make that decision:

Ideas

- How urgent is it to get this issue resolved?

- Do you have other job opportunities that are much more appealing and about to turn from warm to hot?

- How extreme and urgent are your personal and financial stresses?

- To what degree are these troubling aspects of the job uncomfortable to you?

- To what degree do you think you will be invited back to Round #2?

- Getting the hiring manager to reconfigure the job more to your liking is one element of negotiations. Would it be better to bring up your concerns after an offer is made and merge the negotiations of job responsibilities and compensation?

Whenever you decide to raise the subject, this is something to discuss with the hiring manager, not with other interviewers. Also, you want to discuss the issue in positive terms as to what you would like see in the job, not in negative terms as to what you don't like. An un-alarming way to broach the subject is by posing questions. Start off by stating two or three things you like about the job and then say something like "I was hoping for more (or less) _____ with the job. Is that a possibility?" You are now negotiating the job responsibilities. Based on the hiring manager's response, you will get a signal as to whether to bring up another troubling aspect of the job or whether it's hopeless.

The second case is the one in which there are one or more aspects of the job which are so objectionable to you, no matter how much they would pay you, <u>and</u> so unlikely to be re-configurable. There are three things to consider in this situation.

- <u>When</u> do you tell the hiring manager? The bottom line is the longer you wait, the more upset the hiring manager will be when you turn down the job. Even if you are not his/her #1 candidate, he/she will feel that you wasted his/her time. I suggest that you not wait until Round #2 of the interviews. Cut bait no later than near the end of the Round #1 when you conclude this job isn't for you.

- <u>What</u> do you say? The most important thing to keep in mind is that there may be some other job opening within this organization that you don't know about yet, which is exactly what you are looking for. Whatever you do or say now, you want the hiring manager to connect you to that job. I suggest you be candid and specific about those aspects of the job that are troubling to you. This isn't the time to manufacturer some false reasons. They will likely cause you problems later. Clearly tell the hiring manager your concerns and then give him/her a pregnant pause. There is the small chance that he/she is absolutely in love with you and will, in fact, make a dramatic change in the job to your satisfaction. This will also give him/her the chance to consider referring you to another job opening. If neither happens, then express your appreciation to the hiring manager for his time and consideration of you. Then, gracefully make your exit.

- <u>How</u> do you say it? I suggest that you do it face-to-face with the hiring manager. Don't do it in a letter. Why? Because if there is another job opening, the hiring manager is more likely to mention it to you, if you meet with him/her face-to-face.

L. <u>Follow-Up After the Interview</u> – It is *absolutely* essential that you follow up in writing after the interviews, all rounds. This is an excellent and relatively simple way for you to distinguish yourself in the mind of the hiring manager. Decades ago, everyone sent thank you notes. Now, only a small portion of the job seekers do. There was a two-year period in which I interviewed some 35-40 people for a couple different jobs. Guess how many sent me a thank you note? The answer is four and I still remember each one of those people. I even hired one of them.

The first thing to do is to write and send a thank you note to *each* person with whom you met, even the HR person. Get these in the mail within 48 hours after the interviews. One of our CVJS members mastered this part of the follow-up. She carried blank thank you notes and stamped envelops with her in the car. After the interviews, she sat in her car in the employer's parking lot and wrote the thank you notes. She dropped them in the mail on the way home. Now that's both efficient and effective!

Short notes are fine. Using those small thank you notes that fold up and small envelopes are OK. They will even stand out in the recipients' mail slots. The messages to include are few and simple:

- Thanks for meeting with me about the _____ position and answering my questions.

- If I can answer anything else about myself, please don't hesitate to contact me.

- I am quite interested in the job.

- I hope to have the opportunity to come in for additional interviews.

Write these messages out in your own style.

One additional message should be included in the thank you note you send to the hiring manager. Mention that you will be following up with a letter that provides a more complete follow-up to the interviews. What is the point of this follow-up letter to the hiring manager? Here are some ideas.

- Re-state your interest in the job and the desire to be called back for more interviews.

- Re-state your qualifications for the job (now that you understand the job requirements more completely.)

- Re-state a couple very positive things that came up during the conversation between you and the hiring manager.

- Polish off any weak answers that you gave during the interview. (Remember, if you're like most people, you get home and think, "Wow, if only I had said this." Now, you get a chance to say it.)

- If the hiring manager raised a critical subject during the interview that was looking for insight into your capabilities and you have examples of your prior work that demonstrate those capabilities, then reference those in the letter, too, and attach them.

This letter is so important that I've included a template for you in Appendix H.

Get this letter into the mail no later than 72 hours after the interview with the hiring manager.

M. Use Your References Proactively

Now imagine.... you just completed Round #1 of interviews. You really want the job. You got some positive feedback from the hiring manager, but when you inquired about next steps, all you got was the standard answer: "There are other candidates that we will be interviewing. We'll contact you if we want you to come in for more interviews." What are you going to do now? Are going to just sit back and pray that they call you? Are you going to call them once a week and fail to get any response? Now is the time to use your references proactively.

Before explaining how to use your references proactively, let me discuss how references are typically used by job seekers and employers, and why they really don't help you land the job. Understanding this will help you realize that there is a real opportunity for you to do something with your references that will help you.

Here's how it typically goes. A well-prepared job seeker contacts at least two, not more than four people and asks them to be references for them in their job search. Then, the well-prepared job seeker puts a piece of paper together that names these people, provides information as to how to contact them, and, perhaps, describes their relationships to the job seeker. The job seeker then puts this piece of paper among the pile of copies of his/her resume and waits to be asked to produce it. Oh, maybe a job seeker will offer to provide it to an HR person or hiring manager before it is requested, but if he/she does, the response will typically be "We don't need it now," or "Not now, maybe later." When does an HR person or a hiring manager ask to see your list of references? Answer: Right before they are going to make you an offer. (Some may wait until after the offer is made and state that the offer is contingent upon you passing the background check.) Now what happens? Probably the HR person, but maybe the hiring manager, will call your references and ask a variety of, most likely, generic questions like: "The job seeker told us such-and-such. Is that true?" or questions that really only amount to "Is this job seeker a good and upstanding person?" Well, what portion of the time do you think a reference says anything negative about a job seeker? Like never? I mean, you, as the job seeker, picked the references. You didn't pick anyone who would say anything negative about you, did you? So, do references really help you get the job in the typical situation? No, what they really do is keep you from losing it. At best, they are an "after-the-fact" confirmation for the employer that the employer isn't doing anything stupid by hiring you.

How can you use your references proactively? I mean, you've got two to four people who are willing to stand up on your behalf and help you get a job. What can they do to really help you?

This is described below, but you need to have a sense of <u>how often</u> you will do this. In simple terms, you can't do it very often. You will wear your references out. Worst case, they might question their wisdom in saying they will be a reference for you. You also need a sense of <u>when</u> to do it. You do it when you encounter a job that is especially appealing to you. You are likely to be "lusting" for it. It's OK to use your references as described below to help you get the interview, but it is much more effective after you've been though the first round of interviews. Besides, how can you really "lust" for a job until you've had first round of interviews and have confirmed what the job entails? For the sake of the description below, let's presume that you've been through the first round of interviews.

> **Say**

Here's how to use your references. Call each one up. Tell him/her you just found a job that you are very, very interested in. Briefly describe the job and the employer and why you want the job. Tell your reference that you'd like his/her help in landing the job. You want him/her to contact the hiring manger and explain why you are a really good candidate. Tell him/her you would like to meet with him/her and compose a letter he/she would send to the hiring manager.

Now, go meet with this reference. Since a few days have passed since you called him/her, start by again describing the job, the employer, and why you want the job. Then, explain the job requirements. Next, the two of you need to make a list of reasons why you qualify for the job and how you fulfill the requirements. (Using your T-Letter is a good source of information. You did use a T-Letter to get the interview, didn't you?) In the course of this conversation, you and your reference should reflect on your prior work experience together. Think of those things you did / accomplished which remind the reference of first hand experience(s) with which qualify you for the job. Make a list and be sure to leave a copy with the reference. Also give your reference this information, preferably in writing:

- The name of the hiring manager.
- The hiring manager's title.
- The hiring manager's mailing address.
- The job title.

Outline the contents of the letter for your reference. (Note. Sending an email is just as good as a letter. A telephone call is, of course, better.) It should include these parts:

Ideas

- An opening statement that names you and the relationship of the reference to you.

- A statement that indicates you have told your reference you have interviewed for the such-and-such job, are working with that hiring manager, and that you are extremely interested in the job.

- A statement, based on your description of the job, indicating the reference thinks (1) you would be an excellent candidate for and (2) requests that the hiring manager give you serious consideration for the position.

- The reference should then include a description of specific first-hand experiences (two to five should do it) that he/she has had with your work and, preferably, how those experiences and skills will help the hiring managing.

- An offer from your reference to the hiring manager for him/her to call your reference if he/she has any questions.

The above specifics of the letter are, of course, not cast in gold.

While it is important that the letter be in your reference's communication style and say what he/she believes, there is nothing wrong with you "taking the bull by the horns" and leading him/her through this, detail by detail. It may be inappropriate in a courtroom for an interrogating attorney to "lead the witness," but this is one of those times for you to "lead your reference." Unless you clearly see it is inappropriate with a specific reference, don't be afraid to actually paraphrase, or even write, the script of parts of the letter.

The last thing for you to do is to ask your reference to let you know when the letter is in the mail.

In return, you have two things you *must absolutely do* for your reference. First, buy him/her a bottle of wine, or tickets to the opera, or whatever he/she likes, just reciprocate in some manner. Do something for the reference which pays him/her back for this wonderful thing he/she just did for you. The second thing is to keep your reference apprised of how your pursuit of this job is going. In particular, if you get any feedback from the employer about the reference's letter, be sure to pass that back.

N. <u>What to Do When They Won't Call You Back</u> – Not more than a couple of CVJS meetings go by that some job seeker indicates he/she has had one or two interviews with a hiring manager and, while everything seemed to have gone along just fine, with the likely prospect of future encounters, subsequent attempts to contact the hiring manager by phone or email have been unsuccessful. What do you do in that situation? The opportunity looks good enough that you don't want to see it slip away. Yet, you're verging on exasperation at failed attempts to connect with the hiring manager. At the meeting, the job seeker usually asks something like how aggressive can he/she be without coming off as too pushy. . . . . . It's the wrong question. After three to five unsuccessful efforts to get the hiring manager to call you back, the better question is what else can you do other than call and send emails? Remember, "Time kills all deals."

Ideas

Here is list of suggested ideas of other things to do to bring about another discussion with the hiring manager, at least on the phone, if not face-to-face.

- <u>Other Opportunities</u> – If the hiring manager is really interested in you, the thing that is most likely to light a fire under him/her is the recognition that he/she may lose you. Presuming you have other opportunities which are heating up for you, notify the hiring manager of such via phone or email. Close by saying something to the effect that, "While you are really interested in his/her job and would like to push ahead with this hiring manager, you will have to realign your priorities and focus on these other opportunities, given lack of response to your previous inquiries." The most alarming thing you might say is that you have another offer in hand. (Do not lie. If this approach works and you end up talking to the hiring manager and he/she is a decent negotiator, he/she will ask you for details about these other opportunities. If that happens, you will feel compelled to pile a lie on top of a lie.)

- <u>HR People</u> - Call the HR people and see if they can give you any insight as to what is going on. Be open, candid, and clear about what you are hoping to find out. Fish for information as to whether the hiring manager is continuing to interview other people.

- <u>Research</u> - Research the hiring manager's company, send him/her notes / emails / whatever telling him/her what you found. News about customers, competitors, suppliers, and/ or the industry are all possibilities. Actually, meeting with customers, competitors, and suppliers and sharing what your heard is even better.

- <u>Proactively Use Your References</u> – I discussed this in detail in the prior section.

- <u>Inside Advocate</u> - Find someone inside the company who knows you and ask them if they can intervene, be a front for you, vouch for you, deliver a note from you, and/or find out what is happening.

- <u>Contractor</u> – Send the a hiring manger a letter indicating you would be willing to discuss with him/her the possibility that you would consider coming on board as a contractor and give the hiring manager a "try and buy" option. (Note: This approach comes from a pessimistic position. That is, don't use it, unless you think your chance of getting called back is slim.)

O. Handle Turn-Downs

OK, you did everything I suggested and then some. Yet, you got a "Dear John" letter or, if you were lucky, someone actually called you.

No doubt, you are really disappointed, if not quite upset. All right, this is not the time to let your anger come out. This is exactly the time when you need to pick yourself up off the floor and send the hiring manager a follow-up letter that demonstrates you are a classy person so he/she keeps you in the back of his/her mind.

Why? Here are some reasons:

- It's the right thing to do.

- How can you continue to complain about no one ever you calling you back during your job search, unless your standards are higher than theirs?

- When the hiring manager gets your letter, you will have distinguished yourself in his/her mind. He/she may then consider you for another job in his/her organization. (Yes, that really happens sometimes.)

- The #1 candidate may not show up on day one and the hiring manager will want to contact you. (Yes, that really happens sometimes, too.) If he/she thinks you're upset about not getting the job, he/she may skip you and call their #3 candidate.

- Even if the #1 candidate shows up, after a few weeks, he/she or the hiring manager may decide it isn't working out and the #1 candidate leaves the organization. Again, in this situation, you want the hiring manager to be comfortable about calling you. (Yes, that really happens sometimes, too.)

If the news came via a letter or an email, then you need to send the hiring manager what is called a "Thank You for Not Hiring Me" letter. (The name is tongue-in-cheek. I've discussed this several times at CVJS meetings. One time, a member indicated this was the name he gave this type of letter and the name has stuck.) It is such an important letter to send that I've provided a template in Appendix M. Use it when you need it.

(Note: If the "Dear John" message came over the phone, then you have to express your disappointment and then deliver the messages in the "Thank You for Not Hiring Me" letter.)

Five to six days after you send the letter to the hiring manager, call him/her. Start off by asking if he/she had received your "Thank You for Not Hiring Me" letter. If not, paraphrase what your letter said. Then, try to make this "turn-down" situation into a networking opportunity. Presumably, you liked the company. There may be other job opportunities, some not even posted anywhere, that you might also be interested in. The hiring manager might be your contact to those other opportunities. The additional messages to convey on the phone with the hiring manager are:

- You are still interested in working at his/her company.

- Can he/she provide any help in your pursuit of any other positions with his/her company?

- If you interview for any other jobs, can you give his/her name as a reference? (Of course, only do this, if you think he/she will give you a good reference.)

- Does he/she know of any other opportunities with other employers?

Basically, the idea is to use the hiring manager as a networking contact in the same way you would use any other networking contact. Tell them how they can help you and ask for help.

There is one final thing to do in a "turn-down" situation. Sit down and write out a post-mortem. That is, write out statements as to what you did well during the interview process and what you didn't. During any one set of interviews, anyone may have a bad day. Save your post-mortem notes, though, and look for things which happen frequently. Maintain the good things and brush up and eliminate the bad things.

P. <u>Ace the Round #2 Set of Interviews</u> – Everything I suggested for the Round #1 interviews applies to Round #2. There are a couple of things you need to focus on and firm up during Round #2 and any subsequent rounds.

First, as you are likely to be meeting with higher ranking people during Round #2, you need to remember that your personal characteristics are even more important now than Round #1. You've got to sell yourself and convince the interviewers you have the personal characteristics which are appropriate for the job. Personal characteristics are typically things like, being energetic, creative, hard-working, personable, communicates well, and so on. They will vary from job to job, so hopefully, you figured out during Round #1 which ones are critical to this job. Second, you must have a complete and accurate understanding of the job requirements. Third, and most importantly, you must have a clear idea as to whether you want the job or not, or at least, how you are going to figure it out.

Chapter 16 – Negotiate Your Compensation and Benefits

The fun starts now. When salary comes up, you can be reasonably sure the hiring manager has begun to seriously think about making you an offer. It is a critical time, though, and you need to make sure you don't accidentally say something that will cost you thousands of dollars.

The first thing I need to explain to you is "How to <u>Not</u> Answer the Salary Question." In the last section in this chapter, I provide a lot of detail as to how to successfully get though the compensation and benefits negotiation.

A. Don't Answer the Salary Question

If you haven't gotten "the salary question" yet, then you haven't been looking for a job for very long. You should expect about every other person you interview with is going to ask you this question, so you had better be prepared with a solid answer. The question may take on a variety of forms, such as:

- What is/was your salary?
- What is your salary history?
- What are your salary requirements?

Whatever form it takes, do *not* explicitly answer "the salary question," at least not the first time an interviewer asks it. Why not? That's simple. If you explicitly answer the question, you've lost the first round of negotiations. It's just like selling your house. No buyer expects to pay the number you put in the advertisement. If you name a number, not only do you just put a lid on the maximum offer you might get, worse yet, you may just eliminate yourself from consideration.

What do you say? I'll give you 29 ideas later in this chapter.

Not more than one or two CVJS meetings go by, before someone asks a question such as "What do I say when they ask me what my past salary was?" or "Do I fill in my salary history on the application form?" The subsequent discussions then go on for 20-30 minutes, with several folks sharing their experiences and offering advice. The discussions have demonstrated there are almost as many views on this subject as there are people. The answers range from "definitely yes", to "definitely no", to several "special case" answers, and general tips.

The information in this section is presented from the perspective of, and benefit to, the job seeker and not the hiring authority. It is intended to help the job seeker. It is the culmination of ideas and opinions of the leaders of the CVJS group, its members, and guest speakers at CVJS meetings. In this section, I am going to tell you how to respond to the question without answering it. In addition to the sources just cited, there are three specific cases / stories that surfaced which support this approach when dealing with the question.

- I always ask CVJS members who land jobs to come back to a meeting and tell the other job seekers about their success and how it came about. One person who did so said the only reason he got the job was because he followed our advice and did not answer the "What are your salary requirements?" question. He said he got the question during the interview with the HR person and with about every other person who interviewed him. His last interview was with the CEO. The CEO made the offer, they negotiated, and they reached agreement. Afterwards, the CEO told him if they had known earlier in the interviewing process what his salary requirements were, they would have screened him out long ago. As it was, the job seeker convinced so many people along the way how much he could do for the company, they raised their expectations as to what they should pay him before the salary negotiations actually started.

- About once a year, I bring in four to six internal HR managers and directors and feature them as a panel in a room full of jobs seekers. Sometimes they make opening and closing comments, but the bulk of the time is spent with job seekers asking questions of the panel. The question always comes up "How should we respond to the salary question?" The response from the panel is nearly always unanimous. They tell the job seekers not to answer it. One HR Director put it very succinctly in one word: "Dance." In other words, don't answer the question. Now, think about this. This is a panel of HR people who ask job seekers during interviews "What are your salary requirements?" and they are bold enough to come to a meeting of job seekers and tell them not to answer the question. - - That says tons. Consider the implications.

- Back in 2001, I was looking for a job with another employer. I had done my salary research, but I hadn't gotten any feedback from "people-in-the-know" to confirm that my salary expectations were consistent with what hiring managers might think. One morning, I got a call from an external recruiter. He talked to me about a job I wasn't interested in. Before we ended our conversation, he asked me what my salary requirements were. I thought this might be a good time to test out the market, so I threw out a range to him ($X thousand to $Y thousand), where upon, he nearly screamed at me over the phone "Don't ever answer that question." Now, think about that. He's a person who needs to match jobs and job seekers, both in terms of functionality and compensation. Many of his customers probably tell him they won't talk to any candidates, unless he can tell them beforehand how much money the candidate wants. Yet, this external recruiter is telling me not to answer "the salary question." That spoke volumes to me.

It is also observed that a large portion of the job seekers appear to feel (at least in a tough job market) that they are in a situation in which they have to explicitly answer the question . . . . . to an extreme, from an almost "spineless" position. This is probably due to one of two reasons. First, the job seeker has concluded (rightly or wrongly) there are many qualified candidates for the position and that he/she will face immediate rejection, if he/she doesn't answer the question right up front. Secondly, the job seeker is not prepared with comfortable responses to the question which explicitly answer the question. However, those inexplicit answers may be what keep him/her "in the running."

Many job seekers realize that answering the question means you've lost the first round of negotiations, if a job offer does materialize. It's like selling your house. No buyer expects to pay the number you first name.

The questions posed and the subsequent conversations at the CVJS meetings suggest people presume there is one set of good answers for these questions, when in fact, the best answer varies, depending on the situation and circumstances. Unfortunately, this makes it challenging for the job seeker to get his/her arms around the issue and develop a strategy for answering the question and preparing responses.

The primary purpose of this section is to provide the job seeker with a comprehensive framework from which to determine how to respond to the question and what answers might be given.

You should take the following factors into account (long before the question is asked) when deciding how you are going to answer the question when it does come up:

- The "Demand/Supply" situation for the job.
- Your personal situation.
- <u>Who</u> is asking the question.
- The reason the question is being asked.

The next few sub-sections address these issues one by one.

The "Demand/Supply" Situation for the Job - The "Demand" side is the number of job openings and how urgently the employer perceives the need to be to fill the job. The "Supply" side is the number of "qualified" candidates. You want to come out of this analysis with a sense for whether the situation is "favorable," "neutral," or "unfavorable" for you, the job seeker. This level of breakdown is sufficient to explain the concepts, principles, and recommendations that come later, but as you become more experienced and adept at dealing with this question, you may want to add "Strongly Favorable" and "Strongly Unfavorable" as possible assessments.

Your assessment of the "Demand/Supply" situation needs to be done at a couple of levels. The first is the regional situation. (Ignore the national situation. There's so much variation from region to region in this country the national is irrelevant to your situation.) The second is the employer's company situation. The third is the specific job. The "farther" the level is away from the specific job, the less important it is. For example, if you conclude the regional situation and the employer's company situations are unfavorable, but there are three openings for a specific job and you are the only qualified candidate for a thousand miles, it behooves you to conclude that the "Demand/Supply" situation is "strongly favorable" for you.

Your assessment of the "Demand/Supply" situation also needs to be done from two perspectives. One is from your perspective and the second is from the employer's. The employer's perspective is probably never going to be explicitly stated. You need to listen and read between the lines of what you hear the employer's people say. If your assessment is "favorable" and the employer's is "unfavorable," even if you are right, you are going to meet resistance and you are going to have to spend time "educating" the employer on the what the situation really is. If your assessment is "unfavorable" and the employer's is "favorable," you'll get the job, but you're probably going to end up with a lower starting salary, without knowing it, regardless of who is right.

The specific job "Demand/Supply" situation is very simply translated to how many jobs there are and how many candidates there are. On the "Demand" side, while it's common an employer only has one opening for a specific job, there may be other employers who have the same job and maybe an opening. On the "Supply" side, you may be the only viable candidate or you may be only one of ten. Size it up. Act accordingly.

The most extreme situation I ever heard was from a fellow who told me he was one of only 50 people in the entire USA who could do a highly technical software job. He did the software quality control analysis on MRI machines, to ensure the images of our bodies which the machines provide to the radiologists, are accurate. Initially, this sounded like a situation in which the demand / supply situation was highly favorable to this person. Then, I asked him how many such jobs were there in the USA. He told me 25!!!

Here's a more elaborate way to make your assessment. Look over the chart below. The Demand/Supply situation improves for the job seeker as you go from left (-3) to right (+3).

	Supply Exceeds Demand				Demand Exceeds Supply		
	-3	-2	-1	0	+1	+2	+3
Candidates * for the job	More than 25	15-25	10-15	5-10	3-5	2-3	1
Elapsed Time to land a job	10-14 Months	> 6 Months	3-6 Months	2-3 Months	1-2 Months	4-6 Weeks	Days to Weeks
Importance of Networking	Ex-tremely	Ex-tremely	Very	Consid erably	Some-what	Hardly	Not at all
Importance of Planning	Ex-tremely	Ex-tremely	Very	Consid erably	Some-what	Hardly	Not at all
Your new compensation	Lower	Likely lower	Maybe lower	Same as old	Maybe higher	Likely higher	Higher

This grid is based on the collective experience and judgment of a variety of people. It is not the result of a survey, but it does serve to give you a reasonable perspective on the situation.

Let me provide an example, so you will understand how to read the grid. Consider the row labeled "Candidates for the Job." If there are "more than 25," this is an extremely unfavorable situation for the job seeker. Supply exceeds Demand by a whole lot and as far as this factor goes, it's a -3 situation. The asterisk (*) on the word "Candidates" means I'm talking about "qualified" candidates. I'm not talking about the other 300 people who send their resumes in to just about every job posting they come across.

The second row, "Elapsed Time to Land a Job," gives you some estimates. A couple of decades ago, there was an old rule of thumb that a job seeker would spend one month looking for a job for each $10,000 he/she makes. Forget that. Times and inflation have extended the elapsed time.

The third row gives you a sense of the "Importance of Networking." While basically every job search consultant and every job search book stresses networking, you can see that in an extremely favorable environment for job seekers (+3), you won't need to do much networking. The employers will be calling <u>you</u> every day.

The same goes for the "Importance of Planning."

The final row gives you a sense of what "Your New Compensation" will be, compared to your last job. Again, these are just estimates and your situation may play out differently.

To give you some perspective, 1998 was a +3, here in northeast Ohio. I remember a job search consultant who quipped "Back in 1998, you could get a job, as long as your prison record wasn't longer than a year!" At the other end of the spectrum, 2001 and 2002 were a -3 environment for job seekers.

The good news is that the demographics experts say a skilled worker shortage is coming, due to all the baby boomers who are going to be retiring. In maybe four to six years, we'll be back to a +3 environment and the employers will again be calling job seekers all the time.

In summary, you need to develop a reasonable sense of the environment in which you will be searching for a job.

Your Personal Situation - Again, you want to come out of this analysis with a sense for whether your personal situation is favorable, neutral, or unfavorable, regardless of your assessment of the "Demand/Supply" situation.

An extreme "strongly unfavorable" situation would be that you may have such financial, medical care requirements, and/or personal pressures on you so you must land a job fast. Your definition of an acceptable job is very broad, and you would settle for a huge pay cut.

An extreme "strongly favorable" situation would be you already have sufficient financial resources to carry you through retirement, outstanding medical coverage, and a loving/supportive family. The only reason you are thinking about working is that there is some activity you love to do which you can't do by yourself as a hobby.

Who is asking the question – The question may be posed in a variety of ways, and isn't necessarily asked directly by a person. Here is a fairly complete list:

- An ad in the newspaper that asks applicants to also include their salary history.
- An employer's application form.
- An external recruiter.
- A Human Resources person, working for the employer.
- Peers of the hiring manager.
- The hiring manager.
- The CEO of the hiring company.

The "closer" you are (both physically, psychologically, and in terms of agreement about the job) to the hiring manager, the more detailed information about yourself and your compensation you should consider revealing. Obviously, the opposite is true, too. The farther you are away from the hiring manager, the less you should reveal about yourself. The above list is roughly sorted from "far away" to "very close."

The reason the question is being asked - There are a variety of reasons. Here are some:

- The questioner or organization is researching salaries and really isn't trying to fill a job opening right now.

- To make sure they don't waste too much of their time on you.

- To determine whether the compensation of the position and a candidate's salary expectations are sufficiently close for the questioner to continue the interviewing process.

- To negotiate compensation.

- To make sure they don't make you an offer significantly higher than your last job.

This is a difficult one, because the reason is rarely revealed. You're going to have to make a judgment call, based on limited information.

Before responding to "the salary question" and addressing specific situations, here are some basic philosophies / principles a job seeker should try to adhere to, regardless of the situation.

- Reasons - There is really only one reason to explicitly answer the question: that is, you've concluded you are on the only path which leads to the job and you are sure you will be eliminated as a candidate, if you don't explicitly answer the question right now. (On the flip side, of course, you need to acknowledge to yourself that if you explicitly answer the question, it may be "deemed" the wrong answer and you may still be eliminated. You never get the chance to demonstrate that your capabilities more than warrant any perceived variance between your desired compensation and the job's). Recognize though, it is easy to conclude that the path you are on is the only one which leads to getting the job. If the *hiring manager* is asking the question, that is probably true. But, if it is an ad that asks the question or a recruiter, there are, more than likely, other avenues for you to try to stay in the running. "To answer" or "not to answer" is a judgment call that you have to make for each and every situation in which you are confronted with the question. You need to arm yourself with experience, facts, and options that will help you make the best judgment.

- Obligation - Understand you are not under any obligation to explicitly answer the question. Even our justice system and courts do not require an accused person to make statements that tend to incriminate him/her. You explicitly answer the question, only when you conclude that it is in your best interest to do so.

- When - You do not need to explicitly answer the question the first time it is asked. Professional, external recruiters who have participated on the CVJS Recruiter Panel unanimously agreed that any question can be "deferred" (or side-stepped) at least one time with an interviewer.

- Advantage/Disadvantage - Far more likely than not, it is to your disadvantage to explicitly answer the question the first time it is asked. It's like selling your used car. You've got a prospective buyer in the driveway. The first one to name a figure loses. (If you still don't think this is frequently the case, ask yourself why most ads and most employers don't tell you up front what the salary is!)

- <u>Proximity</u> - The "closer" you are to getting the job, the more information you should consider sharing. The farther away you are, the less. "Close" means physically, psychologically, and in terms of time. For example, you are very "close" if you are on your third interview with a hiring manager who doesn't need anyone else's approval to hire you and the two of you have agreed to all other aspects of the job. "Far away" would be when you are sending material to a blind ad/ posting.

- <u>Self Esteem</u> - You also want to acknowledge that really good employers who want to hire good employees do not want someone who is going to "roll over and play dead" when confronted with a challenging question. This is particularly true for higher paying jobs (say $75,000 and up). <u>Effectively</u> not answering the question may be one capability the employer is looking for. (Really good external recruiters will chastise a job seeker for answering the question. Experienced ones can handle a non-explicit answer, because they can determine quite closely what you have been paid, based on what you have done. If a recruiter can't get a good idea what you have made in the past based on what you did, your experience and skills, then that recruiter is new to his/her job or just outright incompetent.)

- <u>Confidants</u> – There are people you have known for a long time and would keep confidential information about you to themselves. They will be able to more effectively help and advise you in your job-hunt, if they have more details about your compensation history and goals. However, while many external recruiters are very helpful to job seekers, remember they are being paid by the employer. Answering their salary question is just like giving the answer to an employer. You are probably best served if you just think of the recruiter as someone in the Human Resources Department in the employer's organization.

- <u>Completeness of an Answer</u> - If you conclude that you will explicitly answer the question, first consider whether your compensation will be perceived as "too low" or "too high." If "too low," then be sure to include all parts of your compensation (e.g., commissions, profit sharing, bonuses, cars, etc.). If "too high", then respond initially with just your salary and then determine where to go next. If your salary alone is perceived as "too high," the overall gap will be difficult to overcome. If you are still "in the running" after revealing your salary, then your other forms of compensation will be available as negotiating chips, if you get an offer *you* judge to be too low.

- <u>Two Chances to Answer</u> – It is hard to believe any job seeker ever got shown the door right after not explicitly answering the question the first time it was asked. If that happens to you, you probably would not want to work with that person, anyhow. After a non-explicit answer, worst case, you might get a terse, harsh restatement of the question with a tone which carries a "veiled threat." If such is the case, reassess the situation and decide if it is time to explicitly answer the question.

Now, here are some details about how to <u>not</u> answer the question.

<u>Preparing for the Question</u> - It's easy to say what you need to do.

- Do a lot of salary research to know what you are worth and what the job which you are interviewing for is worth. This is very important, so you can answer the question with responses like #8 & #9 below. (There are many sources for salary information. Go get them.)

- Review the list below of 29 non-explicit answers (in the following section) to the question and determine which you are comfortable with, and which fit the job situation at hand. Memorize your planned response. Have it ready on the tip of your tongue.

- Read this chapter thoroughly every month until you "get it" and are no longer afraid to avoid answering the question.

- Read Section B, "Negotiating Compensation and Benefits," in this chapter.

- If you conclude you are going to explicitly answer the question, always carry your old pay statement with you to share, in case you are asked to show proof or you decide it is in your best interest to prove it.

Non-Explicit Responses - How can you respond to "the salary question" in a manner that doesn't explicitly answer the question? Below are 29 examples of responses which "side-step" the question. They fall roughly into these approaches:

- Ignoring the question
- Answering some other question
- Answering with a question
- Asking for something in exchange. (Quid Pro Quo)
- Implied refusal to answer
- A direct challenge to the asker
- A frontal attack. (Don't bluff.)

The more favorably you've assessed your demand/supply situation and your personal situation, the further down this list of approaches / responses you can effectively use.

Here are sample responses for you to use which don't explicitly answer the salary question. Look them over, carry them with you, and decide which one might apply to the specific circumstance you encounter. At the end of virtually all of the suggested statements below, you want to add a sentence to the effect "Can you tell me more about _____ [an aspect of the job]?" This is extremely important to do. The point of this is to deflect the interviewer away from the salary subject.

1. My experience has been that if the job's requirements and the candidate's qualifications match well, then so will the compensation. Let's focus on requirements and qualifications. (Ignoring the question)

2. I'm sure we could reach agreement on a salary, if we can find a good match between your job and my capabilities. (Ignoring the question)

3. I am fortunate. I have a spouse who works, good medical coverage, and I have been stashing cash away for a few years. Money is not my primary driving force and XYZ is at the top of my target company list. (Ignoring the question)

4. I'm not concerned about salary at this point. I'm sure your company pays competitive salaries. Let's focus on the match between your job and my capabilities. (Ignoring the question)

5. I can't comment on my salary requirements for a job, since none has been offered. Let's focus on the job's requirements and my qualifications. (Ignoring the question)

6. [Particularly if a job offer is about to be made] "What do you have in mind?" (Answering with a question)

7. I know I am underpaid right now . . . . . that's why I'm looking to move. I'd rather you give me a range for what you

feel my skills are worth and we'll go from there. (Answer with a question.)

8. I'm sure you have a good idea of what the job is worth. Don't pay me any more or less than that. If I'm the best candidate, make a reasonable offer. (Ignoring the question)

9. If I handle this interview process properly, at the end, you'll be so excited about me that you will take on the challenge as to how you're going to get the money to pay me what I'm worth. (Ignoring the question)

10. How am I going to find out that you are a fantastic boss (or XYZ Company is a fantastic company) and I should take a pay cut, or how are you going to find out that I am a great candidate and you should raise the pay level for this job? (Ignoring the question)

11. My salary requirements are not fixed. They depend on several factors, the most important of which is what specifically the job entails. After a productive face to face discussion in which I can get a more complete understanding of the job, I'm sure we can home in on the compensation subject. (Ignoring the question. Implied refusal to answer.)

12. If you are asking this question because you are concerned that I would accept a job with you and then "jump ship" when a higher paying job came along, then I would be willing to consider making a commitment to you which gives you protection in that regard. (Ignoring the question. Implied refusal to answer.)

13. If a hiring manager needs to know my salary in order to be confident he/she is making an appropriate job offer, then I am willing to put more facts on the table. (Ignoring the question for now)

14. I'm looking for the right company, the right boss, and the right job. How am I going to find that is you, and XYZ Company? You've read my resume and must have some sense of what I'm paid now and what I'm capable of. I would hope these facts give you sufficient comfort to proceed. (Ignoring the question and challenging)

15. Are you making me an offer? (Answering with a question)

16. If you are concerned that you would give me too big of a raise, I am willing to mutually exchange information about my salary history and the job's salary. (Ignoring the question for now. Implying a need for Quid Pro Quo.)

17. If the only thing that is standing between me and getting a job offer is revealing my salary history, then I will do so. But, lets' talk about _____. (Ignoring the question for now)

18. My salary history is personal and confidential. (Implied refusal to answer)

19. I'm sure a person with your experience can determine what I've been paid in the past after reviewing my resume and meeting with me. (A direct challenge to the asker)

20. What are you concerned about? Wasting an hour or two of our time? Remember, I am taking a risk here, too. You may have inflexible constraints on what your company will pay for this job and they may be well below the market value of this job. (A direct challenge to the asker)

21. My last two responses implied it's my principle not to discuss salary at this stage. I'm sure you, too, have some principles important to you which you would want me to honor. How can we proceed to determine what a great job

you have or how capable I am and still honor each other's principles? (Implied refusal to answer)

22. If I tell you my salary requirements, are you going to tell me what you are willing to pay? (Asking for something in exchange. Quid Pro Quo)

23. If you tell me what you are willing to pay, I will tell you whether I am willing to consider that. (Asking for something in exchange. Quid Pro Quo)

24. (To a recruiter) I think it is premature to discuss salary at this point. Why would I want to give you personal and confidential information now? I don't even know yet, whether I would want the job. (Ignoring the question for now, but challenging the asker)

25. (To a recruiter) If they aren't willing to pay at least $X,000, then, I guess, there's no point talking any further. (A frontal attack. Don't bluff.)

26. (To a recruiter) If the hiring manager can't determine what I am worth after reading my resume and meeting me, I don't think I want to work for him. (A frontal attack. Don't bluff.)

After you give one of the above answers, you may get "The Salary Question" again. You can consider giving another one of the answers above as your second response. However, you may conclude that it wouldn't be effective to respond with another one of the responses. You will be able to tell by the body language of the interviewer and the tone and terseness in the way he/she asks the question again.

You can then move on to responses which provide somewhat more information, like the following. The key at this point is to not give a single number. Instead, give a range and make the range as wide as you think you can and still sound reasonable.

```
  Say
```

27. Well, the salary surveys say the 50th percentile is $X thousand and the 75th percentile is $Y thousand. How does that compare to what you are thinking? (Answering with facts and a question.)

28. I have extensively researched the salary for these kinds of jobs in this geographic area and I have concluded that $X thousand to $Y thousand is a reasonable range. (Answering a different question)

29. My salary "requirements" are between $X thousand to $Y thousand. (Answering a different question)

Your objective is to ensure the range you give is somewhat higher than and overlaps the range the hiring manager has in mind. That will help ensure that you remain on the interviewer's short list of candidates and yet, you've positioned yourself for salary negotiations that will come later.

Recommendations for Specific Situations - This sub-section describes a few specific situations and offers recommendations for your first response.

```
 Ideas
```

Situation #1 – You come across the ad/posting for a job for which you want to apply. You find it in a newspaper, magazine, or on the web somewhere. In addition to asking for your resume, it also asks you to provide your salary history.

Recommendation – If the employer is not identified, definitely don't send in your salary information. Chances are, the person/organization who posted the job isn't trying to fill an opening, but is merely collecting information about salaries in the local market. These are called "blind ads." Avoid responding to a "blind ad," unless it is absolutely the "perfect job" and you are the "perfect candidate" or you are really desperate.

Now, the other case is where the employer is identified. First, why are you so quick to respond to an ad/posting? It is far better for you to spend some effort, make some contacts, try to find out who the hiring manager is, and contact him/her directly. Perhaps you tried that and got nowhere. You've decided your only chance is to respond to this ad/posting. Unless you are operating in cell #1 in the above grid, then don't send in any salary information. Be optimistic that your T-Letter (You use a T-Letter, right?), resume, and any other background information you submit will catch their eye and you will hear from them. If you're worried there will be many other qualified candidates who will send in their salary information, then console yourself in the fact that you are not as desperate as they are. Regardless, include a sentence in your cover letter that effectively says "Compensation information could be shared during an interview," or some similar wording.

Situation #2 – You are filling out an employer or external recruiter application form and you get to a section which asks for your salary history or salary requirements.

Recommendation - Do not provide specific salary history or salary requirements information on forms. Don't worry. If it is really important, they will ask for it soon enough. Instead, write one of the phrases below, or some variation thereof, on the application form:

- "Personal and confidential, but discussible."
- "Open" or "Negotiable."
- "Depends on the specific job."

Situation #3 – You're interviewing for a job and, while it sounds somewhat interesting, you're starting to worry they won't be willing to make a salary offer anywhere near what you want.

Recommendation – Don't be the first person to bring up the salary subject, unless you conclude you are in a strongly favorable situation. Focus on selling yourself and increasing their perceived value of you. If you are in a strongly favorable situation, you're in control and there isn't any reason to spend your time pursuing a job, unless you are confident the employer is going to compensate you at a level you consider appropriate.

Situation #4 – You've had several interviews with a company and you're talking with the hiring manager for the third time. He/she loves you. You love him/her and the job. He/she says he/she is about to make you a salary offer but now asks you the salary question.

Recommendation – Remember the grid! Size up the situation. Are you clearly the best candidate? Or one of many? Does it help your situation to explicitly answer the question? Here are a couple other questions for you to consider asking the hiring manager in this specific situation:

- "Have you already decided on a figure?"
- "What are you going to do if my prior salary was appreciably lower than that number?"
- "What are you going to do if my prior salary was appreciably higher than that number?"

Consider if one of the 29 non-explicit responses above is still appropriate. If yes, use it. It no, then before you answer the question ask for quid pro quo. (In this case, a question asking for some quid pro quo would be "I can share such information with you, but are you in a position in which you can share what other people who have had this job have been paid in the past, or what the salary range is for this job?")

B. Negotiating Compensation and Benefits

Think back to the last time you got a job offer. Did you ask for more money? My sense is that the vast majority of job seekers is so happy to receive a job offer and/or is so uncomfortable about negotiating compensation that they don't do it. In this section, I hope to give you the know-how and the courage to do so.

The objective of this section is to explain to you how to get the "right" compensation for your next job. "Right" means not too much and not too little for what the job warrants and what you deserve.

I believe:

- Getting the "maximum" compensation may not be the "right" compensation. I'm promoting a longer term, rather than a shorter term view here. If you end up with the "maximum," the hiring manager will figure it out, feel he/ she overpaid you, and develop a negative attitude towards you. I'm not promoting a "hit and run" tactic. A "win-win" situation is what you want for a result.

- If the job requirements and the candidate's qualifications match, so will the compensation offered and expected. Before and during the interviewing process, a job seeker (and the hiring manager, for that matter) can have some concern as to whether there is going to be a compensation "fit." If you understand and believe this, you will be more comfortable about spending time selling yourself, learning the job requirements, and letting the compensation topic remain on the back burner.

- Quality (your character) is remembered long after price is forgotten. Always remember, you are selling more than your services. You are also selling your character.

The best tip I ever heard was "Ask and you will receive." (Matthew 7:7) If you employ that tip, you'll earn another couple of thousand dollars per year for the rest of your working life.

The best feedback I ever received that support the ideas, thoughts, and suggestions in this section came from a CVJS member who landed a job because he negotiated. He was a regional sales manager. After two or three rounds of interviews, he was in the office of the VP of Sales, his boss-to-be. It just so happened that a couple of his peers-to-be were also in the office (not an uncommon occurrence). The VP made him an offer and the job seeker went into the negotiations mode described in this section. Somewhere along the line, the VP turned to the other regional sales managers and said "Why can't you guys negotiate like this?"

There's a lot of material to consider. Therefore, let me give you a quick overview of where I'm going to take you next.

- Source and Reference Materials
- Compensation Defined
- The Employer's Perspective
- General Tips
- How to Assess the Demand / Supply Situation
- What to Do . . . .
  - Before the interview
  - During the Interview
  - When an Offer is Made
  - When the Offer "Is Fantastic," "Is Just Right," "Is Disappointing"
  - If you and the hiring manager can't agree.
  - After you accept an offer

<u>Sources & Materials for This Section</u> – In addition to my own, the thoughts, ideas, and suggestions in this section are an accumulation of such from a variety of sources such as other job search consultants, external recruiters, HR people, and CVJS job seekers. I've compiled and organized it in a manner that will give you an idea how to proceed when you are in the negotiating process.

<u>Compensation Defined</u> – I believe one mistake made by many job seekers is thinking of compensation as only salary. Doing so is bad because it limits your room to negotiate and reduces the chance of landing a job you really want. There are, in fact, many aspects of compensation.

Money

- Base Salary
- Commission Rates
- Conditions and Levels of Bonuses
- Stock Options
- Signing Bonus
- Amount of next salary Increase
- Cost of Living Adjustment
- Profit Sharing
- Favorable Deductibles for Insurance Coverage
- Deferred Salary

Benefits

- Vacation / Time Off
- A formal, recurring Salary Review
- Relocation expenses
- Health care

- Company matching savings / retirement / 401K plans
- Company car, Computers, cell phones, etc.
- Memberships (Country clubs / trade associations)
- Tuition reimbursement
- Special office arrangements
- Retirement Program
- Retirement medical coverage

Timing of Events

- Start Date
- Date of first salary review (after starting)
- When the scope of your responsibilities increases
- When benefits become effective

The Job

- Job description / function / responsibilities / scope
- Title
- Number of people reporting to you
- Spending authority
- Budget responsibility
- Reporting relationships
- An employment contract

Miscellaneous

- Discounts on company products
- A job for your spouse
- Special child care arrangements
- Link a future compensation increase to achievement of a particular goal/objective
- A company contribution to a charity of your choosing
- A loan
- Free parking

```
Concepts
```

The simple point here is that you may not be able to get what you want in one aspect of compensation, but you may consider the job acceptable, if it is offset by some other form of compensation.

Money and benefits are the typical aspects of compensation which job seekers think about. However, "time" is another important one. It can become particularly challenging, if you and the hiring manager are at an impasse. One solution for moving past an impasse is to get a commitment as to what you want to happen at a later date (time). Here's an example. Twenty years ago I worked in the Information Technology group for a large regional bank. There was an Applications Development Group, a Computer Operations Group, and a Software Technical Support Group. A man was brought in from the outside to lead the Applications Development Group. Months later he told me that when he had been interviewed for the job, he asked to also head up the Computer Operations Group. It couldn't be offered at the time because of the current incumbent and the political situation. However, he convinced the hiring manager to give him responsibility for the Computer Operations Group within six months. Based on that, he accepted the job.

All of the items on the lists above are things you receive, except for some of those listed under "The Job." When you can't get an offer for the salary you want, you can offer to take on more responsibility for more compensation. Typically, the hiring manager can't rationalize offering you more money without getting something more in return.

I have one last point I want to emphasize for you before leaving this sub-section: Which of the compensation items on the above lists are negotiable? If you didn't answer "All of them," then you haven't gotten the point, yet. At the very least, assume they all are, until you find out otherwise.

The Hiring Manager's Perspective – Unless you find out otherwise, assume that the hiring manager is coming from a reasonable position. Here's the way reasonable hiring managers think and operate.

- Hiring managers and HR people ask for salary early on in the process to screen you out and to save time interviewing you, if they conclude that your salary expectations are way out of line. (You and I would do exactly the same thing, if we were them.)

- The level of compensation goes up with the level of responsibility. (This is what I call a BGOTO, a Blinding Glimpse of the Obvious. Since it is obvious, it leads to a potential solution when you and the hiring manager have been unable to agree on salary.)

- Most times, the hiring manager is not making you his/her best offer first. (It's like selling your house or car. No buyer expects to pay your asking price. Likewise, any competent hiring manager will be prepared with a better offer, just in case you don't accept the first one.)

- The hiring manager does not want to bring you on at a higher salary than the people who will be your peers. This will disrupt his/her ability to sustain reasonable and fair salary administration across all his/her employees.

- The hiring manager frequently needs to get you to accept a salary that his/her boss thinks is OK. (This is what happened to me the last time I made a job change. The initial offer didn't meet my expectations and I sensed that the hiring manager couldn't go higher. I gave my boss-to-be three or four reasons why I deserved more money. This helped the hiring manager to rationalize my salary request to others. . . . . . By the way, I got what I asked for!)

- Most medium and large companies have predefined salary ranges for each job. While this may sound limiting, the maximum of the ranges are commonly 30% to 50% higher than the minimums.

- The employer typically makes an offer below the midpoint of a salary range on the assumption that it is still competitive, gives him/her room to raise the offer if you object, and it leaves room for salary increases at a later time, without a job change.

Cases in which there's not much flexibility on salary ranges:

- Government jobs
- Public school teaching jobs
- Union jobs

Cases in which there is much more flexibility on salary ranges:

- Small or less structured organizations
- New organizations
- Top executives (CEO, CFO, COO, etc.)
- Newly created positions

General Tips

Here is a handful of things to keep in mind when negotiating compensation.

- Negotiations start the moment that someone names a salary number (or you put one in a cover letter or on a job application).

- Negotiating never stops, or from a practical standpoint, not until the day you start work. There are some very shrewd negotiators out there. You need to be ready for them. Let me tell you a couple of stories to try to illustrate this point.

Back about 1900, J. P. Morgan was one of the wealthiest people in the world. At that time, tie pins were in fashion. A tie pin was a six inch pin that went through a man's tie to help keep it in place. People put emblems, family shields, and jewels on the upper end of the tie pin. J. P. asked a jeweler to design a tie pin with a diamond on it. They discussed the design and agreed on $10,000. In those days, that was a lot of money. Two weeks later, the jeweler completed the tie pin, placed it in a nice box, and sent it to J. P. The next day, a courier appeared at the jeweler's store. In one hand, he had the tie pin box. In the other, he had a check for $8,000. He told the jeweler that J. P. had given him instructions to offer both the pin box and the check to the jeweler and return with the one that the jeweler didn't pick. Well, naturally, the jeweler was outraged that J. P. would try to extract another $2,000 out of him. He grabbed the box and went into the back of his store. He opened the box with the intention of placing the tie pin in one of his display cases and what did he find? A check for $10,000.

The second story goes like this. Twenty years ago, I was selling my son's old car. A fellow came to my house. He checked the car out and we agreed on $1,100. There was something about the guy that made me not trust him entirely, so I asked for payment in cash. He agreed and said he would be back the next morning with the money. Yes, he showed up, but he pulled only $1,000 in cash out of his pocket. I said, "There better be another $100 in the other pocket." Sure enough, he reached into the other pocket and pulled out $100.

- Avoid negotiating compensation over the phone. This is extremely important. Negotiating compensation is not a two minute project. If you really think through all the aspects of compensation and which ones are important to you, it's going to take more time than that. In addition, you want to give the hiring manager the impression that you are serious about the job. Negotiating face-to-face does this much better than over the phone. (There are a variety of other reasons to negotiate face-to-face which will be addressed later.)

This is what I did, the last time I changed companies. The hiring manager called me on a Friday night at 5 PM and made a salary offer on the phone. At that time in my life, there was something much more important to me than getting a big salary increase. Two of my family members were quite ill, in and out of hospitals. I wanted and expected to need much more time off than what was typically offered to a new employee. In essence, I planned on asking the hiring manager for an undefined and essentially, unlimited amount of time off. I expected that this was going to be a stumbling block for him and a complete explanation from me was going to be needed. When he called, I asked if we could meet on Monday morning. That gave me the whole weekend to prepare my pitch. I went in on Monday and got what was really important to me.

- Never exaggerate (read that as "Never lie") as to what you used to make. The reason you absolutely must adhere to this is because you have to assume that you will be asked to present a copy of your last pay statement at some point.

- The three most important things in negotiating compensation are:
  - Prepare
  - Prepare
  - Prepare

This leads to the obvious question, "What do you prepare?" Here's a list.

```
Procedure
```

- Determine which aspects of compensation are most important to you and which you couldn't care less about. (Refer to the lists in the previous section, "Compensation Defined.")

- Do salary research on the type of job you want:
    - Find out what the local compensation range is for the kind of work you want to do and for a person with your experience and capabilities.
    - Go to the library. Read books. (See below.)
    - Check out Internet sites. (See below.)
    - Hold "Informational" interviews with people "in the know."
    - Contact professional or trade associations.
    - Call five people who already hold a job like the one you want. Tell them you will be negotiating compensation for a similar position. Describe the responsibilities. Ask them if they would be willing to give you a salary range in exchange for results of your survey.

- Determine the maximum salary you are worth and the minimum you will accept.

- *Memorize* your answers to the question "What are your salary requirements?" (Refer to the previous section in this chapter.)

- Determine your sense of urgency (personal and financial stress).

- Assess the demand / supply situation. (See the previous sub-section, "A – How to Not Answer the Salary Question.")

To help with researching salary, here are some sources for you to check out:

- *The American Almanac of Jobs and Salaries*, John W. Wright (book)
- *American Salaries and Wages Survey*, Gale Research Inc.
- *Annually Updated Salary Information on 500 Occupations*, The Career Center
- *U.S. Bureau of Labor National Wage and Compensation Survey*, www.bls.gov/bus/blswage.htm
- For salary information for a variety of jobs - www.salary.com

<u>What to Do Before the Interview</u> – OK, so you've got an interview coming up. Or maybe, even better, you're going into the second interview with the hiring manager. Here are some things you need to keep in mind. (Several of these points were made in the prior section. They warrant repeating.)

Ideas

- Do not reveal your prior compensation or current requirements, unless you believe withholding either will prevent you from getting the interview.

- Do research to determine salaries for a person with your background and experience, for the job you are going to interview for, and for the region where you want to work.

- Contact people you know inside the company to find out the company's salary range for the job.

- Develop an answer to the question "What are you salary requirements?" (It may vary from job to job.) Review the list of 29 non-explicit answers in Chapter 16.

- Call the HR department and become more of an expert about the company's benefits than the hiring manager.

- When responding to a job posting that asks for your resume and salary requirements, do not give them your salary requirements unless you are desperate. In the cover letter you send, include a statement like "Salary is discussible and negotiable, based on level of responsibility."

- When filling out official company job application forms that have spaces for prior salary, fill those spaces with an asterisk (*) and a footnote that has a statement like the one above.

- Try to avoid giving a recruiter or an employment agency an indication of your salary requirements. (If they're any good, they'll know what's reasonable.) If they ask, respond with "What do you think is reasonable?" If they press, they either want to decide if you have reasonable expectations or they are "fishing." If you feel you have to respond, give a wide range ($X thousand to $Y thousand). You do not need to feel obliged to put your actual salary history on one of their applications. That's just like giving it to a hiring manager and losing Round #1 of the negotiations.

<u>What to Do During an Interview</u> – OK, things are starting to warm up for you. You're in a face-to-face interview. It may be with an HR person, a hiring manager, or one of his/her peers. Here are some tips and guidelines that will help you produce better results for yourself when the offer comes.

- Assess the specific demand /supply situation. (Refer to the prior material on this.)

- Ask where the hiring manager is in his/her recruiting process? How many other qualified candidates does he/she have? How many have gone to round 2 or 3?
- Assess the hiring manager's sense of urgency. Ask how soon he/she hopes to fill the job.

- Do not be the first person to bring up the salary topic.

- Never discuss salary until you have been offered the job.

- Never answer the "What are your salary requirements?" question, at least not the first time it is asked. (Have I mentioned this enough times, yet?)

- When the subject comes up, avoid being the first person to name a number.

- If you get forced into answering the question "What are your salary requirements?" question, answer with a range like $X thousand to $Y thousand. After you answer, expect quid-pro-quo. That is, ask for comparable information from the hiring manager. An example of comparable information is "What is the salary range for the job?" If your request isn't granted, excuse yourself politely and leave.

- Express understanding and respect for the hiring manager's concerns and needs.

- Use integrity, logic and passion.

What to Do When an Offer Is Made – OK, things are really exciting now. You just got an offer. You need to respond. What do you say or do?

Well, I need to ask a question. Who did the offer come from? If the offer came to you via an external recruiter or an HR person, you do not want to negotiate with these people. You should only negotiate with the hiring manager. If it came from one of those other people, then:

> **Procedure**

1. Ask for the offer in writing. Tell them that the written offer should include the following:
    *   A statement of what job is being offered. (At minimum, the job title and your boss-to-be.)
    *   A numeric indication of all forms of compensation (salary, commissions, bonuses, etc.)
    *   A statement of what benefits you would receive.
    *   A statement of any contingencies the offer depends on.

2. If they won't provide you the offer in writing, that is a bad sign. Be concerned. In this case, write the offer down as they explain it to you. Read it back to them to make sure you understand it correctly. Then, tell them that you think this is a fine offer, you will consider it, and get back to them.

3. If the offer came via an external recruiter, ask for the recruiter's advice as to how you should respond, but don't immediately act on it. (Remember, the recruiter's objectives and yours don't necessary mesh well. It is not in the best interest of a recruiter to turn you into a tough negotiator. The recruiter is biased and wants you to accept the first offer.)

4. Tell the person that this is a fine offer, you will take it under consideration, and respond shortly.

5. Solicit the advice of your advocate / mentor as to how to proceed.

6. Based on everyone's advice, decide how you want to respond. Formulate your response and write it out in bullet format.

7. Meet face-to-face with the hiring manager. (The next couple sub-sections explain how to proceed when you are face-to-face with the hiring manager.)

8. If you are unable to meet face-to-face with the hiring manager, write a letter, send it to the hiring manager, along with a copy to the person who called you with the offer.

  - If you accept the offer, restate your understanding of the offer and any/all terms and conditions and contingencies, if any.
  - If you do not accept the offer, make a counter proposal, stating the terms and conditions which are acceptable to you.

If the offer came to you directly from the hiring manager on the phone:

- Tell the hiring manager this is a fine offer and you will have to talk to your family about it.
- Ask for the confirmation of the offer in writing.
- Arrange to meet in the hiring manager's office in one to three days.
- Go to step 5 above.

If the offer came to you directly from the hiring manager in a face-to-face meeting, then:

- No matter what the offer is, repeat the salary figure out loud and be quiet. Have a contemplative, concerned expression on your face, and hold it for as long as you can. (Do this, even if you are extremely excited about the offer. This is not a suggestion that you be disingenuous in any manner. I'm trying to protect you from having an excellent offer being withdrawn, to get you a couple thousand dollars added to the offer without a word from you, or to prevent you from making a mistake.) During the time you are thinking:
  - Calculate what the salary offer is on an annual basis.
  - Compare that to your desired salary and to your minimum acceptable.

- Decide how you really feel about the offer.
- A large percentage of the time, the outcome of your silence is that the hiring manager will speak, and you will get a raise on the spot.

- If the hiring manager does not speak first, then you will need to respond. Speak the truth. The truth is the offer is either "fantastic," "just right," or "not enough."

<u>What to Do If the Offer Is Fantastic</u>

While you may be excited they are willing to pay you much more than you hoped, ask yourself "Did I get myself into something way over my head?"

If you have concerns that this may be the case, then go back and review the job responsibilities. Start out by stating your understanding of those to the hiring manager. If the hiring manager and you have the same understanding of the details of the job, then you are on firm ground. Pat yourself on the back, now that you know you are worth more than you thought. If the hiring manager and you have a different understanding of the details of the job, then this is the time to iron out those differences, not during the first couple of weeks on the job. Since the hiring manager offered you more money than you expected, presumably the hiring manager's view of the scope or responsibilities of the job is larger than yours. If that larger scope is OK with you, then go with it. If not, you'll need to try to reduce the scope of the job in the hiring manager's mind. If you are successful doing this, the hiring manager will likely reduce the offer somehow, bringing it more in line with your original expectations.

Once the hiring manager and you are aligned in terms of the job details, responsibilities, and scope, move on to the next sub-section.

<u>What to Do When the Offer is Just Right</u> – OK, you're in a great situation, but your work is not over. Here's what you need to do now.

- Go over all the other aspects of compensation (relocation, benefits, start date, time until the next salary review, etc.) Make sure they are what you think they are. Negotiate these, if inadequate.

- Make sure you know who your boss is going to be. (Yes, I've known job seekers who started a job and found out their boss wasn't going to be who they thought it was.)

- Once you have reached agreement on everything, tell the hiring manager you think it is an excellent offer, that you intend to accept it, and that you want to think about it for 24 hours.

- Evaluate the offer with your advisors. (This excludes the recruiter who led you to the job. A recruiter is not going to help you be a good negotiator. It is not in his/her best interest. He/she only gets paid, if you accept the offer. The few thousand dollars you might be able to negotiate for yourself means peanuts to a recruiter.)

- If you and your advisors think it's appropriate, proceed to "After You Accept an Offer."

- If you and your advisors don't think it's appropriate, develop your negotiating plan, call the hiring manager in the morning, and arrange another meeting in his/her office.

<u>What to Do When the Offer is Not Enough</u> – OK, you've got some work to do, but don't give up hope. Here's what you need to do in this situation.

- <u>Never</u> say you reject any offer. (You might decide to accept it later.)

- First, declare your sincere, intense interest in the job.

- Ask the hiring manager for some facts. It is OK and fair to ask things like:
    - What is the salary range for the job?
    - What is the basis for the offer amount? How was the amount determined?
    - How does the offer compare to others hired for the same job?

- Tell the hiring manager about your extensive salary research and what it reveals. (You did the salary research like I told you earlier in this chapter, didn't you?)

- Make a counter offer. (In other words, name a number that you would accept.) Then, be quiet and listen.

- During this quiet moment, remind yourself how you assessed the Demand / Supply situation.

- If the hiring manager accepts your counter, then go back to "Offer is Just Right."

- Otherwise, if the other, non-salary items have not been agreed to, then say something to the effect of "Well, we'll have to work on the salary. Let's come back to it in a few moments. Let's talk about _____ [another aspect of the job] and see if we can reach agreement on that."

- Remember all the different aspects of compensation. Try to negotiate something better than the standard which would offset the lower salary. If this is successful, then go to "Offer is Just Right."

- If you can't get the hiring manager to agree to a particular salary now, ask for a commitment that it will occur later, preferably at a specific time.

- If the hiring manager says he has three other candidates waiting in the wings who would accept this offer, first, say to the hiring manager, "Well, since you made the offer to me, I presume that you have already concluded that I am more valuable than the other candidates. Isn't that worth something extra to you?" ("Ask and you will receive." Sit back and be quiet.)

- Never believe a statement from the hiring manager that "They don't have that much in the budget." That is probably a ruse to convince you that there is something outside the hiring manager's control which limits the offer. (You can respond to this statement with something like "I've got to think of a way you will be comfortable to tell your boss that you have found an outstanding candidate who is worth more than what is in our budget.")

- If not successful, consider another counter offer.

- If that still doesn't result in an agreement, then …………

<u>What to Do When the Hiring Manager and You Can't Agree</u> – Do *not* panic. Do *not* feel that you have to complete the negotiation at the first meeting when an offer is made. It is OK for negotiation to carry over into one, two, or more sessions. (Remember, the hiring manager may be in a more urgent situation than you.) Here are some ideas of things for you to do at this point.

- Ask for time. Arrange the next meeting. Be sure you both know and agree who will make the next contact with the other.

- Always "Leave the door open." That means, always depart from your discussion with the hiring manager so that he/she understands you are still trying to come up with terms and conditions which you will both agree to and he/she is doing the same.

- Go home. Consult with your advisors. Develop another counter offer.

- Go to the scheduled meeting with the hiring manager and present your counter offer.

- If the hiring manager won't agree, you're pretty much at the end of it. You will either have to accept the hiring manager's last offer or turn it down.

<u>What to Do After You Accept an Offer</u> – Whoa. You're not done, yet.

- Ask for the offer in writing. The letter should include:
    - The compensation, commission structure, benefits, relocation expenses, etc.
    - Any non-standard, special terms or conditions which you and the hiring manager agreed to.
    - Your start date.
    - A statement indicating there aren't any contingencies on the offer (unless there are).

- If the hiring manager refuses to give you a letter, then you write a letter with all of items above and an opening sentence like "I accept you job offer that you made on _____ {date]. I understand the terms of this offer to be _____ _____ {state the terms]"

- If you receive a letter and want to firm things up even more, send a letter saying you accept it and reference the offer letter and date. (I've provided an example in appendix M.)

There's one other thing you need to do with your new boss before you start work. Ask him/her what you can do before your official start date to speed up your acclimation process (like read materials or fill out forms). Why? Here's a handful of reasons.

- It's the right thing to do.
- Your modes operandi should be to deliver more than you promise.
- You want to make a good impression early on in the new job. This is a great way to start.
- You want to ask, before the hiring manager asks.

Don't worry. There's probably only a 10% chance that the hiring manager will take you up on your offer. Even if he/she does, you've got the time. You're no longer looking for a job!

Phase VI – Wrapping Up

Congratulations! You landed a job and you start in a couple of weeks. You feel the great sense of exhilaration and a huge monkey has been lifted off your back. But, you've still got things to do.

Chapter 17 – Notify and Thank Everyone

If you think back, there were many people who helped you during your job search. Now is the time to let them know about your new job, thank them for their help, and offer to similarly help them in the future.

Here's a tickler list of people who probably helped you.
- Your mentor and advocate.
- Your references.
- Anyone who gave you a referral to a job or networking contacts.
- Networking contacts you met with, called, or exchanged emails with.

It's OK to write a standard note to use with many of these people. It's OK to send it by mail. However, there are likely to be people who went above and beyond the call of duty in helping you out and you should do something special for them. Take them out to lunch. Buy them a bottle of wine. (Remember, the cash is going to start flowing in again.) Do whatever is appropriate for these special people.

There also is the chance that you were in the middle of interviewing processes with other employers at the time you accepted a job with your new boss. Notify those other hiring managers. Express your sincere interest in them, their organization, and their job, but inform them you decided to accept a job with another employer. In addition to being the right thing to do, a pessimist would say there is a chance your new job will fall through and you will then want to re-ignite your relationship with these other employers. Don't burn any bridges. Instead, make a professional close with these other employers.

Chapter 18 – Maintain Your Network After Landing a Job

Remember, during your job search how hard you thought it was to find people to whom to network? You should have been updating your record keeping system with the names and contact information of everyone who you encountered during your job search. Well, keep it up, even after you start your new job. _Every_ person you encounter is a potential networking contact for the next time you are looking for a job (and there will be another time). That includes customers, suppliers, colleagues, bosses, government regulators, _everyone_.

Part II – Special Cases & Issues

The following chapters address some special cases which occur during the job search. While they don't apply to every job seeker, they pop up so often, I want to draw particular attention to them.

Chapter 19 – Advantages of Older Workers

I commonly hear job seekers express concern that employers are reluctant to hire older workers. (For your reference, the median age of CVJS members is probably about 45.) The issue is important and it impacts many job seekers.

To that end, this chapter is intended to provide job seekers who think they are older with ways to act, things to say, and ideas for their resume which will help reduce the chance of not getting a job offer because of age.

This chapter is broken into these sections:

- Advantages of Older Workers
- Things to Do
- Things to Say (How to Respond When They Say "You're Over-Qualified")
- Tips for Your Resume and Cover Letters
- Work on Your Attitude
- Act Younger
- Pithy Comments

The overriding message in this chapter is if you encounter employers who are concerned about hiring older workers, do not view it as an insurmountable obstacle. Deal with it. This chapter will give you ideas how to do so.

If it is any consolation, I hear the exact opposite from younger, just-out-of-college job seekers. Their complaint is all they hear from employers is "You don't have any experience." All these younger workers see is a "Catch 22." If they won't hire me, how will I ever get the experience?

Advantages of "Older" Workers – There are many advantages that older workers have over younger workers. Here is a list. Read it closely. Raise these points during interviews if you suspect the interviewer is concerned about your maturity.

Ideas

1. Training Time - Older workers train faster than younger workers.
2. Training Cost - Older workers cost less to train than younger workers.
3. Start-Up Cost – The overall start-up costs of older workers is lower. Assimilation of a new worker is more than just training. There is also the cost of the time to familiarize the new worker with the employer's facilities, customers, suppliers, and other workers. Older workers typically assimilate faster.
4. Productivity - Older workers tend to be more productive, since they have already experienced a variety of different ways of doing things.
5. Work Ethic - Older workers tend to have a very good work ethic. They work harder and longer. They are more interested in getting the work done than in spending energy figuring out how avoid the work.
6. Supervision - Older workers tend to need less direct supervision. They understand the outcome desired and can appropriately perform, turning minimal instruction into desired actions.

7. <u>Loyalty</u> - Older workers are more loyal to employers and will be less inclined to jump, if things get a little tough or the grass looks greener elsewhere.

8. <u>People Interactions</u> - Older workers tend to be effective in working with many, and different types of, people. They've already developed this capability by doing all the jobs they've held in the past.

9. <u>Judgment</u> - Older workers' judgment is more seasoned, resulting in better decisions and appropriate actions.

10. <u>Creativity / Ideas</u> - Older workers tend to be more creative and have more ideas, since they have already experienced so many things. Older workers often have a more global perspective than younger workers.

11. <u>Economic Conditions</u> - Older workers have managed/ worked through economic expansions and contractions, and know how to deal with both, unlike younger workers who have only seen a boom and don't know how to deal with a downturn.

12. <u>Time Off</u> - Older workers tend not to get pregnant, nor ask for leaves of absence. Their family situations are more stable, helping them to stay on the job. They tend to not take off sunny Fridays. They tend to recover from Thursday night parties faster.

13. <u>Reliability</u> - Older workers tend to show up to work no matter how challenging their personal circumstances are.

14. <u>Focus</u> - Older workers tend to be better focused than younger workers.

15. <u>Initiative</u> – Older workers will tend to take more action on their own since they know how to do things.

16. <u>Adaptability</u> – Because of their extensive experience, older workers bring other skills to a job or task and adapt those skills to new objectives.

17. <u>Resourceful</u> - Older workers tend to have more resources (for example: external contacts, organizations, external databases) available to apply to the new job.

18. <u>Mentoring / Coaching</u> - Older workers will tend to help co-workers more than younger workers, since they have more experience doing things.
19. <u>Team Players</u> - Older workers tend more to be team players. They are more interested in getting the job done than rising up the corporate ladder.
20. <u>Credibility</u> – An older person can give instant credibility to a new, small company which only has younger people.

<u>Things to Do</u> – Here are a variety of things to do to help you overcome any concerns about your maturity.

- When interviewing with the hiring manager, make sure you find out what his/her problems, needs, and concerns are. Then, explain how you can help. (A younger person with little to no experience will not know to do this.)

- During interviews, ask questions. Don't be passive. Offer ideas for solutions to problems. (A younger person with little to no experience will not be able to do this.)

- During interviews, emphasize your *capabilities*, not your experience.

- Explain to the hiring manager why he/she should hire you, rather than two twenty-five year old people. Here are some reasons why:

- When his/her department's productivity is calculated and published, he/she will look better with fewer people.

- With two twenty-five year old people, the hiring manager has doubled the flight risk. (Flight risk means an employee will leave.)

- Two twenty-five year old people will take up more of the hiring manager's time.

- There are more on-going expenses to the company with two twenty-five year old people. (Health benefits, desks, offices, airplane fares, supplies, etc.)

- Explain to networking contacts the kind of work you want to do and which employers you want to do it with. (A younger person with little to no experience will not know how to do this.) Don't ask networking contacts to review your resume and figure it out.

- Ask networking contacts for referrals. (A younger person with little to no experience will not think to do this.)

- If you leave an interview worried that the hiring manager will reject you because of your age, consider rattling off a handful of the above list of "Advantages of Older Workers."

- Be sure to use a computer in your job search. Not doing so will give employers and recruiters the impression that you are not computer-savvy.

- Become as proficient executing the job hunting process as you were in doing your last few jobs.

- Visit the local Senior Employment Center.

- Spend more time with younger people.

Things to Say (How to Respond When They Say "You're Over-Qualified") – What you say and the language, grammar, and vocabulary you use can help you overcome concerns that someone may have about your maturity.

Say

- If you find during an interview you are getting asked a series of questions which indicate the interviewer wants to know your age, respond by saying: "I think what you're asking me is 'How long will I be in this position?'" Then, pause and say firmly, "I'm committed to be at your company at least five years. How many young candidates will promise you that?"

- Don't use phrases like: "At my age...," "Years ago...," "Back then...",,When I was younger...," "It used to be that...," "We used to...," "Listen, son...," "...up in years.," "Nowadays...," "The girls in the office...," etc. (BGOTO = Blinding Glimpse of the Obvious.) Seems obvious, but it's hard to break well-ingrained speech patterns.

- If someone comes right out and asks how old you are say "I'm only _____ [your age]." The word only is very important. Without coming out and saying it, the word implies to the other person that you think you've got many productive years ahead of you. Then, mention your career goals and objectives.

- After getting a question, either on an application or during an interview, consider saying "I'll be glad to provide whatever information is needed for employment after accepting a job offer."

- If a prospective employer comes right out and says "You're over-qualified," consider responding with a statement like "Well, you wouldn't feel that way about your surgeon, would you? Don't you want a person in the job who you're confident can do it without requiring a lot of training and your time?" (Pause. Don't panic. Wait for a response.)

- Cite several of the "Advantages of an Older Worker," in particular, the lower training cost and faster learning curve.

- Consider saying "You want the most-qualified person for the job, don't you?" (Pause. Don't panic. Wait for a response.)

- When an employer is concerned that you are over-qualified, that's a "cause." They are not indicating what undesirable "effect" may occur because you are "over-qualified." You can't overcome their objection, unless you understand what the employer thinks is the underlying problem. Consider saying "What problem do you foresee if I were over-qualified?" (Pause. Don't panic. Wait for a response.)

- Consider saying "When you express concern that I'm over-qualified, does that mean you are concerned about what you might pay me? I would be happy to discuss compensation with you. What did you think is reasonable?" (Pause. Don't panic. Wait for a response.)

- Consider saying "I understand your concern; however, I am confident that you will find me a valuable asset in this position. In addition, should you want to promote internal talent in the future, I'll have proven myself and have the years of experience to assume more responsibilities successfully. My sole objective is to prove myself over time."

- If a recruiter says you are "over-qualified" first, find out whether that is the recruiter's opinion or whether he/she heard it from an employer about you. If the latter, ask the recruiter what did he/she say in response to the employer. Regardless, if you are not happy with the recruiter's response to your question, drop him/her like a hot potato.

Tips for Your Resume and Cover Letters – Here are some ideas / changes for your resume.

Ideas

- Your resume is a marketing document. It is NOT an autobiography. You don't need to cite all your prior employers and all your jobs on your resume. At the end of your employment record section, include a statement like "More details available upon request." That way, no one can fairly accuse you of hiding your past.

- Keep your resume short. Minimize details in your employment record. Focus on your achievements, not all the jobs you have had.

- Consider leaving dates off your resume, particularly when you graduated from schools / colleges.

- If you include a "Personal" section on your resume, refrain from referencing your grandchildren. (tongue-in-cheek)

- Avoid statements in resumes and cover letters like "I have 25 years experience in _____."

- Don't put personal information on your resume.

- Don't include a statement like "References are available upon request." (All people in the hiring process presume that.)

<u>Work on Your Attitude</u> – Your attitude comes through with your tone and body language. Here are some ideas to help with your attitude.

- On the outside, appear positive and happy. Don't ever let negative thoughts come out of your mouth, appear in your facial expressions, or in your body language.

- When in an interview, sit on the edge of your chair. That will make you appear energetic and attentive.

- Here are some facts from http://www.careerjournal.com/myc/fifty/20060328-capell.html (a unit of the Wall street Journal).

A recent study of 434 male and female job seekers between June 2004 and November 2005 suggests that older job seekers don't need much more time to land new positions than younger ones. Here's how job hunters' age, search length and pay level correlated in the study:

Age Category	Average base salary in prior job	Average time to find new position in months
35-40	$83,450	5.00
41-45	123,461	4.96
46-50	125,161	5.51
51-55	115,100	6.33
56-60	96,444	5.94
61+	94,600	6.13
All (Average age 50.2)	12,552	5.62

(Tough Love) No doubt, there are employers out there who are concerned about hiring older workers. But, your job is to sell yourself in an interview. If you can't explain enough reasons why the employer should hire you which offset his/her concern about your age, then *you* are the problem. Don't use age as a face-saving reason why you didn't get the job.

- Finally, remember, the really important issue isn't age. It is the set of problems employers need to solve. You've got to tell them what's in it for them if they hire you.

<u>Act Younger</u> – How you present yourself and take care of yourself gives other people a sense of how mature you are. Consider these ideas.

- Energy Level – Show your energy by thinking faster, talking faster, and walking faster. Don't sound sluggish on the phone or in person. Stand up, when you talk on the phone. Use hand gestures, as though the other party was in the room with you.

- Health – Improve your health. Lose weight. Exercise more. Eat the right foods. Build stamina.

- Activities – During an interview, talk about all the things you do on your personal time that demonstrate your high activity and interest level. Mention the marathon you're training for, the mountain biking trip, and your civic and volunteer activities, especially coaching youth sports.

- Appearance – Wear newer clothes fashions. Get newer hair styles. Look up to date.

- Contemporary – Stay up to date about your profession and your industry. Make sure you know and use the current terminology. Read, read, and read about things related to your work and target employers.

- Computer Skills – It is a rare job these days that doesn't require the ability to work with computers. Make sure your computer skills are up to date. (Most county job search agencies offer computer training for free.) Carry electronic devices (cell phones, PDAs, iPods, etc.) with you, even to interviews. However, be sure you turn them off!!!

<u>Pithy Comments</u> – Clever one liners may encourage you and be received well by others, if you use them. Here's a handful.

- During the 1984 debate against Walter Mondale, Ronald Reagan was asked if he thought he was too old to be president. Reagan's response was that he refused to make age an issue in the election by pointing out his opponent's youth and lack of experience.

- Old age is a state of mind. (Dennis Hopper, on commercials)

- I will never be an old man. To me, old age is always fifteen years older than I am. (Bernard Baruch)

- The denunciation of the young is a necessary part of the hygiene of older people, and greatly assists the circulation of their blood. (Logan Pearsall Smith, U.S.-born British writer.)

- Age and treachery will always overcome youth and skill. (While sarcastically humorous, be careful about using this with an employer.)

Chapter 20 – Sustain Your Search During the Year-End Holidays

I commonly hear job seekers express apprehension and a sense of futility about looking for a job from the latter half of November through the first week in January. They think the lack of response from employers which they experience during the rest of the year will only get worse during this time period at the end of the year. The truth of the matter is that for a variety of reasons, discussed below, it is actually a very good time of the year to "rev" up your job search. Read on and get at it.

Here is a list of myths about looking for a job over the holidays. _Don't buy into them_!

- No one does any hiring at this time of the year.

- No one has time for a meeting with all their other concerns.

- There is no turnover in December.

- There are no budget dollars left to do anything else this year.

- Everyone is too busy with year-end projects.

- Everyone goes on vacation out of town.

- Anyone you haven't talked with in a while will feel that you are "using" them if you contact them during the holidays when you need a job.

Here is a list of reasons why you should "rev" it up.

- There is less competition, because many job seekers are pessimistic about the prospects over the holidays and fewer people are actively looking. Those who work the phones have an above-average chance of getting a face-to-face interview.

- Positions advertised over the holidays are ones that companies are very serious about filling.

- Secretaries and other gate keepers are more likely to be on vacation. That increases your chance of actually talking to a hiring manager.

- Executives who travel a lot throughout the year are often in, sorting through end-of-the-year paperwork or finishing business plans for the next year. This is another reason why your chance of talking to a hiring manager increases.

- Employed people who voluntarily leave, typically do so at the end of the year. That creates openings for persistent job seekers.

- Holiday parties are good for networking and you, even as a job seeker, will get invited to more "get-togethers" at this time of the year than any other.

- Business volume increases for many employers at the end of the year due to the seasonal buying pattern of their customers. This creates more job opportunities.

- Employed people tend to want to tie up loose ends before the new year. Hiring managers, human-resource representatives and executive recruiters are like the rest of us who have that feeling of urgency as the year-end approaches. If there are unfilled positions on their staffs, hiring managers naturally want to fill them.

- Headhunters are more motivated to place candidates before the end of the year. "Contingency" recruiters are paid on commission, and sometimes bonuses, for annual level of business they produce. Hence, a recruiter may be motivated at the end of the year to stretch and reach a particular sales level.

Here are some ideas of things you can do to become even more effective during the holiday season:

Ideas

- Make a telephone "holiday" greeting call to the people in your network. The holidays give you another reason to remind them that you are looking for a job.

- Get involved in a year-end charitable event. This will create networking opportunities for you, in addition to doing something worthwhile.

- Send holiday greeting cards with your business card enclosed to hiring managers with whom you've recently interviewed.

- Consider a part-time job (even if it's not your first job objective) with an employer who needs extra help over the holidays. It may turn into a more desirable job and, and at a minimum, it will generate some cash for the holidays. (About 40% of temp workers at Manpower Inc., a temporary-staffing firm based in Milwaukee, end up getting a permanent position.)

Consider the following insights to add to your inspiration to keep at the job search.

- "Why not go out on a limb? That's where the fruit is!" - Will Rogers.

- "I am a great believer in luck and I find that the harder I work, the more I have of it." – Thomas Jefferson.

- "Hope is the dream of those that wake." – Matthew Prior.

- "To have begun is half the job: be bold and be sensible." – Horace, Roman Poet (65 – 8 BC).

- "Choose a job you love, and you will never have to work a day in your life." - Confucius (551 BC - 479 BC)

- "There is more credit and satisfaction in being a first-rate truck driver than a tenth-rate executive." – B. C. Forbes.

Chapter 21 – Tag Team Interviews (Interview by Inquisition)

Concepts

A tag team interview is when more than one person interviews you at the same time . . . . . maybe even four or five people. This can be rather intimidating for a job seeker, particularly the first time it happens. This short chapter is intended to explain reasons why you might get tag-teamed and how to deal with it.

The possible reasons are few. More than likely, it is merely a matter of convenience to the interviewers. It may be a sign of the urgency of the employer to fill the position, which, of course, would be a negotiating advantage to you, if you get an offer. Another possible reason is that working under pressure is an important part of the job and a tag-team interview is a way for the employer to test out your ability to do so.

Basically, all the interviewing ideas and suggestions presented elsewhere in this book are applicable for you in a tag-team interview. Here are some additional things you need to focus on. However, do these things <u>before</u> the questions start coming.

Ideas

- After everyone is assembled, there will be introductions. Be sure you write down *everyone's* name and title. In a tag-team interview, introductions will be offered very quickly. Don't be afraid to slow it down to make sure you get names and titles correctly.

- Ask how the people are related to each other from a functional standpoint and really more importantly, how they might relate to the person who gets hired. This is critical.

Having this information will help you frame responses to their questions.

- Ask for an explanation as to how this interview will be handled and an idea of its duration. This will give you a sense of what to expect.

Consider doing / saying the following during the questioning.

- Even if someone explains that you don't get the opportunity to ask questions, certainly do so anyway, if you want clarification of people's roles. If you're bold enough, ask any relevant question that would be construed as a common sense inquiry. The panel may be testing you to find out if you can break unreasonable rules.

- If you are asked a complex question that you don't feel able to answer quickly, say something like "That is a complex question with a variety of possible solutions. I would want to spend a fair amount of time identifying viable solutions and evaluating them."

Don't forget to "close" like you would in a one-on-one interview. (At a minimum, ask for feedback in regard to how you did.)

Chapter 22 – Get Passed the Gatekeeper

Concepts

Your initial goal is to get an interview with the hiring manager. Many hiring managers have executive assistants, secretaries, and/or administrative assistants. These people are "gatekeepers." One of their roles is to help the hiring manager effectively use his/her time. That includes keeping outsiders from trying to talk to, or meet with, the hiring manager. You're going to frequently encounter "gatekeepers." The purpose of this chapter is to give you some ideas as to how to get through or around them to get to the hiring manager.

The first thing you must do is treat the gatekeepers with respect. They may be annoyances to you. However, they are merely doing their job. You must not allow your frustration to come through in your attitude or tone when talking to a gatekeeper. Another way to show respect is to be straightforward and honest about your intentions. If you fabricate some story, either the gatekeeper or the hiring manager is going to figure out your deceptiveness and then they'll cut you off for good.

The second thing is to get the gatekeeper's name when you first contact him/her. This is essential for a couple of reasons. A gatekeeper wants to be treated like a person, just like anyone else. Using the gatekeeper's name is another way to show respect. This will help you do so. You also will find that the gatekeeper for a hiring manager changes periodically. You'll want to know when that happens and adjust your conversation, accordingly.

The third thing for you to do is to take notes after each conversation. Why? There's a good chance you aren't going to get past the gatekeeper the first time you call. When you call the second and third times, and probably fourth time, you'll want to refer to prior conversations, so the gatekeeper doesn't start you back at square one each time. Each time you call, briefly review the prior calls with the gatekeeper and explain what the next step was going to be. With each conversation, you want to advance a little closer to talking to the hiring manager.

When you first call a hiring manager and get a gatekeeper, identify yourself and explain in simple terms that you want to speak to the hiring manager. If the gatekeeper asks "What company are you with?" respond by saying "In this matter, I represent myself." If the gatekeeper asks, "What is this in regard to?", here are some responses to consider:

- If you got a referral to the hiring manager, then say "_____ ___ [name a person] called the hiring manager and indicated that I would be calling."

- Otherwise, if you previously sent in a T-Letter or your resume and are applying for a job opening, you can say to the gatekeeper, "I sent the hiring manager some material and I'm following-up on it."

- Or say "I would like to talk to the hiring manager about the such-and-such job that he/she is trying to fill."

- If you're hoping for an informational interview, then "I am doing a research on such-and-such and was told that the hiring manager is very knowledgeable on this. I'd like to ask to meet with him/her for 20 minutes."

If the gatekeeper refers you to the HR Department, then hold your ground. Explain that the HR Department probably receives hundreds of resumes and you don't want to get lost in the shuffle. You think you are a good fit for the job and would like the opportunity to make your case directly with the hiring manager. Finish by asking "Is he/she available?"

If the gatekeeper says "He/she's in a meeting," then you're in great shape. That response implies that the gatekeeper may let you through at an appropriate moment. Your response is important. Don't ask the gatekeeper to ask the hiring manager to call you. Say something like "OK, I'll call back later. Can you suggest a time?"

No doubt, you will get stiff-armed on your first attempt. Don't leave the call with the gatekeeper without knowing what the next step is and whether the gatekeeper or you are going to take it. Regardless, don't let more than three business days go by without calling again (unless the gatekeeper told you that the hiring manager will be out of the office for a longer time than that).

When you call back, you are likely to get the gatekeeper again. Before calling, review your last conversation with him/her. When you call, address the gatekeeper by his/her name and refer to the last conversation, and ask again to speak with the hiring manager. Worst case, try again to advance a little closer to the hiring manager by arranging something with the gatekeeper. After enough respectful, courteous calls, the gatekeeper is going to either give you valuable information that will help you pursue the job or let you through to the hiring manager, either because he/she admires your perseverance or has become tired of dealing with you.

In the course of these conversations with the gatekeeper, you want to ask questions that will give you insight into the company, the job, and the hiring manager. Here are some examples of information that can help you.

- How long has the job been open?
- How many people have been interviewed?
- How soon does the hiring manager want to fill the job?

If all of the above prove unsuccessful, then you need to try calling during days/times when the gatekeeper is not likely to be there. Good times are before 8 AM and after 5 PM. Late Friday is frequently good, too. Try holidays. The gatekeeper probably won't be working on the holiday, but the hiring manager may be.

Another alternative is to just show up at the gatekeeper's desk / office. You aren't likely to get to see the hiring manager. However, this will reassure that gatekeeper that you are a normal person with two arms and two legs and that you have extraordinary perseverance.

Finally, if it took several phone calls with the gatekeeper to get through to the hiring manager, you need to do something for the gatekeeper, even if you didn't break through. Sending candy / flowers are obvious choices, but sending something more personal or performing a favor is even better. Aside from the fact that this is the decent thing to do, it might be the act of kindness that does get you through to the hiring manager.

Chapter 23 – Determine Someone's Email Address

```
Concepts
```

There are going to be many times when you identify someone you want to contact. While face-to-face meetings are best and phone calls are second best, sending emails is extraordinarily convenient. Here are some ideas as to how to determine a person's email address. (When you ask for an email address, take the additional minute to get the person's title and mailing address, too.)

- Call him/her, tell him/her that you have some information that you would like to send to him/her, and come right out and ask for the email address.

- Call the main phone number of the company, talk to the receptionist, and ask for the person's email address.

- Identify another person who works at the same company. Call him/her and ask for the email address of your target person.

- Do a Google search on the person's name and company. There are probably references on the Internet somewhere for about anyone. Maybe you will get lucky and find one that includes an email address.

- Get the email addresses of two to four other people who work for the same company where your target person works. Examine the email addresses and figure out what the pattern is that is used for email addresses at that company. Common patterns are (ignore the brackets [}):
  - {firstname}{lastname}@{companyname}.com
  - {firstinitial}{lastname}@{companyname}.com
  - {firstname}.{lastname}@{companyname}.com

- [lastname][firstname]@[companyname].com
- [lastname]_[firstname]@[companyname].com

- Go to this web site: www.networksolutions.com/whois/ index.jsp. This website includes all registered domains. Type in a domain name (like networksolutions.com) and click on the "search" button. Scan what comes up. You will find at least one person with an email at this domain name. Look at the email address and try to determine the pattern for email addresses at this employer. If you think you've got an idea that's close, try it for the person you are trying to reach. Don't worry. If you're wrong, you will get an email back that says your email could not be delivered. Try another pattern.

Chapter 24 – The 20 Best Tips I Ever Heard

I've easily heard hundreds of good ideas as to things to say and do in your job search. I've imparted lots throughout this book and wrapped them into a "process." Here's a quick summary of some of the best tips. Details about most of them are found in one or more chapters in this book. There's a section and maybe a whole chapter devoted to many of them. (The most important ones are at the top of the list.)

Ideas

1. The three most important things in the job search are networking, networking, and networking. (Get off the Internet, out of the house, and meet with people.)

2. Use the document that is more important than a resume (T-Letter) for every job to which you apply.

3. Stop wasting your time applying for jobs through the HR Department and filling out online application forms. (View pursuing a job through those avenues as your last resort.) When applying for a known job opening, initially attempt to identify and contact the hiring manager first.

4. Learn how to *not* answer the "What was your salary?" question (at least not the first time someone asks).

5. Learn how to negotiate compensation.

6. Learn how to respond to objections to meeting with you.

7. Use your references pro-actively.

8. If you're not getting interviews, it's your resume. If you're not getting the job, it's your interviewing skills.

9. Sell your "*benefits*," not your "*features*,"

10. When interviewing with a hiring manager, figure out what his/her problems are and explain how you will solve them.

11. When on the hunt, tell everyone you are looking for a job.

12. Get a mentor, an advocate, and a job search partner. (They may be different people.)

13. Be flexible as to the type of jobs that you are willing to consider, but be focused when encountering an opportunity.

14. Not only are you a sales person when looking for a job, but you must turn everyone that you meet / network with into a sales person for you. (In particular, train your spouse.)

15. Go to Trade Shows, Industry Group meetings, etc.

16. Take some materials with you to the interview to talk about. (It's easier to talk about some object, rather than yourself.)

17. Establish a group of people with whom you have met and discussed your job search and are willing to help you on your job search. Update them every six to eight weeks on your search status.

18. The ways to approach people, from best to worst, are: face-to-face, phone, email, paper.

19. After a job interview, send a handwritten thank you note within 24 hours. Follow up with details in a typed letter to the hiring manager within three days. Call in seven to ten days.

20. When talking on the phone from home, stand up, use hand gestures, emotion, and energy.

21. Create multiple versions resume. Every time you apply for a job, customize your resume for that job. (With a computer, it doesn't take that long.)

22. No one cares about "your" job objective, except you. "Your" job objective must become the "hiring manager's" job objective.

23. Use the "retail" outplacement firms only as a desperate, last resort.

24. Most people have an emotional reaction to losing a job. Get it behind you as soon as you can. There's nothing wrong with you. Based on figures from the Bureau of Labor Standards, I estimate that 30,000 to 50,000 people in this country leave their employer every day.

25. Your dress and appearance probably won't get you the job but, they could easily lose it for you.

OK, you're right. I couldn't keep the list to just 20.

Chapter 25 – Handle Multiple Job Offers

This is a problem which every job seeker wants. However, it takes some deft maneuvering to end up with the outcome that is "best" for you.

Here are some ideas as to how to go about it. The approach outlined below is oriented towards getting you the job that is the "best" fit for you, not necessarily the one that gets you the biggest salary. In addition, this approach is based on the fact that you will get much better results by telling each hiring manager that you have, or are about to have, multiple job offers. Competition is a wonderful thing. However, don't fall into the trap of exaggerating and definitely don't lie. Remember, you're also selling your character and integrity, not just your services.

Pull out the "Your Desired Job" and the "Your Desired Compensation and Benefits" forms. (You filled them out, like I told you to, didn't you?) Read them. Make a list of the three to four most important factors about your desired job and the one to two most important factors about your desired compensation. Now, for each of the two to three offers you have, or will have in hand soon, rate them on your important factors. A simple rating scheme like -2 to +2 or 1 to 10 for each factor is good enough.

If one of the jobs clearly rates higher than the others (even if it isn't "perfect") then focus on landing that job.

Concepts

- Contact the hiring manager and pick up the pace when the offer comes and/or when the negotiations occur.

- For the other one or two jobs, slow them down as much as you can. Try to reschedule them for a day or two after the time you plan on meeting with the hiring manager for the #1 job.

- Meet with the hiring manager for the #1 job. Tell him/her how much you want the job. Tell him/her about the other job offers, but that you prefer his/her her job. Assuming the #1 job is not "perfect," tell the hiring manager what changes you'd like to see in the job or compensation/benefits that would make it "perfect" and acceptable to you.

- If the hiring manager agrees, accept the job and reject the others. If the hiring manager won't agree, express your appreciation for what he/she has done for you, indicate you will give his/her offer serious consideration, that you fully expect to accept his/her final offer, and that you will respond in ___ [a number] days.

- Then, meet with the hiring managers for the other jobs and do the same.

- Accept the offer you think is "best" for you.

If none of the jobs clearly rates higher than the others:

- Then arrange to meet with each hiring manager. No doubt, one is moving too fast and one is moving too slowly. Do everything you can you to line them up, probably one day after the other.

- Again, tell each hiring manager how much you want his/her job. Tell him/her about the other job offers. Tell each hiring manager what changes you'd like to see in the job or compensation/benefits which would make it "perfect" and acceptable to you.

- Don't accept any offers until you have met with all the hiring managers.

Regardless of what happens, always remember that you will get more favorable negotiating results if you meet face-to-face with hiring managers.

Chapter 26 – Overcome Objections to Meeting with You

Concepts

Other than getting a job offer, arguably the most important objective during the job search is to get a face-to-face interview with someone. No one comes out of the blue and offers to meet with you. You've got to contact them and they usually have objections, reasons why they can't or don't want to meet with you. You have to talk them into it. There are three places in this book where I itemize objections and suggest responses to you to overcome them. They were oriented to specific circumstances addressed within the chapters where they appeared. In this chapter, I've provided a summary of these objections. They may not all apply to the specific situation you are currently confronted with at the moment. However, this will provide a single place you can reference to help prepare you for this moment in your job search which will occur many, many times.

There are fundamentally four basic situations in which you would want to meet face-to-face with someone: an informational interview, a job interview, a target company you want to work for, and a networking situation. The objections below may come in any or most of these situations. Consider the suggested responses for these objections and modify them to fit your specific circumstances and communications style.

Say

Regardless of which "response" you use, add another sentence after the response that asks for the interview. Here's a couple of examples: "Would you be available to meet on Wednesday at 10 AM?" or "Would you like to meet over coffee before work on Wednesday morning?" . . . . . This is a critical piece to this verbal exchange. One of the phenomenons of human conversation is that the person who speaks last, usually gets his/her way. (Did you ever have an argument with your spouse?) You need to do everything you can to be the last one to speak and the best thing you can do is to <u>ask</u> for the face-to-face interview.

Finally, remember, the only reason you don't get the interview is because you give up trying to convince them to invite you in.

Objection	Your Response
"I don't have time to meet with you. Call back in a couple of months."	"Presumably, that means that business is good and volume is up. It sounds like now is the time that you could use some additional help. I'd like just 20 minutes of your time to explain how I could help you out. At XYZ Company, I did this-and-that which improved the productivity of the entire such-and-such group."
"I don't have a job for you." Or, "We're not hiring."	"Oh, before I called, I realized that you don't have a job for me. However, I am very interested in working for XYZ Company and I like people to know about me when the time comes to do some hiring."
"You don't have a such-and-such degree or certification."	"No, but I've done this-and-that for x years and that more than compensates for the degree or certification."
"You don't have any such-and-such experience."	"No, but I've done this-and-that for x years. Those experiences and skills will readily transfer over to such-and-such."
"Please contact our HR Department."	"Candidates get lost in the HR Department and you have to rely on them to not screen out someone you might want to hire. I sent you my resume. I am substantially qualified for all the requirements of your job."

"You're over-qualified."	"If you're concerned that I will jump ship too soon, I'll be glad to make a commitment to you in terms of how long I will stay in this position." Or, "My experience in doing such-and-such will only make my training and acclimation fast. I will also be able to help some of my colleagues advance more rapidly." Or, "If by over-qualified, you are concerned that I have been paid more than what is in your budget, I want you to know that I am financially comfortable. I have been saving for several years and do not have any large expenses facing me. I am pursuing this position because I am quite interested in it." Or, "What are you thinking when you express concern that I may be over-qualified? What bad thing do you think will happen if you hire me?" (Play off the answer.)
"We don't have it in the budget to hire anyone at this time."	"Well, that sounds like costs are critical right now. I would be glad to lay out a plan that would explain how I would bring cost reductions to your group." Or, "I would be glad to initially come on as a contractor and prove to you that I can save you money."
"OK, send me your resume."	"I would be glad to. However, what I have done in the past is not as important as what I could do for you in the future. I'd like to have the chance to talk with you to determine how I could help you." Or, "In the time that you could read my resume, I could explain to you in more human terms what I have accomplished and how I could help you."

Chapter 27 – Develop an Employment Contract

Concepts

Employment contracts typically only come in to play for higher paid employers. However, there are other situations, such as employment with a new, start-up company, which has as much chance to fail as succeed, in which a job seeker may want an employment contract to provide some additional protecting.

As important as you might think nailing down your billing rate is, it is also extremely important that you and the other party have a detailed understanding of who will do what and who will pay for what. Here is an example list of items you should address to become confident that you and the other party are in agreement. (Note: *I am not an attorney and I highly recommend that you consult one before entering into an employment contract.*)

Ideas

- What services, products, materials, equipment, etc. will you provide?

- What services, products, materials, equipment, etc. will the other party provide?

- What will the other party pay you as compensation? What is the basis for the compensation? A fixed amount? An hourly rate? Based on the value that is derived from the short term assignment?

- When will you be paid?

- What do you have to pay the other party for?

- If either of you incurs expenses that need to be paid to a third party (like travel expenses), who has the liability for these expenses?

- What good thing might happen as a consequence of this short term endeavor and what benefits might each party have a right to?

- What bad thing might happen and what liability does each party have if it does?

- If the business goes well and you are a success, will you receive additional rewards, such as a stock option, for your contribution?

An employment contract is a written and signed document. There is another document that can be also be effective, although it may not be legally binding. It is a document that lists items like the ones above. It's just that it typically isn't signed. It could be a letter from you, stating your understanding and asking for confirmation or a slightly more formal variation, is a document called a "Document of Understanding."

Some criteria used to decide which method to use are your personal style and how well you know and have experience with the other party.

When this subject comes up, a job seeker frequently asks, "How much can I trust the other party?" There's no good answer that applies to all situations. I usually respond to people that when things do not go as planned or hoped, you can "trust" the other party to do what is in his/her best interest, which may cause you harm. In these days, the less clear you are about details of the agreement between you and the other party and the less control you have over what the other party does, the more risk you are assuming. Consider that the only people you end up in a disagreement with about the terms and conditions of a business arrangement are the ones you trust. That's because you entered into a contract with those you didn't trust.

Chapter 28 – Work in a Temporary/Contract/Interim Position

In the course of your job search, you will likely come across one or more temporary/contract/interim positions. You will consider them for a variety of reasons such as the work sounds interesting, they may lead to a full time position, or they provide much needed cash. However, these situations have a downside, if you are ultimately looking for a full time job. That is, they make it more challenging to maintain your search for that full-time position. However, on the whole, I believe these situations net out to be a positive for job seekers and I suggest you give them consideration when you come across an interesting one.

In these situations, you are more than likely going to end up working for a third party who has effectively brokered the arrangement between you and the ultimate employer who receives the benefits of your services. Given that, you need to recognize that the "contract" that you hear about is probably between the employer and the third party.

Below are some issues to address when considering these types of arrangements.

Assuming there is a third party involved, you want to be absolutely clear about the following:

- How much will you be paid per unit of time (hour, day, week, etc.)?

- What will the process be for recording the amount of time you worked?

- When will you get paid? How often? What is the lag time between working and getting paid?

- What benefits will the third party provide you? (For example: health care, vacation, etc.)

- Will you be reimbursed for expenses you incur? (For example: commuting, parking, travel)

- When or upon what basis do your services begin and end?

In addition, *don't sign* anything that obligates you to pay a fee to a third party. It is standard practice that the *employer* pays any fees due to the third party. The third party is making a profit between what the employer pays the third party and what the third party pays you.

If there isn't any third party involved, then you will need to address the above issues with the employer.

In addition, you need to address the following issues with the employer:

- What services, products, materials, or equipment is the employer expecting you to provide?

- What will the employer provide to help you perform the work? (For example: an office, desk, and/or computer.)

- Is the employer going to ask you to sign confidentiality or non-compete agreements?

- Whom will you be taking directions / orders from?

- What are the criteria upon which it will be determined whether this temporary/contract/interim position turns into a permanent, full-time position? Who makes the decision?

- When will this temporary/contract/interim situation turn into a permanent, full-time position?

How do you achieve this detailed understanding with the other party(ies)? Well, there are generally three ways. Most people handle it verbally. At the other extreme is a written and signed contract. (Please note. *I am not an attorney and I certainly suggest that you consult one if any documents created are going to require signatures*.) The third way is in-between and less common. It is a document that lists items like the ones above. It's just that it typically isn't signed. It could be a letter from you stating your understanding and asking for confirmation or, a slightly more formal variation, is a document called a "Document of Understanding."

Some criteria used to decide which method to use are your personal style and how well you know and have experience with the other party(ies).

Part III – Appendices and Forms

The material in this part does not need to be read from start to finish. Scan the Table of Contents at the start of the book, so you know what is included in this part. Then, when the need arises, go to the appropriate appendix, read the instructions, if any, and use the material found there.

<u>Purpose</u> - The primary purpose of the "Your Desired Job" form is to provide a vehicle by which you can quickly identify and define various aspects of the job you want, think through what your position is in regard to each, and develop solid answers when people ask what your desired job is.

<u>Background</u> - A resume is more of a statement of where you have been, what you have done, and where you are. Granted, even without some type of objective statement at the top, it does imply the kind of work you are looking for (although this is not the case, if you are trying to make a career change). However, the resume typically doesn't answer other aspects of the desired job which job seekers need to have clarity about in their own minds, and should be prepared to address, when another person asks. For example, a common question that job seekers get is "Are you willing to relocate?" That question typically isn't answered on a resume, but a job seeker needs to have an answer, may need to do some soul searching about this issue and eventually, be prepared to present a solid answer. Don't ad-lib. The attached form will help you define the kind of job you would like to have.

<u>Filling Out the Form</u> - Read the form over and write out your answers to the information requested. Writing it down is very important for a couple of reasons. First, most people aren't going to able to remember the details of their answers three months down the road without writing anything down. Second, your answers / positions are probably going to change as the weeks and months go by. You should come back to this form and see if what you thought a couple of weeks ago or a couple of months ago still stands. If it changes, that is OK, but it will be helpful to you to confirm and acknowledge the change. By the same token, if you change it several times over a few months, you should probably be concerned about that and seriously consider obtaining some formal counseling in career planning.

Ninety percent of the people who have been on the job hunt for several months can probably fill out the form within 15-20 minutes. A person who has never had full time employment, who just started looking for a job, or who is considering a career change will not come anywhere close to filling it out completely in the first sitting. That's OK. This task doesn't have to be completed in one session. Come back to it in a couple of days, a couple of weeks, and certainly every couple of months to confirm that your answers still stand. If you continue to have difficulty trying to fill out this form after several serious tries, you probably need to consider contacting a professional who advises people on career planning.

Note: While it is good to be specific to achieve focus in your job hunt, the narrower your definition of your desired job, the longer your job search will probably be. Therefore, you will need to determine the amount of specificity that is right for you.

<u>How to Use</u> – Type up titles for each paragraph on the form, along with your answers. Don't give the completed form to a hiring manager, an HR person, or a recruiter. *It is primarily for your own use.* Here are some ways to use it:

- Use it to help prioritize your job search, so you don't start pursuing jobs which you don't really want.

- Use it to answer people when they ask what kind of job you want.

- Use it as a source of questions during an "Informational Interview" when you are trying to obtain information to help you define your desired job.

- The form asks you to indicate the skills, education, work experience, and certifications which your desired job requires. Compare this to what you have in order to confirm that you qualify. If not, do what you need to do, in order to eliminate that deficiency.

There are, of course, other potential uses. Here are a couple of cases in which you should consider giving it to other people:

- Give a copy to those who you think would be willing to help you in your job search (for example: relatives, friends, networking contacts). This will help give them a clear and complete picture of your desired job.

- Give it to a person you ask to review your resume. These people should evaluate your resume to ensure that it will help you obtain your desired job.

<u>Your Desired Compensation and Benefits Form</u> – This is another form. (See Appendix B.) It goes hand-in-hand with this one. It describes what you "get." This one describes what you "give." The two of them need to be in balance. That is, what you "get" can't be materially more than what you "give" and vice versa. Complete them together.

<u>Goal</u> – Provide a brief description of what you want to achieve with your next job. (Examples are: Sustain your standard of living. Increase your compensation. Obtain health insurance. Change what you do. Work with better people. Work with a better organization.)

```


```

<u>Titles</u> – What are examples of the titles that are used for your desired job? (Provide 2 or 3)

```


```

<u>Employment Type</u> – Provide a brief name/description for the type of employment that you are looking for. Examples are employee of an organization, own a company, independent consultant, and franchiser.)

```


```

<u>Function Type</u> – Provide a brief name for the type of function you want to perform. (Examples are administrative support, advertising, engineering, finance, general management, health care, information technology, law, operations, public relations, sales, supply chain, science)

```


```

<u>Function Description</u> – Describe what you will do. What work will you perform? What will you produce? What service will you provide? What kinds of people, machines, materials, etc. will you work with? (3 to 8 sentences)

```


```

<u>Managing People</u> – Will you be managing people? If yes, how many? (Specify a range.)

```


```

<u>Managing Budget</u> – How big of a budget, in terms of sales, costs, or assets, do you want to manage? (Specify a range.)

```


```

Experience – How many years of experience do people holding this job typically require? (Specify a range.)

```
┌────────────────────────────────────────────────────────┐
│                                                          │
└────────────────────────────────────────────────────────┘
```

Skills – Are there special skills which this job requires?

```
┌────────────────────────────────────────────────────────┐
│                                                          │
└────────────────────────────────────────────────────────┘
```

Education – Describe any specific education requirement for this job.

```
┌────────────────────────────────────────────────────────┐
│                                                          │
└────────────────────────────────────────────────────────┘
```

Certification - Describe any specific certification requirement for this job.

```
┌────────────────────────────────────────────────────────┐
│                                                          │
└────────────────────────────────────────────────────────┘
```

Employment Status – What will your status be? (Examples are: owner of the company, work for an employer, consultancy, and franchiser)

```
┌────────────────────────────────────────────────────────┐
│                                                          │
└────────────────────────────────────────────────────────┘
```

Job Duration – How long do you want the job to be? (Examples are full time, part time, interim / contract.)

```
┌────────────────────────────────────────────────────────┐
│                                                          │
└────────────────────────────────────────────────────────┘
```

Work Schedule – When do you want to work in terms of days and times?

```
┌────────────────────────────────────────────────────────┐
│                                                          │
└────────────────────────────────────────────────────────┘
```

Relocation – Are you willing to relocate (that is, move your primary residence)? How far? Are you willing to move outside the USA?

```
┌────────────────────────────────────────────────────────┐
│                                                          │
└────────────────────────────────────────────────────────┘
```

Organization / Industry Types – What types of organizations / industries are you focused on? (Examples are any, chemicals, consumer products, education, energy, financial services, government, health-care, manufacturing, non-profits, pharmaceuticals, technology, and transportation)

```
[                                                                    ]
```

Organization / Industry Targets – Name any specific organizations or companies you are very focused on. (Only name those that you intend to target for several months.)

```
[                                                                    ]
```

Organization Culture / Environment – Briefly describe the key characteristics or qualities of the culture / environment within the organization that you want to work in. (Examples are: level of openness, level of expectations, level of fame, financial status, growing, mature)

```
[                                                                    ]
```

Organization / Industry Size – How big of an organization or company do you want to work for (in terms of number of people, or sales dollars, or facilities. Respond with ranges.)

```
[                                                                    ]
```

Organization / Industry Location – Describe where, geographically, you want to work. (Name cities, states, regions, countries.)

```
[                                                                    ]
```

Travel – What percent of your time are you willing to travel? (Specify a range.)

```
[                                                                    ]
```

Purpose - The primary purpose of this form is to provide a vehicle by which you define what your desired compensation and benefits are, think through what your position is in regard to each, and develop solid answers when people ask you questions about these topics.

Background – There are a couple of very good reasons to have a firm definition of your desired compensation and benefits:

- You need a base against which to compare offers that you get.

- You need to be very clear in your mind and in the words you speak about your desires when negotiating compensation and benefits after an offer is received.

- You need to be fairly specific to ensure that your expectations are close to what the local job market thinks.

Filling Out the Form - Merely look it over and fill in the information requested.

Writing it down is very important for a couple of reasons. First, most people aren't going to able to remember the details of their answers three months down the road without writing anything down. Second, your answers / positions are probably going to change as the weeks and months go by. You should come back to this form and see if what you thought a couple of weeks ago or a couple of months ago still stands. If it changes, that is OK, but it will be helpful to you to confirm and acknowledge the change. By the same token, if you change it several times over a few months, you should probably be concerned about that and consider formal counseling for career planning.

Ninety percent of the people who have been on the job hunt for several months can probably fill out the form within 15-20 minutes. A person who has never had full time employment, or who just started looking for a job, or who is considering a career change will not come anywhere close to filling it out completely in the first sitting. That's OK. This isn't meant to be developed in a one-time session. Come back to it in a couple of days, a couple of weeks, and certainly every couple of months to confirm that what you previous said still stands. If you continue to have difficulty trying to fill out this form after several serious tries, you probably need to arrange some "Informational Interviews" to get some facts to help you fill it in.

<u>How to Use</u> – This form is for your use only. *Share it with only your closest confidants.* Here is how you use it:

- Review it before you go into compensation negotiations. Be sure to note the level of importance of each item so that you know which ones to compromise on and which not to budge on.

- Compare what you have filled out to what you hear from other people and to what you read. Update, accordingly.

<u>Your Desired Job Form</u> – This is another form. (See Appendix A.) It goes hand-in-hand with this one. It describes what you "give." This one describes what you "get." The two of them need to be in balance. That is, what you "get" can't be materially more than what you "give" and vice versa. Fill them out together.

		Impor- tance*	Desired	Minimum Acceptable

Compensation

		Importance*	Desired	Minimum Acceptable
Base Salary	How much do you want to make per year? (Specify a range.)			
Salary Review	When do you want the next one to occur?			
Commission	On what do you want the commission to be based? What would the rate be? (Specify a range.)			
Bonuses	How much? (Specify a range) When available?			
Stock Options	Why type? For what value? Based on what?			
Signing Bonus	How much? (Specify a range) When received?			
Cost of Living Adjustment	Depending on what? How much? (Specify a range.)			

* <u>Importance</u> – Use a simple scale like 5 = Extremely Important, 4 = Important, 3 = Neutral, 2 = Not Important, 1 = Not Important at All

Benefits		Impor-tance*	Desired	Minimum Acceptable
Health In-surance	What types? How much?			
Company Matching Savings Program	How much matched? (Specify a range.) When does it start?			
Vacation Days	How many? How soon usable?			
Use of Company Resources	Examples: Leased car, office space, equipment in you home, etc.			
Relocation Expenses	For what? How much? (Specify a range.)			
Member-ships	Examples: Country Club, professional organization.			
Retirement Program	How much? When vested? When obtainable?			
Retirement Medical Coverage	Portion paid by employer.			

* Importance – Use a simple scale like 5 = Extremely Important, 4 = Important, 3 = Neutral, 2 = Not Important, 1 = Not Important at All

Put Your Name Here

Put Your Street Address, City, State Zip Here

Phone: 999-999-9999 eMail: Put Your Email Address Here

Profile / Professional Summary

Put A Job Title Here - Put 3 to 6 sentences here that summarize what you are, the kind of work you want to do, and your key strengths and/or accomplishments. What you put here is critical. Many people who review applicants' resumes decide in the first 15-30 seconds whether they are interested in the person and whether they want to read any more of the resume. What you put here must attract the reader's attention and lead you to the job you want.

- Put A Key Function Name Here
- Put A Key Function Name Here
- Put A Key Function Name Here
- Put A Key Function Name Here
- Put A Key Function Name Here
- Put A Key Function Name Here
- Put A Key Function Name Here
- Put A Key Function Name Here

Employment History

Company/Organization 1 Name: City, State. From Date - To Date.

Job Title: Put a one to three sentence description of your primary responsibilities for this job. Follow this with a list of your accomplishments.

- Put the description of an accomplishment here.
- Put the description of an accomplishment here.
- Put the description of an accomplishment here.

Job Title: Put a one to three sentence description of your primary responsibilities for this job. Follow this with a list of your accomplishments.

- Put the description of an accomplishment here.
- Put the description of an accomplishment here.
- Put the description of an accomplishment here.

<u>Company/Organization 2 Name</u>: City, State. From Date - To Date.

<u>Job Title</u>: Put a one to three sentence description of your primary responsibilities for this job. Follow this with a list of your accomplishments.
- Put the description of an accomplishment here.
- Put the description of an accomplishment here.
- Put the description of an accomplishment here.

<u>Job Title</u>: Put a one to three sentence description of your primary responsibilities for this job. Follow this with a list of your accomplishments.
- Put the description of an accomplishment here.
- Put the description of an accomplishment here.
- Put the description of an accomplishment here.

Education

<u>College/University 1 Name</u>, Put Your Degree Here, Graduated Fill In Date Here, (or say "In Progress" or "Not Completed,") Put Your Major Area Of Study Here

<u>College/University 2 Name</u>, Put Your Degree Here, Graduated Fill In Date Here, (or say "In Progress" or "Not Completed,") Put Your Major Area Of Study Here

Special Skills / Certifications / Awards Describe and/or list anything that an employer would consider valuable. Example skills are technical, language, and public speaking. Example certifications are CPA, 6-Sigma Black Belt, and CE.

Associations / Professional Memberships Describe and/or list organizations you lead or in which you are a member. If you have an official capacity in the organization, such as treasure, then indicate so. If you lead or are a member of an organization that would contribute to your job performance, name it for sure. If you lead or are a member of an organization that reflects your virtues or character, then consider naming it. If you lead or are a member of an organization that is racial, national origin, gender, age, etc. specific or restrictive, then don't name it.

Introduction

A "T Letter" is used when you are applying for a specific, known job opening and you have the job description in hand.

The assumption behind the need for a "T Letter" is that there is someone (like an HR person or a recruiter) who is going to screen hundreds of resumes before they ever get to the hiring manager (and most don't). Hence, this screener is only able to spend 10-30 seconds on any one resume. You've only got that long to catch his/her attention.

The goal here is to get past the screener and get your resume in front of the hiring manager who will, hopefully, spend 10-30 minutes on it and give it the attention you feel it deserves.

What are these screeners trying to do? They're trying to determine how well you fit the job requirements. Are you qualified? If you don't use a "T Letter," you are relying on the screener to read your resume (and here's the usual deal-breaker) to determine how well you fit and whether you are qualified for the job.

Do you really want a screener with perhaps only two to four years of experience (who probably doesn't understand the job requirements as well as you do) to take only 10-30 seconds to figure out whether you qualify?

The obvious answer is "no."

Sit down. Take 30–45 minutes, analyze the job description, identify the four to six most important requirements of the job, and figure out how you qualify for each "requirement." Then, fill out and construct the table in the middle of the "T Letter Template." Finally, modify the opening and closing paragraphs of the letter to suit your personal style and circumstances.

If you can't convince yourself in writing that you are "qualified" to do the job, how could some "screener" conclude that you "qualify?"

If you aren't willing to spend 30 minutes on it, how can you expect a "screener" to spend more than 30 seconds on it?

Also, consider sending in just a T-Letter, without a resume. Experiment. Figure out what works best for you: T-Letter only, resume only, or both.

I frequently get positive feedback from job seekers that their response rate dramatically improved when they started to use T-Letters.

Put Your Address Here
Put Your City State Zip Here
Phone: Put Your Phone # Here
Email: Put Your Email Address Here

Put The Date Here

Put The Name of The Person Here
Put The Person's Title Here
Put The Company Name Here
Put The Mailing Address Here
Put The City State Zip Here

Dear Mr/Mrs/Ms/Miss/Dr/Sir/Madam Put The Person's Last Name Here,

I am responding to your job entitled "_____" (Reference #_____). I have included a copy of my resume for your review. You will find that I have extensive experience in _____, _____, and _____.

In addition, here is a comparison of your job requirements and my qualifications:

Your Job Requirements	My Qualifications
Put a description of a requirement here.	Put a description of a qualification here. Put a description of a qualification here. Put a description of a qualification here.
Put a description of a requirement here.	Put a description of a qualification here. Put a description of a qualification here. Put a description of a qualification here.
Put a description of a requirement here.	Put a description of a qualification here. Put a description of a qualification here. Put a description of a qualification here.

I would welcome the opportunity to discuss your job requirements and my qualifications with you. I will contact you in a couple of days to follow up. Thank you in advance for your consideration.

Respectfully yours,

Put Your Name Here

Put Your Address And Street Here
Put Your City State Zip Here
Phone #: Put Your Phone Number Here
eMail: Put Your Email Address Here

Put Date Here

Put Person's Name Here, Put Title Here
Put Organization Name Here
Put Address And Street Here
Put City State Zip Here

Dear Mr./Mrs./Ms. Put Last Name Here,

I am a Put Your Job Title Here. My goal is to obtain employment with Put Organization Name Here.

Over the last six weeks, I have been doing extensive literature research on your company, meeting with its customers, suppliers, past employees, and visiting its facilities. I have also met with Put Person's Name Here, Put Person's Name Here, and Put Person's Name Here, who are current employees. I am impressed with company's Put Reason Here, Put Reason Here, and Put Reason Here.

I am offering to share what I have heard and seen with you.

I am interested in finding out more about the company and which departments may have the type of position I am seeking. I hope you would be willing to meet with me, share some information, and give me some direction. I realize that you do not have a job for me.

I will call you in a couple of days to arrange a meeting.

Thank you in advance for your time and consideration.

Respectfully yours,

Put Your Name Here

Put Your Name Here
9999 Any Street, Any City, Any State 99999
Home: 999-999-9999, Cell: 999-999-9999
eMail: Put Your eMail Address Here

Target Job Titles Provide a list of the possible titles of the job you are seeking. Examples are VP of Sales, Director of Sales, and Regional Sales Manager. (3 to 15 words.)

```

```

Target Job Provide a description of the job you are seeking. Consider including the key attributes of the job, key functions you would perform, number of people reporting to you, the size of your budget, customer accounts, the kinds of people you would be working with, etc. (4 to 10 sentences.)

```

```

Employment Type – Provide a brief name/description for the type of employment you are looking for. Examples are employee of an organization, own a company, independent consultant, and franchiser. (2 to 5 words.)

```

```

Professional Summary / Areas of Expertise Provide a description of your experience, background, skills, capabilities, and/or education which substantiate that you can handle such a job. Bulleted lists of key words, topics, projects, specialties, etc. are fine. (4 to 10 sentences or bulleted items.)

```

```

Accomplishments This is a list of your significant achievements which support your ability to handle the job you are seeking. (3-6 bulleted phrases or sentences.)

```

```

<u>Target Employer Size</u> Quantify, in terms of people, revenue, number of facilities, etc. the size of the employer with whom you want to work. Use ranges. Examples are "Fortune 100 to 500 company." "1,000 to 5,000 employees." (5 to 15 words.)

```
┌─────────────────────────────────────────────────────────────┐
│                                                               │
└─────────────────────────────────────────────────────────────┘
```

<u>Target Industry or Field</u> Name the industries or fields on which you are focusing your search. Examples are manufacturing, non-profits, education, and technology. (2-10 words.)

```
┌─────────────────────────────────────────────────────────────┐
│                                                               │
└─────────────────────────────────────────────────────────────┘
```

<u>Target Employer Profile</u> This describes any other aspects of an employer that are important to you. Examples are growth objectives, culture, and community involvement. Avoid statements such as "An employer who cares about its employees." Or "An ethical organization." (2-6 items either as sentences or bulleted items.)

```
┌─────────────────────────────────────────────────────────────┐
│                                                               │
└─────────────────────────────────────────────────────────────┘
```

<u>Target Employers</u> Name specific employers you are likely to focus on for an extended period of time. Examples are Microsoft, Vanguard, and United Way. (2 to 10 employers in a sentence or bulleted list.)

```
┌─────────────────────────────────────────────────────────────┐
│                                                               │
└─────────────────────────────────────────────────────────────┘
```

<u>Target Location</u> Provide a description of the geographic area you will consider. If true, state that you are open to relocation. Examples are "Prefer northern California." "Open to large metropolitan areas." (5 to 15 words.)

```
┌─────────────────────────────────────────────────────────────┐
│                                                               │
└─────────────────────────────────────────────────────────────┘
```

<u>Travel</u> Describe your desire or willingness to travel. (5 to 20 words.)

```
┌─────────────────────────────────────────────────────────────┐
│                                                               │
└─────────────────────────────────────────────────────────────┘
```

Put Your Address And Street Here
Put Your City State Zip Here
Phone #: Put Your Phone Number Here
eMail: Put Your Email Address Here

Put Date Here

Put Person's Name Here, Put Title Here
Put Organization Name Here
Put Address And Street Here
Put City State Zip Here

Dear Mr./Mrs./Ms. Put Last Name Here,

Thank you so much for _____ {insert a description of what the other person did for you] last _____ {indicate when it occurred]. I certainly appreciate your time, the information that you shared, and your advice.

During the course of our meeting, you suggested that I _____ _____ {insert a description of something specific that the person suggested that you do]. I followed through and _____ {insert a description of what you did or will do and what came about as a consequence.]

{Insert a sentence or two here that describes the next step you will take to sustain this relationship. It may be as simple as keeping the other person apprised of your job search process.]

If there is any way that I can ever reciprocate, certainly let me know.

Thank you for your time and consideration.

Respectfully yours,

Put Your Name Here

Put Your Address And Street Here
Put Your City State Zip Here
Phone #: Put Your Phone Number Here
eMail: Put Your Email Address Here

Put Date Here

Put Person's Name Here, Put Title Here

Put Organization Name Here
Put Address And Street Here
Put City State Zip Here

Dear Mr./Mrs./Ms. Put Last Name Here,

Thank you so much for meeting with me and discussing the _____
_____ {insert the job title] position and my qualifications last
_____ {indicate when it occurred]. I certainly appreciate your time and the information about the job that you shared.

During the course of our meeting, there were a few subjects that came
up that I would like to elaborate on.

- {Insert a couple sentences here.}
- {Insert a couple sentences here.}
- {Insert a couple sentences here.}

I am quite interested in the position and would very much like to
move on to the next stage.

{Insert a sentence or two here that describes the next step you will
take to sustain this relationship. It may be as simple as indicating you
will call the hiring manager in about a week.]

Thank you for your time and consideration.

Respectfully yours,

Put Your Name Here

This is a list of questions which interviewers ask, the reasons they ask them, and in many cases, example answers or an explanation of how to answer them. They apply to the situation in which you are interviewing for a specific, known job opening. Review this material. Then, prepare answers to many of the most common questions. Make written notes. Carry them with you. Practice, practice, practice in front of a mirror or with someone else. Review them before you go into an interview.

The time is going to come when you get a question you are not sure how to answer. There are two ways to handle this. One way is with humor. Another way is to respond with a question. Either approach will possibly deflect the questioner off the subject or they will, at least, give you more time to think about a response.

The questions below are grouped by subject matter. Within each group, there is no particular order.

Opening and Introduction at an Interview

Question: "How are you?"

The Reason it is Asked: More than likely, this is just an innocent greeting to start the conversation. However, analytical interviewers are interested to see if it prompts anything negative from you.

How to Respond: No matter how physically or emotionally badly you feel at the moment, you must come back with a positive response. Whatever you do, don't talk about how stressful your job search is or how difficult it was to get this interview. A simple answer is better than a long one. Then, return the favor.

Example Responses: "I'm fine. How about you?"

Question: "Did you have any difficulty finding us?"

The Reason it is Asked: Again, this might be an innocent question. However, you have to assume it's not and it's a small test to see if you can manage minor things.

How to Respond: Even if you got lost three times on the way to the interview, you need to provide a simple and positive response.

Example Responses: "No problem at all. The directions that I received were right on the mark."

Question: "Can I get you something to drink?"

The Reason it is Asked: Again, this may just be a polite courtesy, but you need to assume there is an ulterior motive. Maybe the questioner wants to see if you expect others to take care of you or whether you need stimulants, like caffeine.

How to Respond: Always refuse. They want you to serve them, not the other way around. Don't start off asking them to serve you. You also don't want to be bothered by a glass or cup during the interview, so, politely respond in the negative.

Example Responses: "No thank you. I'm fine for now."

Question: "Tell me about yourself." Or "Describe yourself."

The Reason it is Asked: This is a common "getting down to business" starter question. If it is the first question, it suggests an interviewer who isn't very well-prepared or isn't comfortable interviewing people. The interviewer is looking for a high level summary of your professional background and whether you can verbally communicate in a comfortable and appropriate manner. This is not a request for your entire history.

How to Respond: Be prepared with a specific answer to this question. Don't ad-lib. Keep your answer to less than a minute. Hit the highlights of your professional stature. Paraphrasing the "Professional Profile" in your resume is a good way to respond. Avoid talking about your personal status, unless you sense that such matters are key to landing the job.

Example Responses: "I'm an excellent financial analyst with extensive experience in capital expenditure budgeting and forecasting. I also have a CPA. I have led teams of financial analysts. I am a husband and a father with many interests and hobbies. I volunteer with two community organizations."

Questions About Your Education

Question: "What college courses did you enjoy the most or least?"

The Reason it is Asked: This question is intended to assess your aptitude and fit to the job.

How to Respond: Unless there is a serious difference between the types of courses you took and the requirements of the job, make your answer demonstrate the similarity of the two. Virtually every job requires working with numbers to some degree. Don't say you hated math courses, even if you did. However, if asked explicitly about how you liked math courses, it's time to be candid.

Question: "Tell me about your most enjoyable college experience."

The Reason it is Asked: This is a loaded question. The interviewer is trying to determine how hard of a worker you are.

How to Respond: This is not the time to discuss the wildest party you went to. Wrap your answer around an educational experience which you enjoyed that would contribute to your ability to do the job.

Question: "What portion of your college expenses did you pay for?"

The Reason it is Asked: The interviewer thinks people who paid for a portion of their college expenses make better workers.

How to Respond: If you did indeed pay for some of your college expenses, state that. If you didn't, but you worked during the summers, state that. If neither, describe something you had to do, some effort you had to expend, in order to stay in college.

Question: "Tell me about your extra-curricular activities."

The Reason it is Asked: The interviewer is looking for a well-rounded person.

How to Respond: Again, this not the time to discuss the wildest party you went to. Name college-organized teams or groups in which you participated. Some description is needed, but keep it relatively brief. The interviewer really doesn't care about every varsity football game in which you played.

Question: "How good were your grades?"

The Reason it is Asked: This is really a "fit" question. Good grades are usually desired, but great grades may not be.

How to Respond: Accuracy, such as "My GPA was 3.45" is OK, but not needed. Also, a relative answer (how you stacked up against similar students) is more important than an absolute statement. However you respond, don't lie. They will find out in their background check.

Example Responses: "My grades were above average compared to the other students, but most of my courses were in the honors college."

Questions in Regard to Why You are Looking for Another Job

Question: "Are you currently employed?"

The Reason it is Asked: If you answer "Yes," that will lead to questions about why you want to leave. If you answer "No," that will lead to the next question.

How to Respond: You must tell the simple truth here. Another question will be forthcoming to which you can provide details.

Example Responses: "Yes" or "No."

Question: "Why did you leave your last employer?"

The Reason it is Asked: An optimist asks this question to get confirmation that you make good judgments and decisions. A pessimist asks this question to find out if your last employer thought you were a troubled or problem employee.

How to Respond: You need a response that reassures the interviewer that the reason you left makes immensely good sense. Either the reason you left your last employer had nothing to do with you or you couldn't achieve your career goals through your last employer. If your last employer terminated you because of your performance, you have a serious problem. You are not under any obligation to explain to the interviewer what happened and why. However, you need to have a simple, solid answer that is not a fabrication of the truth. (That's a euphemism for a "lie.") Finally, by all means, do not complain about your last employer, not matter how much it is warranted. If you do that, the interviewer is going to be concerned that you would complain about him/her when you leave him/her. You also need to provide a good reason for why you left your last employer, before you landed a new job. If you don't, the interviewer will worry that you are impulsive and you will leave your new employer at the drop of a hat.

Example Responses: "The company went through a major downsizing. I was one of over a 1,000 people who were laid off." "I want the focus of my career search to be _____. This is something that my last (or current employer) is not able to offer."

Question: "You say that you are looking for a job that has more opportunity. Couldn't you find that where you last worked?"

The Reason it is Asked: The interviewer suspects that there is another reason that you left your last employer.

How to Respond: This is not the time to mention another reason why you left. Doing so with only reinforce in the interviewer's mind that you are, or were, withholding something negative about you. You need to explain why the opportunities that you are seeking could not be fulfilled or not be fulfilled anytime soon with your last employer.

Example Responses: "I could have achieved my next job objective at my last (or current) employer. However, it would have taken years. There is an entrenched seniority system within my last employer's organization and there were many people ahead of me. In and of itself, there isn't anything wrong with a seniority system. However, my last (or current) boss has told me I am more than qualified to handle the next job step up. I didn't want to wait."

Question: "Well, I understand your reasons for wanting to leave your last employer, but why didn't you hang in there and look for another job while you were still employed?"

The Reason it is Asked: This is a direct attack and is now a critical question. This is usually asked when the interview suspects something negative.

How to Respond: You've got to respond with something that reassures the interviewer that you made a good decision to leave, before having another job.

Example Responses: "I was working over 75 hours a week. I definitely wanted to refocus my career and devote much time to making it happen. I decided the best way was to go into a full-time job search."

Question: "Were you ever fired?"

The Reason it is Asked: The interviewer is trying to find out if you are a problem employee.

How to Respond: If you were ever terminated in a mass layoff or downsizing event, describe that situation. If you were ever fired in a one-person event, you may need to describe that. Just don't use the word "fired." You need to describe the situation in the best terms that you can that minimize the possibility of giving the impression that you were a problem employee. If that was the case and you can't make it appear otherwise, then at least explain how you learned from that experience and most importantly, convince the listener that that won't happen again. Note: During their background check of you, they will contact your prior employers. With all the lawsuits, the vast portion of employers do not give reasons why a person no longer works there.

Your Personal Characteristics

Question: "What are your strengths?"

The Reason it is Asked: There are multiple reasons for this question. First, it is for the interviewer to determine if what you think are your strengths match what the interviewer is looking for. Another reason might be to assess whether you are psychologically comfortable "tooting your own horn", particularly if it is warranted.

Another might be for the interviewer to determine whether you have a reasonable assessment of yourself.

How to Respond: Again, be prepared with a specific answer to this question. Don't ad-lib this one. Your answer should be short . . . . . either a few words or phrases that describe your professional and personal characteristics. Make your response relate to the job, as best as you can judge as this point in the interview.

Example Responses: "I have a strong work ethic. I am very analytical, thorough, and have a good balance of technical and personal capabilities."

Question: "What are your weaknesses?"

The Reason it is Asked: This is a loaded question. Not only is the interviewer wanting to know if you have some weakness that will harm you ability to perform the job, he/she is also wondering if you are careless enough to mention a serious weakness.

How to Respond: Again, be prepared with a specific answer to this question. Don't ad-lib this one. The best way to respond to this question is to name a weakness that might, in some circumstances, be actually construed as a strength. Keep your answer brief and simple. (Also, if the interviewer interprets your answer as a strength, then be prepared for the question again by having a different response.)

Example Responses: "Well, sometimes I expect too much of myself." Or "I've come to appreciate the personal computer as a tool for organizing and performing my work. I'd like to take a couple courses to become more proficient at using it."

Question: Tell me about a time you made a big mistake.

The Reason it is Asked: In addition to seeking insight into your work experience, the interviewer is probing to see if you have a fatal flaw.

How to Respond: This is not the time to explain how you lost millions of dollars for your last employer. True confessions are good for the soul, but they won't help you here. You need to recall an incident that maybe had an unfortunate outcome, but one in which the interviewer could conclude that, based on what you knew beforehand, the action that you took was reasonable. This, too, is a loaded question. Be prepared with a specific answer to this question. Don't ad-lib this one.

Question: "What is your sexual preference?"

The Reason it is Asked: You think they can't ask this question. Just wait. . . . . . What legitimate reason could an interviewer possibly have to ask this question? It could be that, in the course of performing the job, people (customers?) may contact you and ask absurd questions like this. The interviewer is looking for some indication as to whether you can handle a question like this without offending the questioner.

How to Respond: Do not respond by saying "You can't ask that question" or "It's none of your business." Respond either with something humorous or benign seriousness.

Example Responses: Chuckle, then say "Well, I'm flexible! What works best around here?" A serious and inquiring response would be "Well, that's a surprising question. Will that come in to play in this job?"

Question: "Tell me what you were doing in this time gap in your work history."

The Reason it is Asked: Many people don't want to work and take months and maybe years off to just wander around. The hiring manager is looking for someone who will work. He/she needs confirmation that you really want to work.

How to Respond: Give an answer that explains what you were doing when you weren't working and which reassures the interviewer that you would have gladly been working. Excellent answers are that you were raising your family, were taking care of a seriously ill family member, or doing volunteer work. It is also OK to say you were looking for a job during that time period. Any employer who is familiar with the job market now knows that it commonly takes many months to find a job. (If this is a question that you frequently get during interviews or that the time gap prevents you from getting interviews, then add information to your resume to eliminate the gap.)

Example Responses: "I set my career aside to raise my children." Or "During that time period, I was looking for a full time job. To keep myself busy and my skills fresh, I did some part-time work for _____ [example employers]"

Question: "What characteristics are you looking for in a boss / manager?"

The Reason it is Asked: This might be "the" most loaded question. The interviewer, probably the hiring manager, is trying to get a reading as to whether he and you are going to be compatible.

How to Respond: If you already really like the hiring manager, then pick some of his apparent positive characteristics. If you really dislike the hiring manager, you've got a problem. This isn't the time to be too candid, yet, you need to speak the truth. If you're not sure, then you need a response that covers both ends of the spectrum for a couple of characteristics.

Example Responses: "I prefer a boss who will give me detailed specifications when they are warranted and, at other times, give me lots of rope when he/she can afford to do so."

Question: "Tell me about a time that you disagreed with your boss. How did you handle it?"

The Reason it is Asked: This is another heavily loaded question. No boss wants an employee to make him look bad in front of other people. By the same token, in today's complex business world, there are fewer and fewer bosses who have all the answers and just want "yes-men" around them. The interviewer may be looking for confirmation that you will eventually be able to do it his/her way in a professional manner, even if you initially disagreed.

How to Respond: You need to demonstrate you can think on your own and have helpful ideas, offer your boss ideas different than his/hers, yet go along with his/her way if that's what it takes. Cite an example from your past that demonstrates all of these elements.

Question: "How much day-to-day direction do you need?"

The Reason it is Asked: If the hiring manager intended to give you day-to-day direction all the time, he/she wouldn't have asked this questions. That's the tip-off that you're going to need to be able to do this job with little day-to-day direction.

How to Respond: Tell the hiring manager you're used to working on your own with little direct supervision. By the same token, you need to reassure the hiring manager that he/she will always know what you are doing. Try to cite an example from the past.

Question: "What makes you angry?"

The Reason it is Asked: The interview wants to make sure you don't need anger management.

How to Respond: "I never get angry" is not an acceptable answer. Everyone gets angry sometimes. Cite a case, an extreme case, in which anyone would have gotten angry. Make it brief and close with a statement that indicates you keep your anger to yourself.

Question: "Do you prefer to work with information or people?"

The Reason it is Asked: Clearly, one or both is important.

How to Respond: If you tend towards the extreme of one or the other, speak the truth. If there is not a "fit," you want to know it now, not later. Most jobs require both, these days. Give a sincere answer that reflects your desire to work with both.

Questions About Your Interest in the Employer's Organization or the Job

Question: "Why would you want to work for our company?"

The Reason it is Asked: This is more than a casual inquiry. The interviewer would like to hear that you think there is something special about his/her company and that you are lusting to work there.

How to Respond: You did research the company, didn't you? Wrap your answer around aspects of the company that you find appealing. Examples are: the company is growing, is profitable, is innovative, is functionally focused on what you love to do. Avoid giving answers that suggest the company is convenient for you, like "Well, your office is only a five minute drive from my home." Shorter, generic answers are better. The more elements you include in your answer, the more chance you will describe something the interviewer knows is not true about the company.

Example Responses: "The company deals with large complex numerical challenges and that's the kind of environment that I want to be in."

Question: "Tell me what our products/services are."

The Reason it is Asked: Many job seekers just go from company to company for interviews and the company is immaterial. The interviewer is looking for a signal that you are actually interested in his/her company and/or that you were willing to spend the time to do some research about it.

How to Respond: You did research the company, didn't you? Tell him/her what you found out. Be as specific as you can. Tell him/her what you did to find the information.

Example Responses: "The company underwrites insurance for personal and commercial vehicles, both through agents and directly through its Internet site. It operates in all states, except New Jersey and Massachusetts. I also talked to my insurance agent who sells policies for _____ [name of company] and he gave me a lot of information, too."

Question: "What could you do to help us out at our company?"

The Reason it is Asked: This could be just an attempt to get the conversation going or it could be a question looking for a solid answer.

How to Respond: Assume the interviewer is looking for a solid answer. The best way to answer the question is in relation to the company's objectives. Hopefully, when you prepared for the interview, you researched the company. In that case, respond by describing what you do with an explanation as to how that would help the company. Otherwise, explain how your background and capabilities will contribute to successfully performing the job.

Question: "Tell me what your understanding is of the job."

The Reason it is Asked: There can be several reasons for this question. The questioner may just be trying to get confirmation that you are at the right interview. It may be a question to assess your interest level in the job. It may be to determine if you understand the job and whether you understand the terminology in the job description.

How to Respond: Answer with energy, enthusiasm, and excitement. Your answer needs to explain what you read in the job description and what other people in the company have told you about the job. Cite the sources for your answer. At the end of your response, ask for confirmation.

Example Responses: "From the job description, I understand the job to be _____ {describe the duties} and requires _____ _____ {describe skills needed} Also, in an earlier interview with _____ {name a person}, he/she told me that the job would also entail _____ {describe other duties or responsibilities}. Is my understanding correct?"

Questions About Your Fit to the Job and Company

Question: "Why should we hire you?"

The Reason it is Asked: This may be a question to simply determine whether you are confident about yourself. It may be because the interviewer thinks you don't "fit." It is more likely looking to establish a fair description of what you can contribute.

How to Respond: This is a critical question. You *must* ace this one. If you can't explain why they should hire you, they aren't going to figure it out on their. Don't ad-lib here. Prepare a solid answer for this specific job and interview. Explain how your background and capabilities will contribute to the job. Describe your qualifications for each of the two or three key requirements of the job. A short answer can't effectively answer the question. A long, windy, wandering answer is also bad.

Example Responses: "My sense is that one of the key requirements of the job is _____ [name a requirement]. Well, I did _____ [describe your relevant experience] for x years and accomplished this and that. Another important requirement of the job is _____ [name another requirement]. I previously held a position as a _____ [name a job title] in which I did this and that. I think this background and experience will make help me successfully perform this job."

Question: "Where will you be in five years?"

The Reason it is Asked: This may be a simple question to determine if you have any ambition. It may be a question related to your career goals / objectives. However, more than likely it is an attempt to determine how well you will fit and will be happy with the opportunities that this job will offer. Also, hiring managers usually do not want to hire people who are going to run over or around them. The questioner may have anxiety about that.

How to Respond: You want to wrap your answer around what you think are realistic possibilities for this job and the group in which it exists. By the same token, if you have concerns that this job will not provide you with the opportunities in the longer term that you are hoping for, then it may be the time to discuss this. (Round #2 of interviews is a better time.) It is best to respond with a simple and benign answer that sounds like what any job seeker may hope for. Examples are expansions in the scope of job, or expansion of the responsibilities or your authorities.

Example Responses: "I hope to have mastered the job's functions and have taken more of a leadership roll with other people within the group." Or "Ultimately, I would want to be recognized as a company expert in _____ [name a role or subject matter]." Or "I'd like to think that I have advanced to a level in which I manage people performing these functions."

<u>Question</u>: "Why did you apply for this position?" or "What interested you in this position?"

<u>The Reason it is Asked</u>: This is not just a "ho-hum" question. The questioner wants to assess your *level* of interest in the job and the fit.

<u>How to Respond</u>: You must respond with energy and enthusiasm. That's almost more important than what you are going to say. Provide an answer that explains how your interests, background, and capabilities are directly related to the requirements of the job.

<u>Question</u>: "Tell me about your management style."

<u>The Reason it is Asked</u>: This is a question to determine if your style "fits" the organization and the people you would be supervising.

<u>How to Respond</u>: Taken literally, the question is about "style." Style has to do with how you manage people and how you manage the work. Management activities include things like planning, resource acquisition, delegation, directing, leading, monitoring. Wrap your answer about those types of things. If you have a pretty good sense of your potential boss's style and it is consistent with yours, then elaborate on those "style" elements.

Questions About Your Career

<u>Question</u>: "What are your career goals / objectives?"

<u>The Reason it is Asked</u>: This is fundamentally a "fit" question.

<u>How to Respond</u>: Don't make something up. If you don't know the answer to this question, then it's too soon to be interviewing for specific jobs. Answer the question directly and briefly. Tell the truth. You want to get a sense as to whether you can reach your longer term goals / objectives with this employer. If not, now is the time to find out. It's OK to answer the question by naming a job title, a functional area, an authority level, responsibility scope, or anything else that you aspire to.

Question: "Why? When did you decide on these goals / objectives?"

The Reason it is Asked: This question is probing to see whether you just made up the prior answer or how committed you are to those goals / objectives.

How to Respond: Speak the truth. Convince the interviewer of your conviction. If they conclude that, because of your answer, you don't "fit," then you probably will be unhappy accepting their job offer.

Question: "What is your plan to achieve these career goals / objectives?"

The Reason it is Asked: Again, this is a test for commitment and reasonableness.

How to Respond: OK, let's assume that you're like most people and you don't have a plan. You're going to have to ad-lib. A reasonable plan is one which has a few steps, slow progress, and advancement is "earned," not given.

Questions to Assess Your Knowledge, Experience, and Capabilities to Handle the Job

This is a great time to use the PAR method explained in Appendix K.

Question: "What do you feel is the greatest challenge in your field?"

The Reason it is Asked: This question is designed to determine if you just perform the job and are oblivious to what's going on around you or you are aware of pending changes and anticipating how you will have to deal with them.

How to Respond: Provide as much detail as you can. Cite examples of changes and how you dealt with them in the past.

Question: "You've performed a similar job in the past. How do you view the government controls that have impacted this job?"

The Reason it is Asked: This question is simply intended to assess you technical knowledge about the job and field. A job's functions are commonly defined by external constituents like governments, customers, and suppliers, and not just internal management.

How to Respond: Provide as much detail as you can. Cite examples of changes and how you dealt with them in the past.

Question: "Tell me about your work history."

The Reason it is Asked: The interviewer is looking for a high level summary of your experience and a sense of your verbal communications capabilities and style.

How to Respond: Speak for about one to three minutes. Do not give a blow-by-blow account for everything that happened in your career. Name the organizations which you previously worked for. Name the job titles you have had. Focus on your accomplishments. You want to demonstrate you've successfully done many of the functions that this new job requires and that you have been advancing / learning, and taking on more responsibility.

Question: "How much are you able to travel?"

The Reason it is Asked: Traveling is clearly a requirement of the job. The interviewer is looking for confirmation that is going to be OK with you.

How to Respond: If you have a sense for how much travel is required, then, you can respond with an acceptable answer. If you aren't sure, then give a response with a range that is as wide as you think you can get away with.

Example Responses: "Well, 5% to 15% would work for me."

Question: The interviewer takes a pen out of his/her pocket and says "Sell this pen to me."

The Reason it is Asked: Clearly, the need to sell things to other people (or to convince them about something) is important to be successful in this job.

How to Respond: This is easy to respond to. I explained how to do it in Chapter 15. Tell the interviewer what the "benefits" of the pen are.

Example Responses: "The pen is small and light weight. (Feature) That will allow you to easily carry it with your wherever you go. (Benefit) The pen has a refillable cartridge. (Feature) When you run out of ink, you will be able to get another cartridge without having to pay for a complete, new pen. (Benefit)

Questions About Your Work Experience

Question: "Tell me which of your prior jobs you liked the best."

The Reason it is Asked: This question isn't about you. The interviewer is trying to determine to what degree you are interested in the job that he/she has to offer.

How to Respond: Assuming you are interested in the interviewer's job, pick a similar job that you previously did and describe it with energy, enthusiasm, and excitement to the extent that you legitimately can.

Question: "Tell about two of your most important accomplishments."

The Reason it is Asked: There can be multiple reasons for this question. One is to see how you verbally communicate. Another is to get an indication of your capabilities.

How to Respond: Prepare for this question in advance. Don't ad-lib. You probably included some of your important accomplishments on your resume, so speak to them. Preferably, speak to an accomplishment that relates closely to the job for which you are interviewing. Speak to each of the accomplishments for a minute or two. When you do, you will no doubt have to provide the interviewer with some background information about the nature of the business, work, and your functions. However, what the interviewer wants to hear is "What did *you do*" and "Why was this important?" Be sure that at least 50% of what you say answers those unspoken questions. Also note: Much of what we do is within a "team" setting and the ability to work on a "team" may be very important to the hiring manager. If you describe such an accomplishment, consider minimizing the "I" portion of your response and focus on your contribution to the team's objective and results. (Regardless, this is another situation in which to use the PAR method to respond to a question.)

Question: "Tell me about a situation in your prior experience in which you reduced costs."

The Reason it is Asked: Business performance is measured in financial terms. That alone is a good reason for the question. But the fact that the question was asked is a signal of what you are going to be expected to do if you land this job.

How to Respond: A strong case can be made that a person is either focused on generating revenue for a company or reducing costs. If you have only been in revenue generation roles in the past, then you may have to say so and try to get by on that. Otherwise, you're going to need to come up with at least one, preferably two, really good examples of how you've contributed to cost reductions. Provide details and be absolutely sure you quantify how much (thousands or millions of dollars) you reduced the cost. Estimates are fine. Keep your answer to six to ten sentences and one to three minutes.

Example Responses: "I did an analysis of a plant's operating processes and capacity and determined a new process sequence that expanded capacity by 20% and forestalled a $10 million plant expansion for three years."

Questions About How Well You Work with People / Team Work

Question: "Do you work well on teams?"

The Reason it is Asked: Team work must be needed for this job.

How to Respond: You must provide a response that is an emphatic "yes," not literally, but clearly. Cite two to three examples of teams that you have worked on, what your role was, and how you interacted with the other people.

Question: "What type of people do you work best with?"

The Reason it is Asked: This is a loaded question looking for a bad answer; someone who can work with only a particular type of people.

How to Respond: You need to convince the interviewer that you are not hung up on the particular types of people that you work with.

Example Responses: "I've worked on so many different teams with so many different types of people that I don't think about types any more. It all about collaborating our efforts and getting the project completed successfully."

Question: "Are you a leader or a follower?"

The Reason it is Asked: More than likely, the interviewer is looking for one or the other, but maybe he/she is looking for a versatile person.

How to Respond: If you know at this point in the interviewing process which is desired and you are good at it, your response should focus on that. If you don't know yet whether you will be called upon to be one or the other and you are good at both, then say so, to demonstrate your versatility.

Example Responses: "On one team in the past, I found that other people had far more leadership skills than I had. In that case, I was comfortable being a follower. On another team, I was assigned the role of a follower, but I found that the leader was weak and I had to take on some unofficial leadership tasks to help move the project along."

Question: "If someone were to attack you personally, how would you react?"

The Reason it is Asked: There could be several possibilities. This may be a signal that you will have to deal with offensive people in this job and the interviewer wants to find out if you can. Or the interviewer may sense that you have an inferiority complex and is testing you.

How to Respond: You want to demonstrate that you can handle such a frontal assault. The best way to do so is to respond in a matter-of-fact tone and inquire why the attacker accused you of something. Then, you respond with information that counters the claims of the attacker.

Example Responses: "Wow, that's not the case. What makes you think that?

Question: "How did I do as an interviewer?"

The Reason it is Asked: This is a test to see if you can provide constructive criticism or whether you brow beat people.

How to Respond: No matter what you think, you're only going to say positive things about the interviewer. This isn't the time to take a risk and say something that he/she will consider as too candid.

Question: "How would you feel about working for a person who is much younger than you and making more money that you?" Or if you are a man (woman) "How would you feel about working for a woman (man)?"

The Reason it is Asked: It is a really good sign if it was the hiring manager who asked this question. This means he/she's already thinking about making you an offer and is starting to "dot-the-I's." He/she is just making sure that this isn't going to be a troublesome issue in your mind.

How to Respond: It's all in the answer.

Example Responses: "Well, apparently your boss has already concluded that you are competent and deserve what you have earned. I'm sure that after I worked for you for a few weeks, I would draw the same conclusion."

Question: "Tell me about the worst boss you ever had."

The Reason it is Asked: This question is to assess how diplomatic you are, whether you hammer people when they're not around, and/or whether the interviewer should worry about what you will say about him/her.

How to Respond: Use an example of a boss who had unreasonable pressures placed upon him/her. Explain what he/she did that was troubling, but then close with a fair rationalization of his/her behavior.

Questions About Your Management / Leadership Capabilities

Question: "Describe a situation in which you were a project leader."

The Reason it is Asked: Clearly, the interviewer thinks leading people and managing work and schedules are important.

How to Respond: You need to provide a really good example. Describe it with energy, enthusiasm, and excitement. No doubt, you will have to provide the interviewer with some background information about the nature of the project. However, what the interviewer wants to hear is "What did *you do*." Be sure that at least 50% of what you say answers that unspoken question.

Question: "Do you delegate well?"

The Reason it is Asked: Well, you better be able to!!! Clearly, this interviewer thinks it's important for this job.

How to Respond: You need to provide a response that sounds like an emphatic "yes." Cite an example or a story to convince the listener. There are several good reasons for a manager to delegate: It keeps him/her from doing work that is below his/her salary level, to develop his/her subordinates, to keep the progress coming. Include something in your response that indicates why delegating is important.

Question: "What do you look for when you hire people?"

The Reason it is Asked: The obvious answer is someone who meets the technical requirements of the job. However, this question was not posed about a particular job. The interviewer is looking for an indication of the personal characteristics that you look for.

How to Respond: Think about the positive characteristics of people, things like: strong work ethic, accuracy, great communications skills, energy, and independence. Pick some positive personal characteristic(s) that you tend to look for and talk about it. If appropriate, make the case that you have found that if people are really well-developed with this trait, it usually overcomes any short term deficiency in the technical requirements of the job.

Question: "Tell me about a time you had to fire someone."

The Reason it is Asked: On one hand, the interviewer may just be looking for insight into your level of experience managing people. On the other hand, it may be a "Red Flag." If you land this job, are you going to have people working for you that will require some form of disciplinary action?

How to Respond: Play it straight. Provide an example or two. You don't want to sound like you are too good at this.

Example Responses: Cite an example in which the need for the firing was clear-cut and quick. For example, someone who worked for you stole company property.

Question: "How do you get people to do what you ask?"

The Reason it is Asked: This is a straight forward question looking for evidence of your ability to lead.

How to Respond: Describe 2 to 4 different methods you use to demonstrate your flexibility to deal with different people who are motivated differently.

Analytical Questions

Question: "Give me an example of your problem solving skills."

The Reason it is Asked: Clearly, problem solving skills are important with this job.

How to Respond: You need to describe a specific case with a fair amount of detail. There are many different types of problems. Pick one that is similar to the type of problem which you expect to encounter in this job. In the course of the explanation, be sure to name or describe the problem solving methodology you used. There are many. You will have to provide the interviewer with some background information about the nature of the problem. However, what the interviewer wants to hear is, "What did *you do?*" Be sure at least 50% of what you say answers that unspoken question.

Question: "Describe the most complex analysis you've done."

The Reason it is Asked: Clearly, the job is going to require the ability to do complex analysis.

How to Respond: This isn't the time to ad-lib. You should have prepared a well-thought-out answer to this question. Hopefully, you picked an analysis example that is similar to the types of analyses that will be required by the job. Be sure to elaborate on what *you did* and the *positive consequences* of the result, not just a description of the complexity of the problem.

Brain Teaser Questions

Question: "How many gas stations are there in the USA?"

The Reason it is Asked: The answer is not important. An accurate answer is irrelevant. The interviewer wants to hear how you think and how to resolve things when definitive information is not available to help you.

How to Respond: Come up with a logical way to estimate the answer. The example numbers you use are immaterial.

Example Responses: "Well, I live in a city of 10,000 people. It has 10 gas stations. There are about 300 million people in the USA, which is 30,000 times the city I live in. So, there are about 300,000 gas stations in the USA."

Question: "Let's say, hypothetically, that you own and operate a local grocery store. You do a fairly good business, seven days a week. Suppose the city council passes a law that no local commercial businesses can be open on Sunday. What would you do to recover your lost business?"

The Reason it is Asked: This is a question looking for insight into your creativity, perseverance, and ability to overcome obstacles.

How to Respond: Cite as many things which you could do as possible, eight at a minimum, twelve to fourteen is even better.

Example Responses: "I'd send flyers to my customers about specials on Saturdays." "I'd start delivering on Sundays." "I'd move my store to a location where it's still OK to be open on Sunday." "I'd organize the local merchants and petition the city council to rescind the new law." "I'd raise prices." "I'd cut back on my employees' hours." I'd upgrade my products to those with higher margins." "I'd open a second store in another neighborhood." (You get the idea?)

Question: "Two men have old, worn out horses. The men constantly argue about whose horse is the slowest. One day, they finally come up with a solution that will resolve the argument, once and for all. What was the solution?"

The Reason it is Asked: It's merely a puzzle to test a candidate's creativity and analytical thinking.

Example Responses: The answer is "They rode each other's horse in a race. The one whose horse came in second was the winner of the argument."

Question: "How would you weigh a Boeing 747 without using scales?"

The Reason it is Asked: This question may be more for an engineer or a scientist, but any analytical person can probably come up with an answer. (There are probably several answers.)

Example Responses: "Put the jet on a large boat and paint a mark on the hull where the water line is. Now remove the jet and the boat rises. Finally, load the ship with items of known weight until it sinks to the line you painted. The total weight of the items will equal the weight of the jet."

Questions About the Amount and Place of Work

Question: "How much are you able to travel?"

The Reason it is Asked: Traveling is clearly a requirement of the job. The interviewer is looking for confirmation that is going to be OK with you.

How to Respond: If you have a sense for how much travel is required, then, you can respond with an acceptable answer. If you aren't sure, then give a response with a range that is as wide as you think you can get away with.

Example Responses: "Well, 5% to 15% would work for me."

Question: "Can you work overtime?"

The Reason it is Asked: Clearly, you're going to be expected to put in extra hours.

How to Respond: "No," is not an acceptable answer. Give as candid an answer as you can, by providing a range that is OK for you. Or, answer with a question.

Example Responses: "I typically work five to ten additional hours per week without being asked. Is more than that expected?"

Questions About Your Outside Interests

You may think that an interviewer can't ask questions about your personal life, but wait until the hiring manager takes you out to lunch. Make sure you recognize that no question about your personal life is innocent, casual, or off the record. They all have a purpose.

Here are some general guidelines for responding to these questions. Refusing to answer on the grounds that the question is not work related will likely hurt your chances. By the same token, you don't need to provide a huge volume of information about your personal life. Find someplace near the middle which you are comfortable with. You want to appear open and comfortable talking about personal things, but also maintain your privacy. If you feel that the interviewer went way overboard with a question, maybe asking something that is clearly unlawful, then start by pushing back with something like "Does it make a difference?" or "How does that issue relate to performing the job?" If the interviewer doesn't get the message and persists, then it's probably time to become indignant, if not just walk away.

Question: "How do you spend your private time?"
The Reason it is Asked: This is a "fit" or a "compatibility" question.
How to Respond: Hopefully, when you were in the interviewer's office, you looked around for pictures or objects that indicate what he/she likes to do. If that works for you, that's the obvious first thing to mention.

Question: "Do you drink?"
The Reason it is Asked: Again, this is a "fit" or a "compatibility" question.
How to Respond: You have to assume that the extremes are bad. Never drinking and drinking all the time aren't likely to be OK. Give a response somewhere in the middle. If you are a recovering alcoholic, you're under no obligation to indicate so.

Question: "Do you belong to any organizations?"
The Reason it is Asked: Again, this is a "fit" or a "compatibility" question.
How to Respond: It's good if you can cite an organization. However, avoid citing organizations that have restrictive membership requirements like religious, racial, or ethnic organizations.

Questions to Assess Your Performance on Your Prior Job

Question: "What were you told on your last performance evaluation that you should improve?"
The Reason it is Asked: The interviewer is looking for a problem.
How to Respond: You need to dispel the thought in the interviewer's mind that there was something wrong with your performance. Describe something you were told with the intent of making you better at the job and not to correct something that you were doing.

Questions to Assess What It Might Take to Hire You

<u>Question</u>: "Are you interviewing with other companies?"

<u>The Reason it is Asked</u>: If the interviewer wasn't interested in you, he/she wouldn't likely ask this question. It's a good sign, if you get it. The questioner is trying to get a reading on how quickly he/she might need to move in his/her interviewing process, if he/she is going to end up making you an offer. It can also be an inquiry to determine how strong the interviewer's negotiating position is.

<u>How to Respond</u>: Unless you have some reason to want this interviewing process (rounds #1, #2, etc.) to move slowly, give as strong a statement as you can that you are actively looking at other opportunities. If another opportunity is about to blow open for you and you consider it less interesting than this job, then mention that to spur the interviewer to move things along quickly.

<u>Example Responses</u>: "Yes, I've been actively looking for a couple months now and there are two other opportunities which I expect to warm up considerably in the next few days." Or "Yes, as a matter of fact, I believe that I will be getting an offer in a couple of days. However, I am far more interested in your position. If you are feeling positive about me, I'd hope that we can move this process along."

<u>Question</u>: "Does your current employer know you are looking for another job?"

<u>The Reason it is Asked</u>: This question is likely a small step to lead up to the question whether the interviewer can contact your current employer for a reference.

<u>How to Respond</u>: If you are confident that your current employer thinks highly of you then it's OK to say "Yes" to this question (presuming you will be OK saying "Yes" to the interviewer contacting your current employer). However, this is a very risky thing for you to let happen. Your current employer has a vested interest as to whether you stay with him/her or leave. Also, he/she may not have been completely candid with you as to how he/she really feels about you. Therefore, I suggest that you give a negative response to this question and offer an alternative.

Example Responses: "It would be detrimental to my situation if you were to contact my current employer. If are you looking for references, I have three people who are quite familiar with my work. You are welcome to contact them."

Question: "How soon could you start work?"
The Reason it is Asked: Unless this question came very early in the interview, this is a wonderful question for you. The interview is already starting to think that you are "the one" and he/she is searching for any last minute obstacles.
How to Respond: If you still have a job, you need to give your current employer reasonable notice. Two weeks is the typical minimum. If you have made commitments to your current employer which will take longer than that, don't worry about stating that now. You can explain that you could work to negotiate an earlier release. If you are not currently employed, then a bad answer is "Right now" or "Tomorrow morning." Why? For a couple of reasons. Everyone has some loose ends to tie up. You may not know what those are, yet, but they'll become apparent later. Second, a response that sounds too eager is going to cost you a couple of thousand dollars in the offer.
Example Responses: "I would prefer a couple of weeks. However, if you are looking to fill the position quicker than that, I can make some arrangements to do so." (If the hiring manager responds with a statement that suggests "sooner is better than later," you should feel really good about how things are going.)

Question: "Are you willing to relocate?"
The Reason it is Asked: Clearly, relocation is required for this job.
How to Respond: Even if you are willing, the best response here is a question with a positive ring to it.
Example Responses: "Yes, I can relocate. In what city might I need to work?"

Question: "What are your salary requirements?"
The Reason it is Asked: If this is asked early on in the interview, the questioner is just trying to confirm that there is a "fit" in regard to

compensation and that he/she isn't wasting his/her time with you. If it is asked late in the interview, that's a really good sign that he/she is giving you serious consideration.

How to Respond: Do not answer the question with a number, at least not the first time it is asked. This is such a critical topic that I've devoted an entire section in Chapter 16 to it. You will even find over 25 responses to use that *don't* explicitly answer the question.

Behavioral interviews have a particular characteristic. You will get questions about how you handled things, particularly yourself. The questions almost always start with the phrase "Tell me about a time when you ...." More times than not, it will be HR people who ask these kinds of questions. They are commonly trained in this form of interviewing, although the time will come when a hiring manager will ask you a behavioral type question. Behavioral interview type questions don't require detailed knowledge about the specific job opening. These questions apply to almost all jobs.

There is another common characteristic of behavioral interview questions. That is, there is a formula for what an appropriate response looks / sounds like. The HR people know what this is. They have forms to fill in the elements of the answer to confirm that it was complete. Here's the formula. Problem. Action. Result. In other words, in your answer, you need to describe the *problem*, the *action* that you took, and the *result* that occurred because of your action. To help you remember the formula, think PAR, for Problem, Action, Result.

Behavioral interview questions are difficult to anticipate and, hence, difficult to develop answers for in advance. About the only thing you can do is mentally review many of the events in your job experience, make them fresh in you mind, and use them in an answer to a behavioral interview question.

Nevertheless, you need to practice to get the hang of responding to a question with a PAR.

Below are examples of behavioral interview questions. Try a couple and formulate a response.

- "Tell me about a time you solved a problem."
- "Tell me about a time you were innovative."
- "Tell me about a time you had to fire someone."
- "Tell me about a time you made a big mistake."
- "Tell me about a time you disagreed with your boss."

- "Tell me about a time you recognized one of your employees for exemplary work."
- "Tell me about a time when you were confronted with a problem and had no idea how to proceed."

Are you getting the idea?

An interview is also an opportunity to ask questions. In particular, you need to ensure that you have a thorough understanding of the job, the company, and the people you would be working with.

Below are several lists of questions. Each list is designed for a particular person that you will encounter during an interview process. The questions are primarily oriented to Round #1 interviews. Since you're likely to focus most of your time selling yourself and learning about the job during Round #1, it's OK to hold some of these questions for Round #2.

The questions on the lists are generally in a good sequence. However, bring them up at a time and in the order which you think is appropriate.

There are some questions or information that you want to solicit after you meet with each person. They are listed next.

Common Questions

- Did I answer all your questions sufficiently? Is there anything else I can tell you?

- How well do you feel I meet the job requirements? Did you hear anything or read anything in my resume which suggests to you that I wouldn't be one of the final candidates under consideration?

- What is your understanding of the interview process? Sequence? Schedule?

- How many other viable candidates are there?

- What is the next step?

- May I have one of your business cards? (You want this to send a thank you note.)

<u>Questions for the Person Who Arranges the Interviews</u> - Here are examples of questions for you to consider asking the person who is setting up the interviews. In large organizations, this is not likely to be the HR Recruiter or the hiring manager. Review the list and pick out the ones that are important to you.

- What are the names, titles, locations, and directions to each person with whom you will be meeting? (Be sure you get the correct pronunciation of the name of each person who you will be meeting with.)

- What are the date, time, and location of each meeting?

- What are the name, phone number, and email address of the person making the arrangements, in case you need to contact him/her?

- Who should you contact, in case you become ill or you have a family emergency?

<u>Questions for an External Recruiter</u> - If there is an external recruiter involved, here are examples of questions for you to consider asking him/her. Review the list and pick out the ones that are important to you. (Also, see the list of questions in Chapter 14 "How to Work with Recruiters.")

- What information do you have about the employer's organization?

- Can you tell me about each of the people with whom I will be interviewing, in particular, the hiring manager?

- Do you have any particular advice as to how I should handle things? (You don't need to take it, but it might, at least, be insightful.)

- Have you submitted any other candidates for this job?

- Do you know whether there are any other candidates, especially internal ones?

- Do you know what the employer's interviewing process and schedule are?

Questions for an HR Person- Here are examples of questions for you to consider asking an HR person during an interview. Review the list and pick out the ones that are important to you.

- What is your understanding of the job?

- Could you provide some information about the entire company?

- What is the culture of the group where the job is?

- What are the titles and roles of the other people with whom I will be interviewing? (You may think you have this information already. However, this question may produce more information than you could appropriately ask for, like "What is the hiring manager like?")

- Whom should I contact, if I have questions about benefits? (More than likely, it will be this person. He/she may offer documentation / brochures on the company's standard benefits. Unless there is a large amount of time to kill, don't spend much time asking for details about the benefits program. You will get that chance another day. You do not want to be perceived this early in the process as one who is overly concerned about benefits.)

- Why should I want this job?

- Ask the "Common Questions" earlier in this appendix.

<u>Questions for the Hiring Manager</u> - Here are examples of questions for you to consider asking the hiring manager during an interview. Review the list and pick out the ones that are important to you.

- Could you please give me your view of the culture of the entire company?

- Could you please describe the culture of the group where the job is?

- Could you please describe the responsibilities of the job?

- What would I be doing day-in, day-out?

- What key education, skills, knowledge, and experience are you looking for in a candidate for this job?

- What are the key personal characteristics (like speed, integrity, accuracy, personal interaction skills) that this job will require?

- How do you think I measure up?

- Who would I be taking orders from? Who would be my official boss?

- Who would be working for me? How many people?

- What are the products or services that the group provides? For whom?

- What groups or facilities do I have to depend on to supply resources / materials to get the job done?

- What objectives have been established that I need to contribute to?

- What problems are there that I can help solve?

- What portion (%) of your time over the next year would you expect to spend with the person who fills this job?

- Who would I be working with in terms of peers, other managers, other departments?

- What authorities (expenditures, hiring / firing people, etc.) would I have?

- Where would I work? What would my working conditions be?

- When would you want me to start work?

- Is this a newly created position? If there was a person previously in this position, what happened?

- Is it an approved, open position or are you planning / anticipating?

- Why should I want this job?

- What are the key characteristics / traits of the group of people I would be part of?

- What is your interviewing process? (number of rounds, who might be future interviewers, etc.)

- How long might it all take?

- How far along are you in your interviewing process?

- Is there anything about my background that would prevent you from hiring me?

- Ask the "Common Questions" listed earlier in this appendix.

- Last question: What are the next steps? Who makes the next move?

<u>Questions for the Hiring Manager's Peers or Other Leaders</u> - Here are examples of questions for you to consider asking the hiring manager's peers or leaders in other departments during an interview. Review the list and pick out the ones that are important to you.

- Could you please give me your view of the culture of the entire company?

- Could you please describe the culture of the group where the job is?

- What would you relationship be to the person who fills this position?

- What is your understanding of the responsibilities of the job?

- What are the key personal characteristics (like speed, integrity, accuracy, personal interaction skills) that this job will require?

- Why should I want this job?

- Ask the "Common Questions" listed earlier in this appendix.

<u>Questions for People Who Would be Your Peers or Colleagues</u> - Here are examples of questions for you to consider asking people who would be your peers or colleagues during an interview. Review the list and pick out the ones that are important to you.

- Could you please give me your view of the culture of the entire company?

- Could you please describe the culture of the group where the job is?

- What is your understanding of the responsibilities of the job?

- What is the hiring manager's managing style?

- What are their expectations for the person who gets the job?

- How can I best help them?

- Ask the "Common Questions."

Questions for Your Boss's Boss - Here are examples of questions for you to consider asking your boss's boss. (This is not likely to be a Round #1 interview.) Review the list and pick out the ones that are important to you.

- Could you please give me your view of the culture of the entire company?

- Could you please describe the culture of the group where the job is?

- What are your expectations for the group?

- What is your understanding of the responsibilities of the job?

- What are your expectations for the person who gets the job?

- What portion (%) of your time over the next year would you expect to spend with the person who fills this job?

- Why should I want this job?

- Ask the "Common Questions."

Put Your Address Here
Put Your City State Zip Here
Put Your Phone Number Here
Put Your Email Address Here

Put The Date Here

Put The Hiring Manager's Name Here
Put The Hiring Manager's Title Here
Put The Hiring Manager's Organization Name Here
Put The Hiring Manager's Address Here
Put The Hiring Manager's City State Zip Here

Dear Mr./Mrs./Ms. Put The Hiring Manager's Last Name Here,

Over the last couple of weeks, I had _____ {put a number here] interviews with you and other people within your organization in pursuit of your _____ {name the position] position. I was quite interested in the position. I thought there was a good match between your requirements and my qualifications. Also, I had the impression that I was one of the final candidates.

I have now been informed that you have chosen another candidate. While disappointed, I certainly understand that you must go with whomever you judge to be the best candidate.

If the other candidate does not show or work out, certainly contact me. If you are aware of a similar position within your organization, I would be glad to hear about it.

Since I am still actively involved in a search for a new opportunity, I would like to ask for your help in identifying whom I might call for additional advice, guidance, and direction. I will follow up with you within the week and hope we will be able to connect.

Again, thank you for your time and consideration.

Respectfully yours,

Put Your Name Here

cc: Put The Name Of The Recruiter Here, If Any

Put Your Address Here
Put Your City State Zip Here
Put Your Phone Number Here
Put Your Email Address Here

Put The Date Here

Put The Hiring Manager's Name Here
Put The Hiring Manager's Title Here
Put The Hiring Manager's Organization Name Here
Put The Hiring Manager's Address Here
Put The Hiring Manager's City State Zip Here

Dear Mr./Mrs./Ms. Put The Hiring Manager's Last Name Here,

[Note: If you received the offer in writing and it included a description that is satisfactory to you of the job, compensation, and benefits, then you can refer to that letter in the first paragraph below and eliminate the material below that describes those aspects of the job.]

I am confirming my acceptance of your offer for the _____ ____ [job title] position.

I am extremely excited about this opportunity and eager to get started on _____ [your start date].

I outlined below my understanding of the job and compensation.

Job Description [List those aspects of the job that are important to you. Examples are shown below.]

- [List job title, job responsibilities, number of people reporting to you, etc.]
- [Job location, name of boss, etc.]

Compensation & Benefits [List those aspects of compensation and benefits that are important to you. Examples are shown below.]

- [Salary per month, hourly rate, etc.]
- [Commission structure and rate, stock options, relocation expenses, etc.]
- [Benefits: Health care, vacation days, company car, etc.]

I will contact you to determine if there is anything I can do in advance to be well-prepared on my first day.

Thanks you so much for this opportunity.

Respectfully yours,

Put Your Name Here

As a former job seeker, Jim became a real student of the process. Today, when he talks about a job search issue, it is with the voice of one who knows about it, not just from the books he read when he was in the midst of career transition, but from his own experiences of working for four companies and changing jobs internally 15-20 times and from personally counseling many of the Chagrin Valley Job Seekers (CVJS) members. He stretches your mind and provides you with valuable insights which will help set you apart from other seekers in the job market.

At a networking breakfast in early 2002, the seed was planted to create the CVJS organization, a job search support group for professionals in transition, which Jim co-founded and continues to co-lead. Six years later with over 2,000 registered members and 65-85 people at each meeting, CVJS is one of the largest and most successful job search support groups of its kind in the country.

Jim has a bachelor's degree in mathematics and a master's degree in quantitative methods. He has worked for a small computer services firm and a large regional bank, where he was part of the IT and operations organizations. From there, he went to a large manufacturer where, after 20 years, he and 3,000 of his closest friends were laid off when the company went into bankruptcy for the second time. He completed his career with a large casualty insurance firm. Over his career, he did analytical, programming, and financial work, moving up to middle management.

Jim now spends his time leading the CVJS organization, doing stock analysis and investing, analyzing baseball statistics, playing Texas Hold'em poker, researching genealogy, collecting coins, and spoiling his grandchildren. He and his wife live in northeast Ohio.

Index

4854803R0

Made in the USA
Charleston, SC
26 March 2010